Organize Your Finances

with Quicken® Deluxe 99

DIANE TINNEY

PRIMA TECH

A DIVISION OF PRIMA PUBLISHING

A Division of Prima Publishing

Prima Publishing, In a Weekend, and colophon are registered trademarks of Prima Communications, Inc. Rocklin, California 95677.

Publisher: Matthew H. Carleson
Managing Editor: Dan J. Foster
Acquisitions Editor: Jenny L. Watson
Senior Editor: Kelli R. Crump
Assistant Project Editor: Kim V. Benbow
Editorial Assistant: Rebecca I. Fong
Technical Reviewers: Franni Ferrero
Copy Editor: Hilary Powers
Interior Layout: Jimmie Young
Cover Design: Prima Design Team
Indexer: Sharon Hilgenberg

Intuit, Quicken, QuickBooks, TurboTax, and EasyStep are registered trademarks and/or registered service marks of Intuit Inc. Billminder, Quicken.com, QuickenMortgage, InsureMarket, EasyQuote, Investor Insight, Intuit Marketplace, QuickFill, QuickTabs, Quicken Financial Planner, and Financial Newsstand are trademarks and/or service marks of Intuit Inc. or one of its subsidiaries.

IMPORTANT: If you have problems installing or running Quicken Deluxe 99, go to the Quicken Web site at http://www.quicken.com. Prima Publishing cannot provide software support.

Prima Publishing and the author have attempted throughout this book to distinguish proprietary trademarks from descriptive terms by following the capitalization style used by the manufacturer.

Information contained in this book has been obtained by Prima Publishing from sources believed to be reliable. However, because of the possibility of human or mechanical error by our sources, Prima Publishing, or others, the Publisher does not guarantee the accuracy, adequacy, or completeness of any information and is not responsible for any errors or omissions or the results obtained from the use of such information. Readers should be particularly aware of the fact that the Internet is an ever-changing entity. Some facts may have changed since this book went to press.

ISBN: 0-7615-1786-3
Library of Congress Catalog Card Number: 98-67610
Printed in the United States of America
99 00 01 II 10 9 8 7 6 5 4 3 2

*This book is dedicated to my husband, James Keene, and my son,
David Keene, for their never-ending patience and support
for my seemingly never-ending work. Here's the proof
that the work really does end somewhere!*

CONTENTS AT A GLANCE

CONTENTS

SATURDAY AFTERNOON

ACKNOWLEDGMENTS

I'd like to thank the folks at Prima for providing me with the opportunity to work on this wonderful *In a Weekend* series title. Thanks to Jenny Watson for remembering my prior works with favor, and to Debbie Abshier for letting Jenny steal me away for a few weeks (that turned out to be a few months). And a special thank you to editors Kelli Crump, Hilary Powers, and Franni Ferrero for reading and rereading the text as it went through many revisions. Your careful review is what gives this book its shine in the end.

ABOUT THE AUTHOR

Diane Tinney has authored more than a dozen computer books about computer software applications, programming languages, and operating systems such as Access, Windows 95, VBA, Windows NT, Paradox, and dBASE. Diane's business, The Software Professional, keeps her busy teaching, creating business applications, and managing Web sites. Her favorite client (other than Prima Publishing) is ACT, a nonprofit computer user group for corporate tax accountants.

Prior to becoming an author and business owner, Diane whittled the time away working for a big 5 public accounting firm, KPMG Peat Marwick, as a senior manager in the corporate tax area, and developing corporate tax applications.

INTRODUCTION

Congratulations! Not only have you purchased the best-selling personal finance software, you have also decided to dedicate a weekend with this book to learn how to use the software effectively. Too often, computer users purchase software with good intentions, but the software lies on a shelf, unused. Or new users buy huge books that weigh more than the software and find—after the first ten chapters—that they still don't know how to do even the most basic tasks. Not so with this book. In one weekend, you will learn the most important skills and features of Quicken. And you'll learn to use those new skills in a real-world setting.

Is This Book for You?

Organize Your Finances In a Weekend with Quicken Deluxe 99 is for anyone who wants to use Quicken, but needs some help learning the ropes. Think of this book as a personal tutorial, a one-on-one class with an expert user of Quicken. What a deal! You get to stay in the comfort of your home and learn how to:

- Automate your checkbook
- Reconcile your accounts
- Computerize your bill payments
- Track and analyze your cash payments
- Perform banking transactions online
- Control and automate credit card transactions
- Track and analyze investments

- Create and implement budget and savings plans
- Gather tax return data
- Project income tax expenses
- Plan for major financial events such as retirement and college
- Print reports that present your financial information as you need to see it

How Much Time Will This Take?

This book is organized in sessions from Friday evening to Sunday evening. Each lasts about three hours, with a break in the middle so you can get a cup of coffee or go for a quick walk. If you have the time, you can cover this entire book in a weekend.

On the other hand, you don't have to limit yourself to a single weekend. The flexible design of this book permits you to spread the book over a week, a couple of weekends, or even a month. You can do each of the sessions on a separate night, or split the sessions over a few days. Tailor the book to your schedule and preferred learning pace and you're sure to be successful.

Some sessions, such as Banking Online, may not interest you at this time. Feel free to skip these for now, knowing that at any time in the future you can spend just a few hours learning them. However, I do recommend that you read the introduction to the sessions you decide not to tackle.

What's Covered in This Book?

- **Friday Evening: Setting Up Your Checkbook** introduces you to the core features of Quicken. If you are new to Quicken, you set up your Quicken data file and create a checking account. Those upgrading from a prior version of Quicken learn how to open their Quicken data file and access their checking account (or create a new checking account if needed). You discover what's on the screen as well so you can navigate the program menus, toolbars, and built-in Help system. Also, this session teaches you how to enter common

checkbook transactions and ends with reconciling your automated checking account to a bank statement.

- **Saturday Morning: Automating Your Account** teaches you how to have Quicken do the work for you every month. You learn how to memorize transactions, schedule recurring transactions, and use the interactive financial calendar. You also set up automatic reminders, use the Quick Entry feature, and Alerts so Quicken tells you when a financial task needs to be done. Then you learn how to set up and automate other financial accounts such as savings, loans, credit cards, and personal assets.

- **Saturday Afternoon: Banking Online** takes you to the World Wide Web of financial automation. You learn what it takes to get online, how to connect to the Quicken Financial Network, and what online features Quicken provides. You pay bills online, download credit card transactions that automatically post to categories you assign, and even stop payment on checks. You learn how to have the Internet deliver to you the financial information you need to manage your finances and shop for the best prices for items such as loans and insurance plans.

- **Saturday Evening: Automating Investments** shows you how Quicken can be used to track and analyze investments such as 401(k) plans, stocks, bonds, and mutual funds. You set up investment accounts and enter common transactions such as dividends, purchases, and sales. You learn how to manage and track your portfolio. This session builds on the prior Banking Online session in that you use the online investment tools that come with Quicken such as Market Watch and news updates. At the end, you learn how to create your own investment watch list so you can plan for the future.

- **Sunday Morning: Reports and Graphs** takes you through the flexible, easy-to-use reporting features of Quicken. You learn how to generate on-screen and printed reports for home, business, and investment use. You customize the reports, save them for future use, and learn how to export data from Quicken to other systems.

✿ **Sunday Afternoon: Managing Your Taxes** helps you turn Quicken into a tax data collection and reporting tool. You learn how to tag everyday transactions for tax purposes and then electronically send that data to tax programs such as TurboTax. You use the Tax Deduction Finder tool to generate tax savings. And you learn how to use Quicken to plan for next year's taxes and prepare estimated taxes.

✿ **Sunday Evening: Planning for the Future** teaches you how to prepare and follow a budget, and shows you how Quicken can help you stay on the budget. You plan for retirement, set up a college fund for the kids, analyze loan options, and start your savings plan. This session also covers many extras included in Quicken, such as the insurance investment, debt consolidation, and mortgage refinancing tools. By the end of this chapter, you will consider what's next with an eye to the year 2000 and beyond.

What Do You Need to Begin?

All you need is Quicken Deluxe 99 installed on your computer (see the appendix for help installing Quicken Deluxe 99) and the following personal financial items:

✿ Your current checkbook register—or if you use duplicate carbon copy checks, just the checkbook you've been using since the last bank statement ending date.

✿ Your last checking account bank statement with the cancelled checks.

✿ A recent credit card statement.

✿ A paycheck stub that shows your gross pay and details of deductions and taxes withheld.

✿ A few recurring bills such as car payments or rent.

✿ For each outstanding loan, a loan statement that shows the principal, interest rate, and payment details.

✿ If you have a mortgage, a mortgage statement that shows the principal, interest rate, and payment details.

⚙ The most recent bank statement for other accounts such as savings or money-market accounts.

⚙ The most recent statement for each of the financial investments that you have: stock, bond, mutual fund, and retirement plan (such as a 401(k) plan).

⚙ The purchase slips for a few major appliances or valuables in your home.

⚙ Any budget plan that you may have tried to implement in the past.

The focus is to get you started with your own financial data this weekend. That is why I don't ask you to enter all your data for the past year. Most Quicken users start today and instantly reap the benefits of automating their finances. Unless you have a need to produce reports for a full year of data, you do not need to enter all of it.

On the other hand, if you have the time and want to, you can enter as much data as you would like. Or, if you don't want to use your own data, you can use the fictional data in this book. Again, feel free to tailor this book to meet your needs.

Looking Forward to a Lifetime of Organized Finances

Imagine being able to find out instantly if you already paid a bill that just came in the mail, to quickly search for the best deal on automobile insurance (and purchase it at your computer), to anticipate the cost of your child's college education and set aside enough money each month to reach that goal, to find out which checks have cleared your bank, to print out a report that will help you prepare your tax return, and to create a useful budget and stick to it—all this and much more is at your fingertips. You're only a weekend away!

FRIDAY EVENING

Setting Up Your Checkbook

- ✿ Setting Up a New User Data File
- ✿ Opening an Existing Data File
- ✿ Getting Help
- ✿ Working with the Register
- ✿ Splitting Transactions among Multiple Categories
- ✿ Reconciling Your Bank Account
- ✿ Backing Up Your Files

If you are following the *In a Weekend* theme, it's Friday night and you have cleared your social calendar for this evening. Quicken will be your date, but you'll have to provide the munchies. With the stresses of the work week behind you, you can now concentrate on organizing and automating your personal finances.

First and foremost, please take a moment to read the introduction at the beginning of this book. Aside from providing you with a good overview of how to use this book, the introduction contains a section named "What Do You Need to Begin?" that lists the personal financial papers you will need this weekend to set up your finances in Quicken.

So grab a soda or a cup of coffee, and get ready to learn how to:

- ✪ Set up a new user Quicken data file
- ✪ Open an existing Quicken data file
- ✪ Set up a new checking account
- ✪ Navigate menus, toolbars, and tabs
- ✪ Use the Help system to find solutions
- ✪ Enter common checkbook transactions
- ✪ Set up and assign income and expense categories
- ✪ Balance your electronic checkbook

Setting Up a New User Data File

If you are a new user of Quicken, you will see the Quicken New User Setup dialog box as soon as you finish installing the program (see Figure 1.1). This set of dialog boxes (which Intuit refers to as EasyStep) walks you through the process of creating a financial data file. If you already have a Quicken data file, this dialog box will not appear, so you can skip ahead to the next section, "Opening an Existing Data File."

If your computer is equipped for sound, you are in for quite a treat! By default, Quicken displays an audio toolbar and begins to play prerecorded voice instructions when you first arrive at a new feature. At any time, you can click on Stop (the button with the square on it) to stop and rewind the audio. The Play button (the one with the arrowhead) toggles to Pause when clicked so that you can pause the audio. Like most features in Quicken, you can customize your copy of Quicken to turn this feature off. But as a beginner, you will probably enjoy the helpful voice instructions.

NOTE In order to play the audio, your computer needs to have a sound card installed with speakers or headphones attached to it. Furthermore, the Quicken CD must be in the CD-ROM drive. Some CD-ROM drives allow headphones to be plugged into the CD-ROM drive so you can listen to music CDs. The Quicken CD will not play audio through the CD-ROM drive headphone connector.

Figure 1.1

New users of
Quicken must first
set up a financial
data file.

Navigating through the New User Setup is easy. Click on Next to see the next dialog box. Click on Back to return to the previous dialog box. Click on Cancel to abort the New User Setup. At any time, click on Help to view context-sensitive help screens.

The New User Setup asks you questions about yourself (see Figure 1.2) so that it can set up commonly used categories for you. For example, if you own a home, Quicken will make sure that expense categories such as mortgage interest and home insurance are set up for you. Categories, as you will learn more about later tonight, are used to control and track finances in Quicken. Although the New User Setup provides a list of commonly used categories for you, you can always add, delete, or edit categories at any time.

NOTE

● ●

To see a list of the predefined categories for each question, click on Help, and then click on the hypertext "click here."

● ●

Next, New User Setup prompts you to name your checking account (see Figure 1.3). Some people use their names (such as Joe's Checking) while others describe the account type. I strongly recommend naming the account by the bank name and type (such as Federal Checking). This allows you to quickly see by the name which account you are working on. Although today you may only have one checking account, in a few years

Figure 1.2

Quicken creates a category list for you based on your personal data.

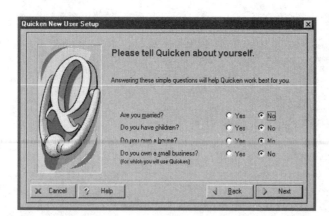

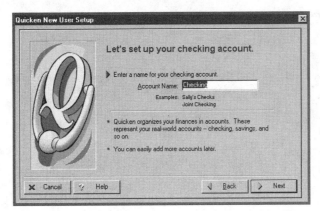

Figure 1.3

You can use up to 30 characters to name your checking account.

you may have several, at several different banks. This approach has saved me more than once.

After you've named your checking account, Quicken asks you if you have your last bank statement for this account (see Figure 1.4). If you do not have a bank statement, Quicken creates the checking account with an opening balance of zero. You will be able to use Quicken right away and adjust the opening balance when you get your next bank statement and reconcile the account.

If you have your bank statement, click on Yes, and Quicken prompts you for the statement ending date and ending balance (see Figure 1.5). The ending balance becomes the opening balance for your Quicken account. But don't enter it yet!

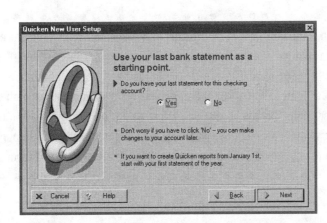

Figure 1.4

You can open your Quicken checking account with a balance of zero or more.

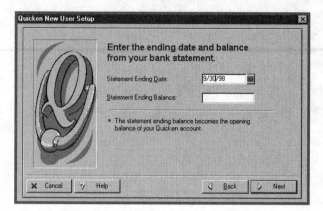

Figure 1.5

You can always change the opening balance and date you enter here at any time.

For tonight's session, I recommend that you follow these steps:

1. Use the beginning balance and date from your most recent bank statement.

2. Use the cancelled checks tonight to practice basic data entry. If there are too many checks to enter tonight, just pull out 5 to 10 checks that you want to enter and adjust the beginning balance. For example, suppose you decide to enter 7 checks that total $500 and the ending balance on your bank statement is $2,000. In step one above you would enter a balance of $1,500 ($2,000 – $500).

3. At the end of the evening, you'll reconcile your account using the same bank statement, so keep it handy.

●●●●●●●●●●●●●●●●●●●●●●●●●●●●●●●●●●●

NOTE   If you want a full year of information in Quicken, just repeat the process you use tonight for each of the months in this year. Only, instead of using the cancelled checks, use your actual checkbook and then reconcile to the bank statement as shown at the end of this chapter. Start with the first of the year and continue month by month until you reach the current date. This might take you a few weeks, but you will have a full year's financial information to use for your planning, tax compliance, or business purposes—you won't have to wait months to build up enough information for useful reports.

●●●●●●●●●●●●●●●●●●●●●●●●●●●●●●●●●●●

The last dialog box shows you the account name, opening date, and opening balance. At this point, you can edit any information or click on Back to move backward and change any of your prior responses. When you are satisfied with your new checking account, click on Done. Quicken will save your new data file to the hard disk (the default name is QDATA).

Next on the screen is Quicken Overviews (see Figure 1.6), which is a part of the Help system. Each topic displays a video with audio (again, the CD must be in the drive and your PC must have sound). Click on the topic "What's new in Quicken 99" to see a short video. The video control buttons work similarly to the audio toolbar buttons. The black arrowhead button plays and pauses, while the black square button stops and rewinds.

You can access Quicken Overviews at any time by choosing Help, Overviews from the menu bar. To close the Quicken Overviews, click on "I'm finished. Take me back to Quicken."

Opening an Existing Data File

If you're a new user of Quicken and just created your first data file and checking account in the prior section, you do not need to do this section. However, if you would like to read along and do this section for extra practice, feel free to continue. Otherwise, new users of Quicken can skip ahead to the next section, "What's on the Screen."

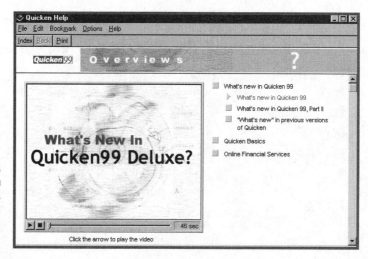

Figure 1.6

Quicken Overviews use video with sound to teach you about new features.

If you've used a prior version of Quicken, you can use that data file for this weekend's lessons. For all prior versions of Quicken for Windows and DOS versions 3 and above, Quicken 99 automatically reads and converts your data file. When you open Quicken 99, your updated data appears. If you have multiple data files, use File, Open to open each data file (Quicken will automatically update the data as the file opens).

Users of Quicken for DOS versions 1 and 2 need a special conversion program to update their data. You can call Intuit to order the program on a disk, or download it from the Internet at **http://www.intuit.com**.

FIND IT ▶
ONLINE

After your existing data file opens, you can use your existing checking account for this weekend, or create a new checking account.

To create a new checking account, follow these steps:

1. Choose Features, Banking, Create New Account. The Create New Account dialog box appears (see Figure 1.7).

2. Choose Checking and click on Next to continue. Tomorrow morning's session covers other types of account creation.

3. Enter a descriptive name (up to 30 characters) in the Account Name text box (see Figure 1.8).

4. Enter a description (optional) for your own use in the Description text box and click on Next to continue.

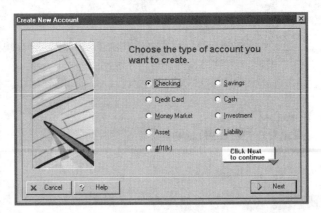

Figure 1.7

At any time, you can create a new checking account.

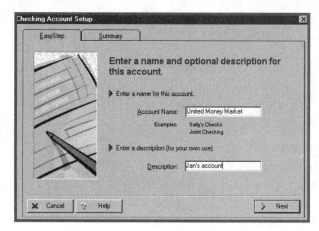

Figure 1.8

Consider using the name of the bank along with the account type as the account name.

5. At this point, the dialog boxes are the same as the New User Setup (see Figures 1.4 and 1.5). Quicken asks you if you have your last bank statement for this account. If you do not have a bank statement, Quicken creates the checking account with an opening balance of zero. You will be able to use Quicken right away and adjust the opening balance when you get your next bank statement and reconcile the account.

    If you have your bank statement, click on Yes and Quicken prompts you for the statement ending date and ending balance. The ending balance becomes the opening balance for your Quicken account. But don't enter it yet!

    For tonight's session, you should enter the beginning balance and date from your bank statement. You will enter the cancelled checks tonight as practice and reconcile your account at the end of the evening. If there are too many checks, just pull out 5 to 10 checks that you want to enter and find the difference to arrive at a new beginning balance. For example, suppose you decide to enter 7 checks that total $500 and the ending balance on your bank statement is $2,000. In step one above you would enter a beginning balance of $1,500 ($2,000 − $500).

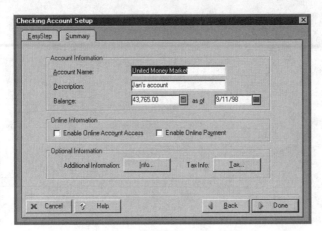

Figure 1.9

The Summary tab
allows you to edit
the setup of
your account.

6. Enter the statement date and ending balance, and then click on Next to continue.

7. The next screen asks if you have applied for online services for this account (this topic is covered tomorrow). For now, leave the selection set to No and click on Next.

8. The last screen (see Figure 1.9) displays the Summary tab for the checking account that you want to create. At this point, you can edit any of this information or click on Back to move backward and change any of your prior responses. (Online and optional information features are covered tomorrow.) When you are satisfied with your new checking account, click on Done. Quicken will create and display the new checking account.

TIP You can access and edit the Summary tab information for existing accounts by clicking on the Edit Account button in the register anytime.

What's on the Screen?

Getting thirsty? Well, just hang in there for a few more minutes. Before you break, take a good look at what's on your screen (see Figure 1.10). Odd as it may seem, this is the biggest stumbling block in computer software education. Folks of all ages, from children and students to adults and seniors, frequently skip over this essential skill and start clicking away into confusion! Explore each of the major screen parts individually, from the top down.

Exploring the Menu Bar

Just below the Quicken Deluxe 99 title bar (notice that the name of your data file (QDATA), the name of your active account, and account type appear in the title bar too), you see the menu bar. Menus have long been the conventional method of providing users with access to a program's

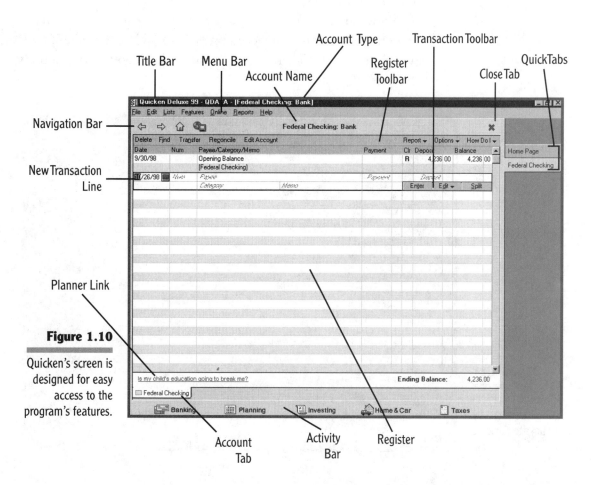

Figure 1.10

Quicken's screen is designed for easy access to the program's features.

features and commands. When you click on a menu bar command (such as File), Quicken displays a list of menu items under that command. You can then use your pointer to highlight a menu item, open submenus (also called cascading menus), and then click on the item you want to use. As you can see in Figure 1.11, menus provide many visual signals that you will want to master.

Here is a quick overview of the visual symbols found on a menu:

⚙ **Underlined letters.** All menu commands have an underlined letter in their name to provide keyboard access to the command. Just press and hold down the Alt key while you press the underlined letter. This opens the menu. After the menu is open, you only need to type the underlined letter of a menu item to invoke it. For example, to open the File menu, you would press Alt+F. (Note that you do not type the plus sign.) Then, to invoke the Backup command, just press the letter B.

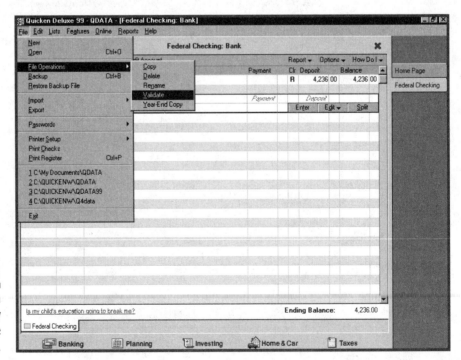

Figure 1.11

You can use menu commands at any time to navigate Quicken.

✿ **Quick Keys.** Some frequently used menu commands have assigned keypress combinations that Quicken calls Quick Keys (also called shortcut keys in other programs). If a menu command has a Quick Key, it appears to the right of the menu item name. For example, the Quick Key for Backup is Ctrl+B (see Figure 1.11). For a complete listing, search Help for the topic Quick Keys.

✿ **Cascading menus.** Some menu commands display submenus called cascading menus. Your visual signal for a cascading menu is a right-pointing black arrowhead. For example, in Figure 1.11, the File Operations menu item displays a cascading menu.

✿ **Dialog boxes.** Some menu commands display a dialog box that requires you to select choices or provide information. For example, in Figure 1.11, the New and Open commands both display dialog boxes prompting you for more information before a command can be executed.

NOTE   Windows 98 programs must adhere to certain common user interface features. All the menu bar actions and shortcuts described here work the same for all your Windows 98 programs.

Take a moment to explore the menus and cascading menus. As I cover each feature and topic this weekend, you will learn the corresponding menu command. Note that the menu is not the only way to invoke commands. The folks at Intuit have done a fine job of providing many easier, quicker ways for you to activate commands. Read on.

NOTE   If you upgraded from an earlier version of Quicken, you might see the Quicken Iconbar (a toolbar) below the menu bar. You can control the display and contents of this Iconbar by choosing Edit, Options, Iconbar. If you are a new user of Quicken, you will probably prefer to use the Activity Bar (discussed later in this section) instead of the Iconbar.

Navigating Quicken Pages

Quicken 99, more than any prior version of Quicken, incorporates the Internet look and feel to the screen design and behavior. Your first glimpse of this is the Navigation bar which appears just below the menu bar. The left pointing and right pointing arrows take you to the prior and next page (which Quicken calls a QuickTab). The house icon takes you to your Quicken Home Page. The icon with the globe and monitor opens the One-Step Update dialog box from which you can download financial information and update your Quicken software. You will learn more about the One-Step Update feature tomorrow afternoon in the Banking Online session.

Click on the Home Page icon in the Navigation bar. Figure 1.12 shows a typical Quicken Home Page for a new user. As you use Quicken features, such as setting up scheduled transactions, alerts, and stock quote watches, you will see this page filled in with your financial data. You can even customize the Quicken Home Page as needed (click on the Customize this page option in top right corner). The Quicken Home Page summarizes the highlights of your finances and provides quick access to key features in Quicken.

NOTE ●

In addition to the Quicken Home Page, each of the financial centers in Quicken (Banking, Planning, Investing, Home & Car, and Taxes) have a similar summary page. You can view the financial centers by choosing Features, Centers, and selecting a financial center to view. The financial centers are also listed on their respective Activity Bar pop-up menus.

● ●

TIP ■

You can quickly move between QuickTabs by just clicking on the QuickTab you want.

■ ■

Using QuickTabs

To the far right of the register, you can see another set of tabs called QuickTabs. Each window you open in Quicken displays a QuickTab labeled with the window name. QuickTabs allow you to easily navigate

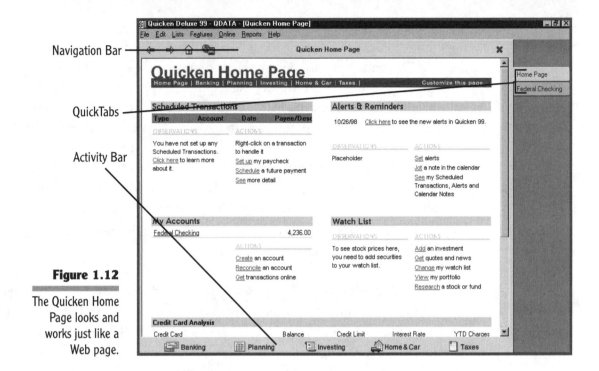

Navigation Bar

QuickTabs

Activity Bar

Figure 1.12

The Quicken Home Page looks and works just like a Web page.

between your financial projects without hunting through menus or memorizing cryptic commands.

Using the Planner

Just above the Account Name tab is a commonly asked financial planning question. When you click on the question, Quicken displays the Planner tab for that financial issue and provides guidance on how to properly plan for it. The Sunday Evening session covers the Planner feature in depth. As you work through Quicken, the question posed will change to pique your interest on key planning issues.

Exploring the Register

Below the menu bar and Navigation bar is the register for your new checking account. As you can see at the top of Figure 1.10, the name and description of the account appear at the top. Next comes the Register toolbar.

You will learn how to use each of the buttons on the Register toolbar tonight and tomorrow morning. The column headings for the register are very similar to the standard headings found in most paper checkbook registers: Date, Num, Payee, Category Name, Memo Payment, Clr, Deposit, and Balance. At the bottom of the register, on the right side, you can see the Ending Balance (which is always up to date—no need to drag out the calculator anymore!). On the bottom left, you can see the Account name on a tab. As you open accounts and work on various activities, each account displays its own tab. Just like a workbook or notebook, you can use the tabs as a quick way to flip back and forth between your accounts.

When you come back from your break, you will spend the next hour using the register.

Exploring the Activity Bar

One of the newest innovations in recent years is the addition of the Activity Bar at the bottom of your screen (see Figure 1.13). The Activity Bar provides easy access to Quicken's most commonly used features. While the menu bar is organized around Windows 98 user interface standards, the Activity Bar is organized around financial activities. Simply move your pointer over an Activity Bar item to view its shortcut menu. Click on an item to start a financial task.

Getting Help

Quicken's Help system contains a complete User Guide, which is even better than the hard copy version. The onscreen User Guide provides

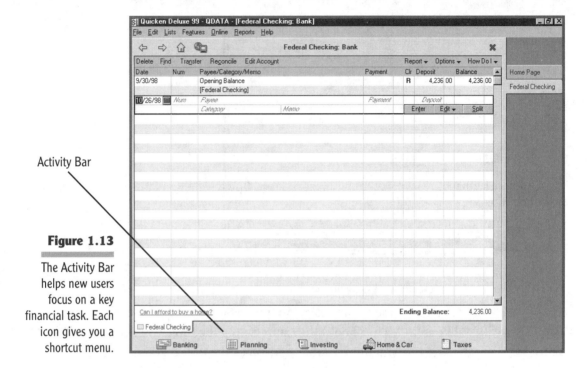

Activity Bar

Figure 1.13

The Activity Bar helps new users focus on a key financial task. Each icon gives you a shortcut menu.

hyperlinks that allow you to jump from topic to topic without looking up a single page number. You can search the Index for keywords or use the Find feature to locate a topic. The Help Contents page lists Show Me audio and video clips.

In addition to the computerized User Guide, Quicken provides you with a How Do I? button that lists common user questions and provides step-by-step instructions on how to complete a task. If all else fails, you can press F1—the Help key—to view context-sensitive help.

Accessing the Help System

The Quicken Help system works the same as any other Windows 98 program. While working anywhere in the program, you can press F1 to receive help on the current task. Or you can choose Help, Index from the menu bar to open the Help window (see Figure 1.14).

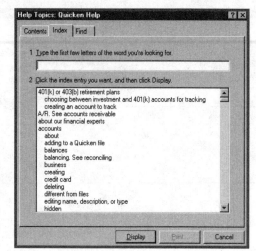

Figure 1.14

By default, the
Help window
opens with the
Index tab
selected.

Using the Index

The Help Index provides an alphabetical listing of the Help topics (just like an index in a book). Just start typing the topic you need help with. The lower box will jump to that portion of the index. You don't need to type in the entire topic name. After you see the topic on which you want more information, double-click on the item. The Help system will either display a short list of related Help topic titles (double-click on one to select a specific Help topic), or provide the requested help text.

TIP   While viewing a Help topic, right-click in the Help topic text window to get easy access to Help commands such as print, bookmark, or annotate, and to customize the Help system to better meet your needs.

Using Find

What if you don't know the exact name of a feature with which you need help? In these cases, use the Find tab in Help. Find allows you to search for words within a Help topic (not just the titles of the Help topics).

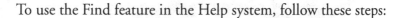

To use the Find feature in the Help system, follow these steps:

1. If you don't have the Help Index window open, choose Help and then Index from the menu bar.

2. Click on the Find tab. The first time you use Find, the Find Setup Wizard appears, prompting you to generate a Find word list. For now, accept the default Minimal word list (you can always change this later) by clicking on Next and then on Finish.

3. In the first text box, type in a word or two that describe what you are looking for. For example, type in **College Fund** and press Tab. Quicken displays a list of similar words in the middle box.

4. Select one or more words in the middle box to narrow your search down. Notice that when you do, the bottom box displays a list of Help topics (see Figure 1.15). Browse through the Help topics listed until you find one that matches your needs.

5. Double-click on the desired Help topic in the bottom box. The Help topic text will appear in a separate window.

6. When you finish with the Help topic, click on Index to return to the main Help window, or close the window to exit Help.

Figure 1.15

The Find feature in Help searches within Help text for the words you specify.

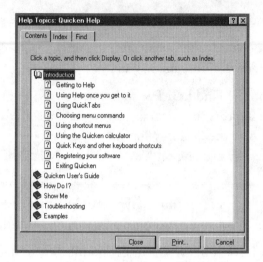

Figure 1.16

Double-click on a Help book to view the chapter titles.

Using Help Contents

The Contents tab in the Help window (see Figure 1.16) is like a set of books on a shelf. Double-click on a book to view the contents page of that book. Double-click on a chapter heading to view the Help text. This is a great place to expand your knowledge of Quicken. Take some time to browse through the books:

- **Introduction.** Basic information such as what's new in Quicken Deluxe 99, how to use Help, menus, and the calculator.

- **Quicken User's Guide.** The text of the entire User's Guide.

- **How Do I?** Step-by-step instructions on how to complete a task in Quicken (such as how to set up a checking account).

- **Show Me.** Video clips that teach you how to use Quicken (requires the CD-ROM).

- **Troubleshooting.** A great guide to help you solve common problems (such as entering transactions into the wrong account).

- **Examples.** A collection of tips, advice, and samples of how to use Quicken (such as a case study for a volunteer service club).

TIP ■
To open a book on the Help Contents page, double-click on the book icon. To close the
book, double-click on the book icon again. Topics appear in the list with a page ? icon—
double-click on that to view the Help text.

■ ■

Getting Product Support

No matter how good a computer program and its Help system are, there
usually comes a time when a user needs extra help from the program vendor's
product support personnel. Quicken makes getting product support easy
by listing it right on the Help menu. Choose Help, Product Support from
the menu bar and Quicken displays the Product Support dialog box (see
Figure 1.17). This dialog box walks you through the key steps in getting
technical support:

- Quicken's Troubleshooting Guide in the Help system.

- Online Help at the Quicken Web site (requires access to the Internet)
  where you'll find an ample FAQ list (a list of frequently asked questions), discussions of known issues, and update notices.

- The phone number for Quicken's Fax-Back service, which contains
  most of the FAQs and known-issues information found on the Web.

- Telephone support phone numbers (and they really do answer the
  phone!).

Figure 1.17

Quicken provides
easy access to
product support.

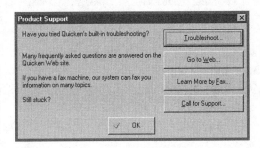

Although you may think that calling someone is the fastest and best way of getting your question answered, don't skip over the Troubleshooting Guide, Web site, and Fax-Back service before you've tried them. More often than not, you will find your question answered—not only the burning issue question, but you will probably run across answers to other less important questions as you browse through the FAQs. This is another great way to learn Quicken!

Using Overviews

If you have the CD-ROM version of Quicken Deluxe, you have access to Overviews (see Figure 1.18), a collection of video clips introducing you to various program features. As opposed to the Show Me video clips that show you how to complete a task, the Overviews video clips take you through an area of the program. For example, in the Quicken Basics Overview you learn about the menu bar, Activity Bar, Help, and the register. To open the Overviews dialog box, choose Overviews from the Help menu.

Take a Break

Wow! Just think of how much you know now, compared to an hour or so ago. Time for you to take a break. Get up, stretch your legs, refill your cup, and get yourself a snack. When you return, you will learn how to use the register and start entering your checks.

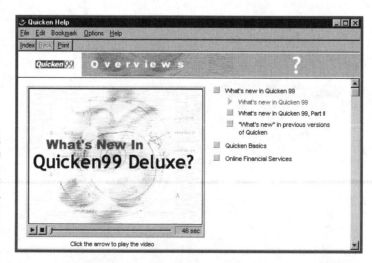

Figure 1.18

Before you venture into a new area of Quicken, consider viewing the Overview video to get the big picture.

Working with the Register

Of all the features in Quicken, you will probably use the Quicken register the most. This is where you will record check dates, check numbers, payees, and amounts. You will also record other checking account transactions such as deposits, automatic payments, and ATM withdrawals. However, unlike a paper check register, the Quicken check register will do the math for you! Never again will you have a check bounce because of a simple math error. Moreover, Quicken will work behind the scenes for you to keep track of your income and expenses. So, get out that last bank statement with the cancelled checks and dive in.

Entering a Check

For tonight's example, you will be entering the cancelled checks that came with your last bank statement. This will allow you to reconcile your account at the end of the session tonight. The order in which you enter the checks does not matter. Quicken will automatically sort them by date (or you can change the default sort order; I'll explain how later). Take a moment to pile the checks up and clear off your work area as needed (but keep the snack handy). For each transaction, you will enter:

1. The date of the transaction.

2. The check number or the type of transaction (such as deposit, ATM withdrawal, and so on).

3. The name of the other party to the transaction.

4. The amount of the transaction.

5. The type of expense or income.

6. A brief memo to describe the transaction further (optional).

Compare this list to the first check in your pile and locate each item.

Now compare this list to the register on your screen. Find the column headings:

1. Date

2. Num

3. Payee/Category/Memo

4. Payment

5. Deposit

NOTE By default, the Tab key moves your cursor from one field to the next. If you prefer, you can change this so that the Enter key moves you to the next field. To change this feature, choose Edit, Options, Register and then select the QuickFill tab. Check or uncheck the Use Enter Key To Move Between Fields check box. In this book, I use the Tab key.

Did you notice that the last line in the register shows today's date and then the rest of the words (in gray) listed above? This is called the New Transaction line. This is where you will enter the information for your first check. The New Transaction line is always the last line in the register. You can also insert a New Transaction line anywhere in the register by choosing Edit, Transaction, Insert, or pressing Ctrl+I.

TIP To quickly move to the New Transaction line, press Ctrl+End.

Look through your check pile and select a check that paid for just one type of expense (say, rent, electricity, or cable TV). You will enter this check first because it's easier to deal with than one that covered a bunch of different things at the same time.

NOTE See those buttons at the far right of the New Transaction line? Enter, Edit, and Split? Well, as you go through this section you will learn how to use each one of these. For now, just know that these buttons are the Transaction Toolbar.

Entering the Date

If you've been clicking and tabbing around, please click back on the Date field in the New Transaction line. By default, Quicken enters today's date in the Date field for you, leaving the month number selected. If today's date is the date of the transaction you are entering, you can just press Tab to advance to the next field.

TIP To quickly move back to the date field for the current transaction, press Home twice.

Unless you're working in a time warp tonight, today's date is not the date of your first check. So you have a few choices:

✪ Type the date without the punctuation (Quicken adds the slashes for you) such as 103098 for 10/30/98.

✪ Type the month number to change just the month, or press the right arrow to select the day or year portion to be changed.

✪ Click on the cute little calendar icon next to the year number. Quicken displays a calendar that you can use to browse through the months and years. Double-click on the exact day and Quicken will enter the date for you.

✪ Use one of the Quick Keys to enter or change a date. To view a list of Quick Keys and other keyboard shortcuts, search the Help Index for Quick Keys. The Quick Keys I use most include the minus key (-) to decrease the date by a day, the plus key (+) to increase the date by a day, and the letter *t* to enter today's date.

TIP To quickly enter a date as the *first* day of this month, press the letter **m** while in the date field. Continue to press **m** to move back a month (still first day). To enter as the *last* day of this month, press the letter **h**. Continue to press **h** to move forward a month (still last day). These shortcuts work throughout Quicken (in the date ranges of Reports and other items).

After the date of your first check is entered, press Tab to move to the next field.

Entering the Check Number

In the Num column, enter the check number and press Tab. Keep in mind that some transactions that you need to enter in your electronic check register will not be checks, but you still use this column to keep track of them. Quicken offers a lot of help with the Num column, both for checks and other kinds of items (available from a drop-down list or by entering specific codes). Here's what's available:

- **Next Check Num.** Quicken increments the last entered check number by one and enters it for you. Default beginning check number is 101.

- **ATM.** Signifies automatic teller transactions such as cash withdrawals. Default code is ATM.

- **Deposit.** Signifies a deposit of funds into your checking account. Default code is DEP.

- **Print Check.** Signifies to Quicken that you want to print a computerized check. After the check is printed, Quicken will enter the check number automatically into your account. Default code is Print.

- **Transfer.** Signifies a transfer of funds from one account to another (such as from a savings account to a checking account). Default code is TXFR.

- **EFT.** Signifies an electronic transfer of funds into or out of your account (such as an automatic payroll deposit). Default code is EFT.

- **Edit List button.** A button that allows you to edit existing code words and create your own code words (maximum of six letters).

TIP Use the plus (+) and minus (-) keys to enter and change the check number by one digit.

NOTE   If you know which transaction type you want to enter, you can begin entering the name. As soon as you type the first letter, Quicken will fill in the rest of the name.

Entering the Payee

After you enter the date and transaction number or type, it's time to enter the name of the person or company who is a party to this transaction. If you are entering a check, this will be the name of the payee on the check. If you are entering a deposit, this will be the name of the person or company writing the check. For miscellaneous transactions such as ATM withdrawals, your payee might be *Cash* or *Withdrawal*. You are free to use any description you want (up to 40 characters).

NOTE   You may notice that after you have entered several transactions, Quicken sometimes attempts to fill in the name of the payee for you, as soon as you start typing. This is a feature known as QuickFill and it is discussed in detail tomorrow morning.

TIP   You can scroll through the QuickFill list by using the up and down arrow keys.

If you make a mistake while entering a name, you can go back and fix it. It's the usual routine: Click at the point where there is incorrect or missing information. Press Backspace if you need to delete characters to the *left* of the cursor. Press Delete if you need to delete characters to the *right* of the cursor. Or just begin typing to insert characters at the cursor.

After you finish entering your payee name, press Tab to advance to the next field. Notice that you will be skipping over the Clr column. This is the column where Quicken records whether a check has cleared your bank or not. You will work with the Clr column when you reconcile your checking account later tonight.

NOTE Keep in mind that at any time in the future, you can come back to any transaction and edit or correct information as needed. That's the beauty of an automated checkbook. No white-out, no cross-outs, and no headaches! However, if you do make a change, be sure to rerun reports that include the altered transaction.

Entering the Amount

Enter checks that you write or payments that you make in the Payment column. Enter deposits or other forms of money coming into your account in the Deposit column. Quicken helps you by placing the cursor in the appropriate column based on the transaction type you indicated in the Num column.

In this case, you need to enter a check amount, so your cursor goes to the Payment column. Type in the dollar amount, making sure you type in a decimal to separate cents from dollars. You do not need to type in punctuation such as the dollar sign or commas. Quicken will add these for you.

TIP If Quicken placed your cursor in the wrong column, you can press Tab to move to the other column, or type a negative sign in front of the amount and Quicken will automatically transfer the amount to the other column.

For now you can ignore the calculator icon in the amount fields; you will use that a bit later. After you enter the amount, press Tab to advance to the next field.

Choosing a Category

The true power of Quicken lies in the assignment of categories to identify where your money goes and where your money comes from. You can think of categories as labels placed on file folders. If you regularly file away receipts and other financial information in a stack of folders, you know the power of categories. Without a label on each folder, it would take you a long time to locate the information you want to use. Quicken uses the categories to which you assign individual transactions as a way of locating, sorting, and totaling financial information.

Take a look at the check you are now entering. What did it pay for? Common examples are items such as dry cleaning, food, rent, donations, or auto insurance. When you set up your first account in Quicken, the program automatically created a list of frequently used categories. If you went through the New User Setup tonight, the list of categories was somewhat tailored to your needs based on your answers to those personal questions.

By default, when you arrive on the Category field, Quicken displays the list of category names (see Figure 1.19). If the category list does not appear on your screen, click on the down arrow in the Category field. Scroll through the list and look for a category that best describes what this check paid for. To enter the category, click on it in the list or start typing the category name (QuickFill will complete the typing for you).

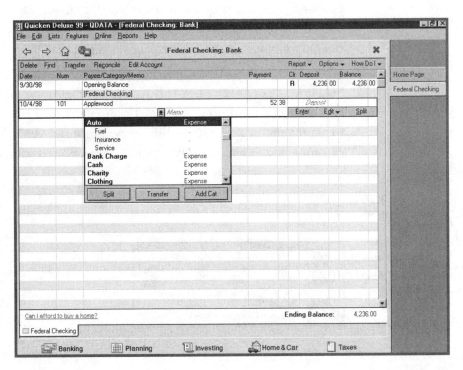

Figure 1.19

The Category List includes all the income and expense categories for classifying your transactions.

CAUTION

◆ ◆

Watch out for the Escape key! If you have a drop-down list open, pressing Esc just closes the drop-down list. However, if you're on a transaction field (with no drop-down list displayed), pressing Esc tells Quicken you want to close the current window without saving the transaction you're working on. Quicken does prompt you to save the transaction before closing the window and does allow you to cancel the Esc key, but it can still be a bit disconcerting.

◆ ◆

TIP

■ ■

If you want to erase what you've done in the current transaction and start over, click on the Edit button in the current transaction line and choose Restore.

■ ■

If you don't see the category you want to use (Dental, for example, is not on the list), you can add a category to the list as you enter your transaction. Category names can be up to 32 characters long. Just type the new category name in the category field of your transaction entry. When you press Tab to move to the next field, Quicken will ask if you wish to add this category to your master list (see Figure 1.20).

When you click on Yes to indicate you want to create a new category, the Set Up Category dialog box will appear (see Figure 1.21). If you don't have any changes or additional information to enter, you can just click on OK to accept the new category. Tomorrow morning, you'll learn how to use category groups and identify expense transactions as discretionary or not.

Figure 1.20

Uncheck the Prompt Before Creating New Categories check box if you don't want Quicken to confirm new category creation.

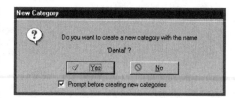

Figure 1.21

Quicken classifies new categories as income or expense based on how you entered the amount—as payment (expense) or deposit (income).

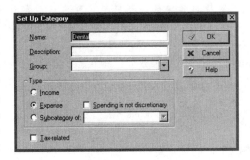

NOTE You may wish to make your new category part of a larger category. For example, you may want the new Dental category to be part of the larger category, Medical. To indicate that you want your new category to be a subcategory of an existing category, click on the Subcategory Of radio button (see Figure 1.22) and, from the drop-down list, select the existing category that will become the parent, if you will, of your new baby category. From that point forward, when you need to assign a payment to the category Dental, you need only type Dental. Quicken will find and fill in the full category name Medical:Dental for you.

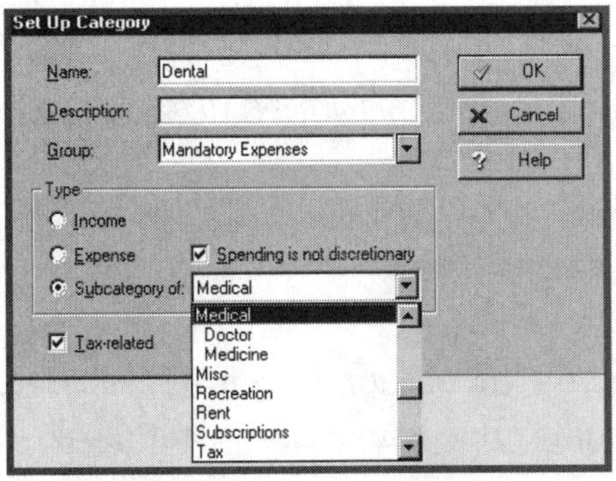

Figure 1.22

Subcategories allow you to break a category down into detailed items.

TIP You can even have subcategories of subcategories! A popular example is accounting for a vacation home. The category would be Vacation Home. One of the subcategories would be Utilities, which would have its own sub-subcategories such as Electric, Gas, and Water. Isn't Quicken's flexibility great?

Entering a Memo

The memo field in your register is optional (you can leave it blank). However, I recommend that you use the memo field to enter as much descriptive information as you can about the transaction. A memo can be up to 54 characters long.

Look at the check you are entering and think about descriptive words (other than the category name) that might describe the transaction. For example, if the check was for a birthday gift, the category would be Gift Given and the memo might be something like "Mom's Birthday."

Another good use for the memo field is documentation on your check for the payee. This is especially important when you have Quicken print your checks (this is covered tomorrow morning). For example, if the check is to the gas company, the category would be Utilities:Gas and the memo might be something like "A/C 987-5566-330."

Go ahead and enter the memo you've decided is appropriate for this transaction.

Recording a Transaction

Now that you have completed all the fields for this check transaction, you are ready to record the transaction in your Quicken register. Notice that the Balance column for this transaction is still blank. Press the up arrow. Note that you can even move up, off the transaction, but it is still not recorded (deducted from your account balance). Press the down arrow to move back to the check transaction line.

To record a transaction in the register, you can either click on the Enter button in the Transaction Toolbar or press Enter. Quicken will record the

transaction and place your cursor on the next line, ready for entry of another transaction. By default, Quicken places recorded transactions in date order. (Tomorrow morning, you will learn how to change the sort order.) Account balances beyond $99,999,999.99 display as asterisks (wouldn't that be a nice problem to have!). Negative balances display in a red color with a minus sign in front of the amount.

If you haven't done it yet, go ahead and record your first Quicken transaction!

NOTE When you advance to the next transaction, Quicken copies the date from the previous transaction. You can always change the date as noted earlier.

Working on Your Own

Pick out another single category check and enter it now. Refer to the past few pages as necessary to help you along. Press F1 Help to get instructions as you work. Do as many single-category checks as you can. Put the checks that paid for more than one category aside for now (you'll learn about them in the next section).

Splitting Transactions among Multiple Categories

Now, look through the pile of checks left and select a check that you used to pay for more than one type of expense. Here are some common examples of checks that paid for multiple expenses:

⚙ A credit card bill payment that includes charges for gasoline, food, clothing, and household items.

NOTE Note that you can create a Quicken account for a credit card and enter each transaction individually as you charge and then pay a group of transactions with a single check. You will explore credit card accounts in further detail tomorrow morning.

- A telephone bill payment that includes charges for your home phone line, your business fax line, and the computer modem line.

- A travel agent bill payment that includes charges for airfare, car rental, and hotel expenses.

- A check paid to a discount store such as Kmart for clothing, music, a book, and some bathroom towels.

- A check paid to an office supply store such as Staples for a work item (for which you'll be reimbursed) and personal items (such as notebooks for the kids).

As you can see, you can use categories to track as much detail as you need. If you don't need or want to know how much money you spend on books versus clothing, you do not need to assign multiple categories. You could just assign your trips to Kmart to a generic household category. But you will lose the detail when you try to budget and see where your money goes. And boy, does it go—you'd think it had legs and walked off by itself! I strongly recommend detailing all your transactions. Tomorrow, you will explore methods that take the drudgery out of this process and make it more automatic.

Quicken refers to the process of assigning a single transaction to multiple categories as *splitting* a transaction. To split a transaction among multiple categories, begin entering the transaction as you did before, starting with the date, the transaction number, the payee or payer, and the amount. When you get to the category field, click on the Split button in the Transaction Toolbar or press Ctrl+S.

The Split Transaction Window opens (see Figure 1.23). On each line you can choose a category, enter a memo, and enter the portion of the total check that applies to that category. Press Tab to move between fields and eventually to the next line. Quicken will keep a running balance at the bottom of the screen so that you can see how much you still have to apply to your categories.

Notice the buttons on the line below where you are working. The Next button moves your cursor down to the beginning of the next line. The Edit

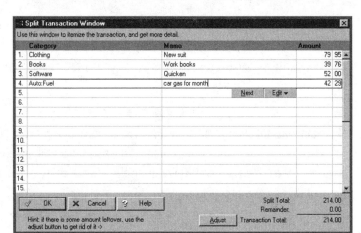

Figure 1.23

You can split a single transaction across as many as 30 different categories.

button displays a drop-down menu of choices. Insert places a new blank line above the current row. Delete erases the current row (note that Quicken does not have an Undo feature, so be careful!). Clear All blanks out of all split transaction rows.

Use the Adjust button at the bottom of the Split Transaction Window to have Quicken change the transaction total to equal the total of your split items. This feature saves you time when you don't know the total of the bills you are paying. For example, I get separate phone bills from the same telephone company. Instead of entering the total payment, I enter the detailed amounts in the Split Transaction Window and use Adjust to let Quicken add them up for me and enter it in the register!

TIP   Here are some Quick Keys that you might find helpful while working in the Split Transaction Window:

- To insert a line, press Ctrl+I.
- To delete a line, press Ctrl+D.
- To close the Split Transaction Window, press Ctrl+Enter.

Click on OK when you finish entering the split transaction information (or click on Cancel if you decide you don't want to use the splits).

Remember to record the transaction by clicking on the Enter button in the Transaction Toolbar, or by pressing Enter. If you try to leave the transaction without recording, Quicken will ask if you want to save the changes in the transaction (click on Yes to save).

NOTE If the amounts that you enter in the Split Transaction Window exceed the Transaction Total entered in the register, the overage amount does *not* appear in the Remainder line at the bottom of the screen. Instead, Quicken displays the overage amount as a red negative amount below your last split row.

If you need to undo a split transaction and assign just one single category to that transaction, just click on the X button in the transaction line of the register (see Figure 1.24). When you click on the X button, Quicken asks if you want to clear all split lines. Click on Yes to delete all split lines. You will then be able to assign a single category name. Be sure to record your updated transaction.

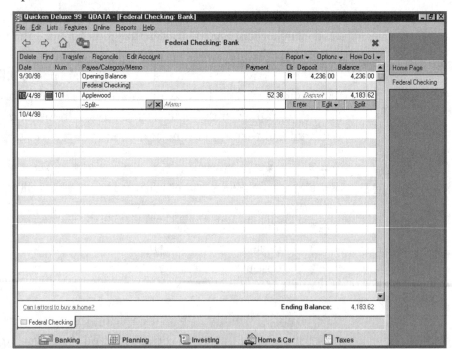

Figure 1.24

Click on the green check mark in the Split field to view the Split Transaction Window. Click on the red X to delete all split lines.

Making Changes

Before you enter any more transactions, first review how to make a change to a transaction and correct errors. Get into the habit of reviewing your work, checking for mistakes or missed items at the end of each data entry session. This extra step will help you learn Quicken faster, but even more importantly, it will reduce your work when it's time to reconcile your account to the bank statement.

Editing Transactions

Accidentally entered the wrong check number? Forgot to split a transaction? Entered a check as a deposit? No problem. It's easy in Quicken to edit a transaction. Just click on the transaction field to be edited. Either type over the existing information, insert new text, or select a new item from the drop-down list.

If, while editing a transaction, you decide not to record the changes, you can revert to the prior unchanged transaction by clicking on the Edit button on the Transaction Toolbar and choosing Restore Transaction. To keep your edits, press Enter or click on the Enter button to record your updated transaction.

■ ■

TIP   Right-click on any transaction field to view a shortcut menu of editing commands such as Cut, Copy, Paste, Move, and Void.

■ ■

Voiding Transactions

Voiding a transaction removes the amount from your balance total, but retains all other details of the transaction being voided. You may need to void a transaction to:

✪ Stop payment on a check.

✪ Handle a lost or missing check.

✪ Reprint a misprinted check (if you use Quicken to print checks).

When you void a transaction, you retain a record of that transaction without an amount affecting your account balance. If you need to permanently erase a transaction from your register, see the next section, "Deleting Transactions."

To void a transaction, click on the Edit button on the Transaction Toolbar and choose Void Transaction. Quicken enters the text **VOID** in front of the Payee name, removes the transaction amount, and places the letter *R* in the Clr field (reconciled). To record the voided transaction, click on the Enter button. To revert to the original transaction and remove the voiding, click on the Edit button and choose Restore Transaction—before you enter it. Once you've clicked on enter, you'll need to edit the transaction by hand if you want to restore it.

TIP ■■■■■■■■■■■■■■■■■■■■■■■■■■■■■■■■■■■■■■

Press Ctrl+V to void the current transaction.

■■■■■■■■■■■■■■■■■■■■■■■■■■■■■■■■■■■■■■

Deleting Transactions

If you inadvertently recorded a transaction that you should never have entered, you can delete the transaction. Deleting a transaction permanently and irreversibly removes all record of that transaction. Do not confuse this function with the Void Transaction function covered previously.

To delete a transaction, click on any field in the transaction to be deleted. Look it over and make sure you want to remove the transaction permanently. Click on the Edit button on the Transaction Toolbar and choose Delete Transaction. Quicken asks you to confirm the deletion. If you want to permanently delete the selected transaction, click on Yes. If you don't want to delete it, click on No.

Working on Your Own

Pull out another multicategory check and enter it now. Refer to the past few pages for guidance as needed. Then, enter all your multicategory checks. Don't forget to check your bank statement for ATM transactions, deposits, and electronic funds transfers. Enter these too. No need to enter bank service fees or bank account interest earned yet (you'll do this in the next

section). When you finish entering these transactions, you will be ready to balance your checkbook and reconcile it to your bank statement!

Reconciling Your Bank Account

You may dread reconciling your checking account and put it off to the last minute (or not even do it at all!). Or you may be the type who heads right for the checkbook and calculator the minute the bank statement comes in the mail, and never gives up until your account balances right to the penny.

No matter how you used to respond to bank statements that came in the mail, from here on you will not only enjoy the experience of reconciling your bank account, you will be able to do it easily, swiftly, and always right to the penny!

You just created a new checking account with an opening balance identical to the one on your last bank statement. Then you entered all the checks, deposits, and other transactions such as ATM withdrawals and electronic fund transfers. Now the ending balance in Quicken should match the ending balance as it appears on your bank statement, except for bank charges and interest earned. Never fear if it doesn't! Quicken's Reconciliation feature will help you find the difference quickly and painlessly!

When you're ready, click on the Reconcile button on the Register Toolbar. The Reconcile Bank Statement dialog box appears (see Figure 1.25).

Figure 1.25

Quicken enters your beginning account balance for you.

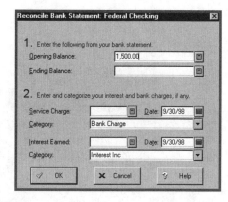

Completing the Initial Reconciliation Dialog Box

In the Reconcile Bank Statement dialog box, compare the beginning balance to the opening balance on your statement. There should be no discrepancy here.

Enter the ending balance from your bank statement. Enter the bank service charge, if such a charge was applied to your account, and adjust the date so that it agrees with the date on which the charge was assessed. Enter interest earned on the account, and adjust that date as well. Then click on OK. The Reconcile Bank Statement window appears (see Figure 1.26).

Presto! You Balanced to the Penny!

All the checks and other withdrawals from your register are listed on the left side of the Reconcile Bank Statement window, in the Payments and Checks column. Deposits are listed at the right. Check off only the items that appear on your bank statement by clicking on each item. You can also

Figure 1.26

Check off checks and deposits that have cleared your bank by clicking on each item. Your goal is to get a 0.00 difference in the bottom right corner of the screen.

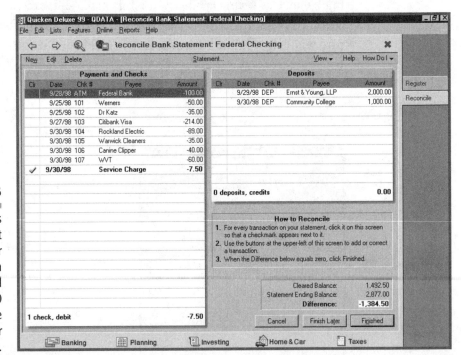

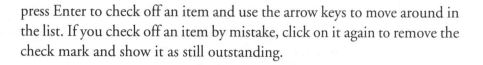

press Enter to check off an item and use the arrow keys to move around in the list. If you check off an item by mistake, click on it again to remove the check mark and show it as still outstanding.

■ ■
TIP By default, Quicken lists your checks in check number order. But what if you want to see them in order of the dates on which you issued them? You can change the ordering of items on the reconciliation screen by clicking on View and selecting Sort by Date.
■ ■

If an amount is wrong, click on the item, and then click on the Edit button at the top of the bank statement screen to go right to the register. Make the necessary change in the register, and then click on the Enter button to record your change. Click on the Return To Reconcile button to go back to the reconciliation screen.

If an item appears on your statement that isn't in your register (I constantly forget to record ATM withdrawals in my account register), click on the New button. You'll be taken to the register where you can enter a new item, click on the Enter button, and then click on the Return To Reconcile button. The edited item will be checked off in the Reconcile screen for you.

■ ■
TIP The statement ending balance shows at the bottom right corner of the reconciliation screen. If you realize that you entered this number incorrectly, you can change it without having to cancel the reconciliation and start over again. Click on the Statement button at the top of the reconciliation screen. Quicken will take you back to the dialog box where you entered your bank statement balance, and you can change the amount.
■ ■

If you have finished checking all items, the Difference at the bottom right corner of your reconciliation screen should be 0.00. If this is the case, pat yourself on the back and click on Finished. If your difference is not 0.00, you need to go back through your bank statement carefully and compare each item to the items checked on this screen. Look at the amounts and make sure everything agrees. There *will* be a discrepancy on this screen if the difference at the bottom does not equal 0.00. When you find the discrepancy, make the appropriate changes and your difference should balance out to the penny!

NOTE   If you still can't find the discrepancy, Quicken allows you to make a balance adjustment. A balance adjustment means that Quicken will create a transaction in your account to force your register to agree with the bank statement. Although you shouldn't do this every month or for significant amounts, it is helpful for small dollar amounts. For example, say your account is off by $1.50 and you've looked everywhere for the difference. Rather than staying up another hour looking for such a small amount, you can let Quicken enter a Balance Adjustment for you.

If you have to get up and leave your reconciliation before you finish it, click on Finish Later and you can return to the task when you have time. Clicking on the Cancel button cancels the entire reconciliation and you'll have to start over again.

When you click on Finished, you will have a chance to produce a reconciliation report. This report shows a summary of your reconciled transactions, along with a list of outstanding checks and deposits. Printing the report is optional.

If you have several bank statements to reconcile in order to get up to date, proceed through the stack one at a time, clicking on Finish after each one.

Closing and Backing Up Your Files

To close Quicken properly, choose File, Exit or click on the Close button (the X) in the upper right corner of your program window.

There is no save feature in Quicken because the program saves your information constantly, while you are working. This means that if you experience a power failure or other untimely shutdown of your computer, your Quicken data should be intact.

There is no excuse, however, for not backing up your files regularly. If your data file is saved on your hard drive and your hard drive crashes (I frequently tell my computer students that a hard drive that hasn't crashed is a hard drive that hasn't crashed *yet*), your data will be lost. Protect yourself from headaches and wasted time recreating lost data by taking advantage of Quicken's backup feature.

By default, Quicken prompts you to back up your data every third time you exit the program. When the prompt appears (see Figure 1.27), place your backup disk in your disk drive and click on OK.

What's Next?

You've done a great job. Believe it or not, you now know the core of Quicken. All the other types of accounts such as savings, credit card accounts, assets, and loans use the same register format and features. You've learned how to create a checking account, enter common checkbook transactions such as checks, deposits, ATM withdrawals, and electronic funds transfers. And you know how to get help when you need it from the Quicken Help system.

Get a good night's rest and tomorrow you'll:

- ✪ Write and print electronic checks.

- ✪ Learn how to put Quicken to work for you by using QuickFill, Memorized Transactions, and Quick Entry.

- ✪ Learn how to schedule transactions and use the Financial Calculator.

- ✪ Learn more shortcuts, tips, and tricks in the register.

- ✪ Create other types of accounts such as cash, assets, and liabilities.

- ✪ Use the Financial Address Book.

- ✪ Track your home inventory.

- ✪ Customize Quicken to better meet your needs.

Sweet dreams!

Figure 1.27

You will be prompted to back up your data every third time you exit the program.

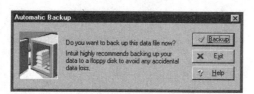

Automating Your Account

- ✪ Saving Time by Writing Computer Checks
- ✪ Tracking Your Paycheck
- ✪ Scheduling Future Transactions
- ✪ Recording Your Assets in Quicken
- ✪ Using Quicken's Home Inventory Feature

Good morning! Depending on how much data entry you performed last night, you may have spent the night dreaming of check registers, categories, and calculators! Now that you've mastered the basics of entering transactions into your Quicken register, you're ready to move on.

In this morning's session, you'll set up all your basic financial information in various accounts, arrange for Quicken to remind you of important events (financial and otherwise), and learn how to customize Quicken to better meet your needs. Specifically, this session covers:

- Writing and printing computerized checks

- Using QuickFill and Memorized Transactions

- Tracking your paycheck details

- Scheduling transactions and setting up reminders

- Speeding up your work with more tricks, tips, and shortcuts

- Using Quick Entry

- Creating other types of financial accounts

- Using the Financial Address Book

- Taking an inventory at home

- Customizing Quicken

So grab your cup of coffee, send the kids off to their friends' house, and give your spouse that list of household chores that need to be done today. You'll be a Quicken Queen or King by lunch.

Saving Time by Writing Computer Checks

I used to spend two hours every other week doing the bills by hand. Sorting them out, going back to files trying to verify the proper amount to pay, and then writing out the checks by hand. Now, with Quicken, it takes less than an hour. If you've been handwriting checks at bill-paying time, you're going to love this feature in Quicken. It will easily cut your bill-paying time in half.

Quicken's check-writing feature not only prints the checks for your signature, it automatically enters the transactions in your register and updates your account balance. When it comes time to reconcile your account to the bank statement, there is no chance that the amount can be wrong. Your cancelled check will match the computerized check register entry.

Ordering Preprinted Checks

To use the check-writing feature in Quicken, you need special computerized checks. You can order your checks from the makers of Quicken (Intuit) or from any forms dealer. See the note for some mail order companies and prices. Generally, computerized checks do cost more than manual checks. You will need to weigh the benefits of saved time and improved register accuracy (most bank reconciliation problems stem from manual entries) against the additional check cost.

NOTE This chapter covers how to order checks from Intuit. However, you can order computer checks from any forms dealer who carries the Quicken check format. Some forms companies that I have used in the past include Nebbs, Quill, RapidForms, and Designer Checks. Prices may be less from these other dealers. For example, my last batch of 250 wallet-sized laser printer checks from Designer Checks was $24.95, whereas Intuit charged $39.95.

TIP

FIND IT
ONLINE

Want to save even more money? Believe it or not, if you have a laser printer or an inkjet printer, you can now design and print your own checks on blank security check paper. Software such as VersaCheck ($19.99 from Mips, **http://www.mipsdia.com**) and MICR ($299 from Nelco, **http://www.nicrchecks.com**) allow you to print checks whenever you need them! With VersaCheck, you print the checks first and then use them as needed with Quicken. With MICR, the software is integrated with Quicken and prints the check while filling in your data from Quicken. Either way, you certainly will save money in the long run.

Regardless of where you get your checks, you will need to provide the following information:

- Usually a voided check that the forms company can use as a sample from which to create your new computer checks. The magnetic MICR codes at the bottom of the check are the most important part the company needs to reproduce correctly.

- The bank name, address, phone number, and fractional number (looks like a fraction—say, 22-3/999—and usually appears under the bank name).

- Your name, address, phone number, and account number.

- Usually, you will be asked to make any changes directly on the sample voided check (for example, you could cross out your phone number if you didn't want it to appear on your computer checks).

- The starting check number (choose something very different from your manual checkbook, such as 3001 (four digits) if your current checks are 101 (three digits). It is perfectly OK to have two sets of check numbers hitting a single account. The bank will not have a problem with this.

- Type of printer (make and model).

- Laserjet or inkjet forms (separate pages) or continuous feed paper (computer paper fanfold).

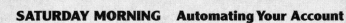

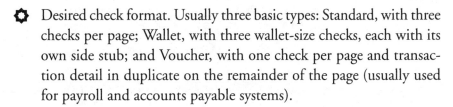

❖ Desired check format. Usually three basic types: Standard, with three checks per page; Wallet, with three wallet-size checks, each with its own side stub; and Voucher, with one check per page and transaction detail in duplicate on the remainder of the page (usually used for payroll and accounts payable systems).

❖ Item number, color, and quantity (from the forms company catalog).

■■

TIP Consider buying the matching envelopes too! You can get envelopes with specially designed clear windows so you won't have to address the envelope by hand. Be sure to get the envelopes that match the check format (standard, wallet, or voucher). Just print, sign, stuff, and stamp. Then go use that saved time to do something fun.

■■

To order from Intuit, you can go the old-fashioned manual route, or if you have access to the Internet, order online. Included in your copy of Quicken Deluxe is a catalog called "Checks Forms & Supplies." Browse through and fill out the order form (in the middle). You can call your order in using the 800 number at the top of the order form. Or, if you have a fax machine, you can fax your order directly to Intuit. Phone, fax, and online orders must be paid for by credit card. Otherwise, write out a check and mail it to Intuit in the envelope provided (no postage necessary).

If you have access to the Internet, follow these steps to order online (the online features of Quicken are covered in depth this afternoon):

1. From the menu bar, choose Features, Bills, Order Checks. After you sign on to the Internet, the Intuit MarketPlace page appears.

2. Click on Shop to enter the online store. The IntuitMarket storefront displays a graphical listing of software and supplies such as checks and envelopes (see Figure 2.1).

3. Click on Checks. The site asks if you've shopped here before or not. The IntuitMarket requires all shoppers to register for security purposes. Click on the number that applies to you. If you're a new shopper, a wizard will lead you through the registration process. Be

Figure 2.1

The Intuit
MarketPlace lets
you order checks,
supplies, and Intuit
software online.

sure to write down your password and store it in a safe, memorable place. If you lose your password, you can send e-mail to Intuit's support folks and request a new password.

4. Select your check type (see Figure 2.2) by clicking on the graphic.

5. Select the printer type, design, color, and quantity from the respective drop-down list fields (see Figure 2.3). Click on the Design Choices button to get detailed descriptions of your check design options. When you've made your selections, click on Next to continue.

6. Intuit shows you your order specifications. Click on Make Change to change or on Next to specify the Imprint information.

7. Read over the explanations, and scroll down to enter the bank routing number (first part of the MICR code), account number, number of signature lines, and first check number. Because Intuit

Figure 2.2

Click on Design Choices for a description of each check type.

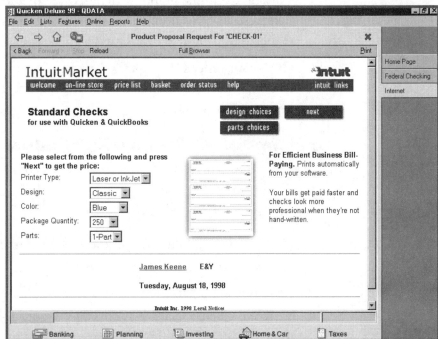

Figure 2.3

When choosing design, color, and quantity, refer back to the catalog for prices.

has such a large database of bank MICR codes, there is no need to send a sample check.

8. Click on Next and Quicken shows you a sample check with your information entered. Scroll down to change how your name and address and your bank's name and address appear on the check. You can even add a free logo or monogram!

 ■■■
TIP Some printers require you to load your check paper upside down in reverse order (the printer takes from the top of the pile). If your printer does this, let Quicken do the work for you by ordering "Reverse Collate" checks (step 8 online, or line 2 on the order form in catalog).

■■■

9. Click on Save Changes to see any changes you made reflected in the sample check.

10. Click on Add to Basket to review what's in your shopping basket. Click on Continue shopping to purchase other items, Empty basket to remove all items from your basket, or Pay to enter payment information and complete your order.

11. Once your order is complete, you can click on the X to close the Internet QuickTab. Choose Online, Disconnect to close the connection to the Internet.

Opening the Write Checks Window

You can open the Write Checks window by doing any of the following (my favorite is the first):

✿ Press Ctrl+W.

✿ Click on the Banking icon on the Activity Bar and choose Write a Check to Print.

✿ From the menu bar, choose Features, Bills, Write Checks.

Once the Write Checks window is open (see Figure 2.4), you can always click on the Register QuickTab to return to check writing.

TIP

■ ■

If, after trying the Write Checks window, you prefer to work in the register, you can. As mentioned last night, you just need to specify Print in the Num field. After you print your checks, Quicken will replace the word "Print" with the appropriate check number.

■ ■

CAUTION

◆ ◆

Like the Register window, the Write Checks window will show multiple tabs when you have multiple accounts. Be sure you are working on the correct account by clicking on its tab. In Figure 2.4, the checks being written will post to the Federal Checking account.

◆ ◆

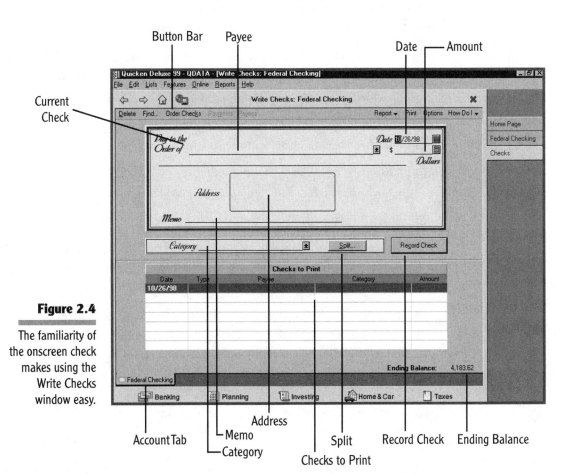

Figure 2.4

The familiarity of the onscreen check makes using the Write Checks window easy.

Take a moment to review the parts of the Write Checks window. Here is a list of the key areas:

- **Button bar**. Provides easy access to commonly used functions such as Delete, Find, Print, Options, and Report.

- **Date**. Same as the date field in your register, complete with the mini-calendar.

- **Pay to the Order of**. Same as the Payee field in your register, complete with QuickFill.

- **Amount**. Same as the Payment field in your register, complete with the mini-calculator. Note that once you tab off this field, Quicken fills in the amount words on the line below.

- **Address**. If you intend to use a window envelope (highly recommended!), enter the payee's address here. Quicken saves addresses so you can edit or access them via the Financial Address Book (covered later in this chapter).

- **Memo**. Same as the Memo field in your register.

- **Category**. Same as the Category field in your register, complete with QuickFill.

- **Split**. Same as the Split function in the register.

- **Record Check**. Same as the Enter function in the register. Check data is saved, posted in the Checks to Print listing, and entered in the register with the Num type Print.

- **Checks to Print**. A convenient listing of all checks to print. You can also page up and down to view the checks to be printed.

- **Ending Balance**. As you record checks, Quicken updates the ending balance for this account and displays it here.

- **Account Tab**. Allows you to select an account from which to write checks.

TIP

To quickly view the first check written, press Home three times when you're on the Write Checks page. To view the last check written, press End three times.

Writing Your First Check

Now I realize that you probably don't have the proper check paper yet, but that's OK. What you will do for this exercise is print a few dummy checks on plain white paper so you know how to write Quicken checks. Grab your current checkbook (checks that haven't been entered into Quicken yet), and get started.

NOTE

If you do have the proper check paper, grab three bills you need to pay and get ready to start saving time!

Follow these steps to write a Quicken check:

1. If it's not already on the screen, open the Write Checks window by pressing Ctrl+W.

2. Select the appropriate Account tab so that the checks you write get deducted from the proper account.

3. Enter the date or select the date from the mini-calendar. Press Tab to move to the next field.

4. Enter the payee or select the name from the drop-down list. If QuickFill found the payee in the list, the amount, memo, and category lines are completed when you press Tab (see Figure 2.5). If you have no changes, you can click on Record Check and go on to the next check. What a time saver!

5. Enter or edit the Amount field as needed. Use the mini-calculator as needed. Press Tab to move to the next field.

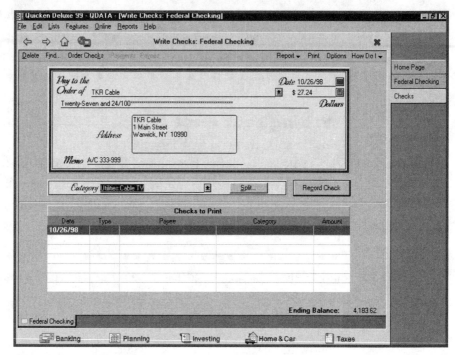

Figure 2.5

The more you use Quicken, the less work you have.

6. If you want to use a window envelope, click in the Address box and enter the mailing address for this payment. Press Tab at the end of each line to move to the next line within the address box. (You can go from line to line within the address box by pressing Enter, but Tab is safer—if you press Enter after the last line, Quicken will send the check off to the print queue and you'll have to fish it out again to enter a memo or category. If you get in the habit of using Tab, you won't have to worry about where you are.) Tab to the next field. This step is optional.

TIP Save even more time! If you want the name of the payee to appear on the first line of the Address box, just type an apostrophe. Quicken copies the name down for you! What a deal.

7. If you want more information on the check, enter a memo (for example, enter a customer number or invoice number as it appears on the bill you are paying). This step is optional.

8. Enter a single category or select one from the drop-down list. Or if you need to assign multiple categories to this transaction, click on Split and complete the Split Transaction dialog box. And yes, you can create a new category from this field the same way you did last night from the register's category field.

9. Review the check as it appears on your screen. If it looks OK, click on Record Check. Quicken displays the check in the Checks to Print listing (see Figure 2.6) and enters it into your register for that account with the Num field set to Print. A new blank check appears ready for action and a To Print field indicates the total amount of the checks to be printed.

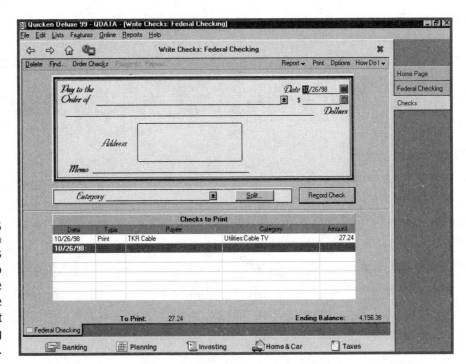

Figure 2.6

Quicken displays a total of checks to be printed at the bottom of the screen, to the left of the Ending Balance amount.

TIP

To see the last check written, press Page Up or click on the desired check in the Checks To Print listing.

To view the register and see the automatic check entry, click on the Register tab and select the proper Account tab. As shown in Figure 2.7, the amount of checks to be printed has already been deducted from your account, even though you have not yet printed or sent the checks. This is the same as writing out a check by hand, logging it into your register, and leaving the check in your checkbook.

Go ahead and enter two more checks. When you are done, you'll print them out.

Setting Quicken Up to Print Checks

Before you can print checks, you need to let Quicken know something about your printer and the style of checks that you are using. Use the Check

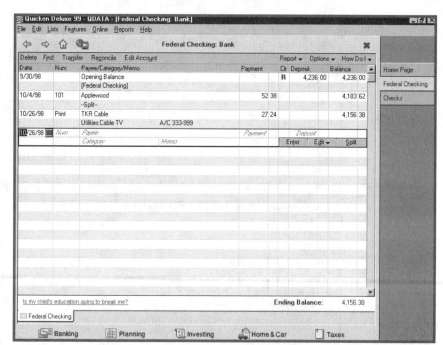

Figure 2.7

Checks to be printed appear in the register in date order with the word "Print" in the Num field.

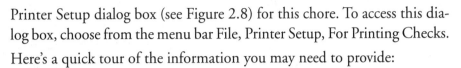

Printer Setup dialog box (see Figure 2.8) for this chore. To access this dialog box, choose from the menu bar File, Printer Setup, For Printing Checks. Here's a quick tour of the information you may need to provide:

- **Printer**. Select from the drop-down list the printer you intend to use.

- **Page-oriented**. Click on this button if your checks are on separate pages.

- **Continuous**. Click on this button if your check pages are connected together in a fanfold.

- **Check style**. Select from the drop-down list the check style: Wallet, Standard, or Voucher.

- **Partial Page**. Click on the button that best describes how your printer allows you to print a single check (you may need to consult the printer manual).

- **Partial Page Source**. Select from the drop-down list where the partial page will be. Options may include Manual feed, Upper tray, Envelope manual feed, or Envelope—they vary by printer.

- **Full Page Source**. Select from the drop-down list where a full page will be: Manual feed, Upper tray, Envelope manual feed, or Envelope—or whatever works for your printer.

- **Font**. Click on this button to change the font settings for your check printing. Default is 9-pt Regular Arial.

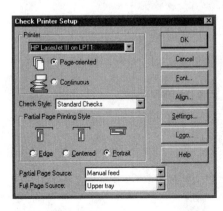

Figure 2.8

Specify the default to print checks in the Check Printer Setup dialog box.

⚙ **Align.** Use Align to adjust the print on checks (usually not necessary).

⚙ **Settings.** Click on this button to change normal printer settings such as paper size and orientation (usually not necessary).

⚙ **Logo.** Click on this button to select a bitmap (.bmp) file with your logo to be printed on the checks. Cool, huh?

⚙ **Help.** Click on Help for more details on what to do in this box.

For the purposes of this morning's example, make sure the printer name is correct, choose Page-oriented, Standard checks, and accept the remaining default settings. Click on OK.

Printing Checks

Return to the Write Checks window (click on the Checks QuickTab), and click on Print or press Ctrl+P. Quicken displays the Select Checks to Print dialog box (see Figure 2.9).

Follow these steps to print all three checks:

1. Accept the First Check Number as 1001 (or your real first check number if you have the proper check paper).

2. In the Print box, leave All Checks selected.

3. Leave the Check Style set to Standard checks.

4. Leave the Checks on First Page set to Three.

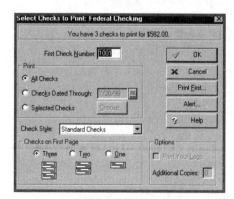

Figure 2.9

You can select to print all or just a few checks.

5. Click on OK. Quicken prints the three checks on one page and displays a dialog box asking if the checks printed properly or not.

6. If some of the checks did not print correctly, enter the check number of the first check that did *not* print properly in the Did Checks Print OK? dialog box and click on OK. Quicken will allow you to reprint those checks. Otherwise, you'll be returned to the Write Checks window.

7. Click on the Register tab to see the check numbers assigned to each of the three transactions (see Figure 2.10).

8. If you entered these transactions from your manual checkbook, take the time now to change the check numbers to the actual check numbers. Be sure to record each transaction change as you work.

9. If you had the proper check paper, and the checks printed OK, rejoice! I'll bet you never knew paying the bills could be so much fun!

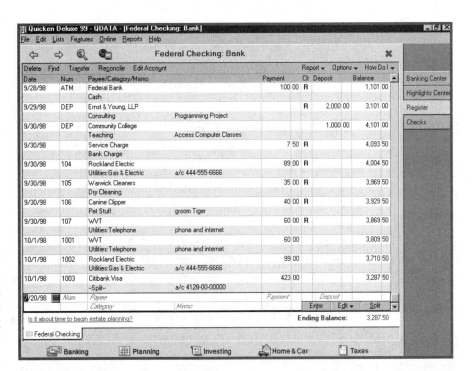

Figure 2.10

Quicken enters the corresponding check numbers automatically.

Automating Data Entry

Quicken has excelled over the past decade as a personal financial application mainly because it really can save you time and do a better job of tracking your finances than a manual method. But you have to know how to use Quicken's time-saving features to realize that time savings. In this section, you'll explore tips, tricks, and traps of the following:

- QuickFill
- Memorized transactions
- Scheduled transactions
- Quicken Reminders
- Financial Calendar

Understanding QuickFill

In the work you did last night and this morning, you saw the power of QuickFill. QuickFill is the feature in Quicken that watches what you do and keeps a list of your transactions. As you type in the Payee field of a check or in the register, QuickFill scans its list and displays matching transactions—completing the payee field for you. As you tab off the Payee field, QuickFill also fills in the other fields: amount, category (including any splits), and memo. You can edit and change any of the information provided by QuickFill. When you record the transaction, QuickFill replaces the entry for that payee with your new information. For example, if you had an ATM transaction in the QuickFill list for the payee Cash and changed the category from Misc. to Travel, the QuickFill list would list one entry for Cash with a category of Travel.

NOTE The first time you enter the Payee's name into Quicken, be sure to spell it exactly as you want QuickFill to remember it. One nice feature in Quicken Deluxe 99 is that Quicken automatically capitalizes the first letter of new payee entries.

You can control the way QuickFill works and even disable QuickFill if you'd like by setting certain options. To set QuickFill options, choose Edit, Options, Register from the menu bar. The Register Options dialog box appears. Select the QuickFill tab (see Figure 2.11). For the QuickFill feature to remember and fill in information for you, both the Complete Fields Using Previous Entries and the Auto Memorize New Transactions check boxes must be checked. Click on Help to learn more about the choices you can make here. Click on OK to save your changes or Cancel to close without saving. In the next section, you will learn how to edit the QuickFill list and teach Quicken a trick or two.

Memorizing Transactions

But what if you need Quicken to remember two transactions to the same payee, but with different amounts, categories, or memos? For example, maybe you get gas from Bill's Sunoco and also pay Bill's Sunoco to do your oil change every three months. QuickFill only remembers the last transaction with Bill's Sunoco.

Enter another great feature in Quicken: Memorized Transactions. Yes, you can have your cake and eat it too! Memorized transactions always reappear just as you asked Quicken to memorize them. And you can have multiple memorized transactions to the same payee.

So why have QuickFill? Well, QuickFill is a great tool for new users. Without you doing anything, right out of the box, Quicken starts doing work for you. Then, after you have the knack of how things work, you can

Figure 2.11

If you'd prefer not to see the drop-down lists during field data entry, uncheck the Drop-Down Lists on Field Entry check box.

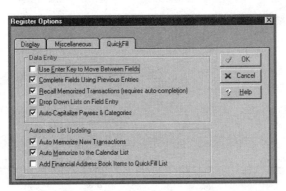

always turn QuickFill off. The downside of turning QuickFill off is that you will have to remember to memorize transactions that you may need to reuse in the future.

A safe compromise is to leave QuickFill on and learn how to turn QuickFill entries into memorized transactions, how to memorize new transactions, and how to clean up old, unused items on your QuickFill/Memorized Transaction List. And that is what you'll learn next.

Using the QuickFill and Memorized Transaction List

Quicken stores all the QuickFill and memorized transactions in a single list called the Memorized Transaction List. Just press Ctrl+T to open the Memorized Transaction List (see Figure 2.12). Familiar window layout, huh? Take a moment to review the Button bar, column headings, and items at the very bottom of the window.

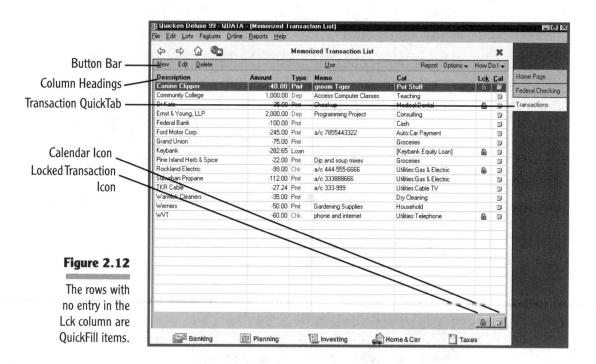

Figure 2.12

The rows with no entry in the Lck column are QuickFill items.

Because you haven't memorized any transactions yet, all the items listed in Figure 2.12 are QuickFill items. Unless otherwise noted, the features discussed here work identically for QuickFill and memorized transactions. For simplicity's sake, I will refer to them from now on as *memorized transactions,* only using QuickFill to point out a difference.

To enter a new memorized transaction here, use the New button on the Button bar. However, it is much easier to memorize transactions as you work.

To edit or change any one of these items, highlight the row and click on Edit in the Button bar. The Edit Memorized Transaction dialog box appears (see Figure 2.13). Change any items as needed and then click on OK to save your changes.

■ ■

TIP The Address button only works if the transaction is a Print Check (a check to be written in Quicken).

■ ■

● ●

NOTE The Amount field in the Edit Memorized Transaction dialog box is grayed out only for split transactions. To adjust the amount of a split transaction, you must click on the Split button (this opens the regular Split Transaction Window) and change the individual amounts. Use the Adjust button at the bottom of the Split Transaction Window as needed to adjust the overall transaction total. Click on OK to update the grayed out Amount field.

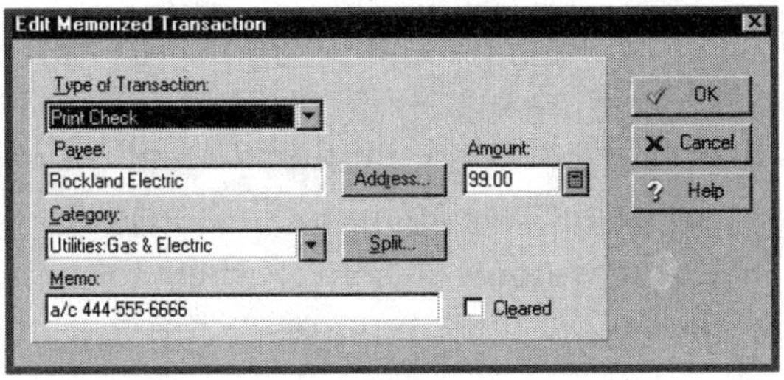

● ●

Figure 2.13

The next time you use QuickFill or a memorized transaction, Quicken will recall your edited transaction.

Sometimes you no longer need a memorized transaction (for example, if you stop using a vendor, or you pay off a debt). To delete a transaction from the list, select it and then click on the Delete button on the Button bar. After you confirm the deletion, Quicken removes the transaction from the memorized list, but not from your register.

To use a particular transaction in the currently active Register or Write Checks screen, select the transaction and click on the Use button in the Button bar.

◆ ◆

CAUTION Before you select a memorized transaction to use, make sure your cursor is not blinking in an existing transaction you want to keep. If the cursor is on a transaction, Quicken will replace that transaction with the memorized transaction you selected. If this happens by accident, just click on Edit, Restore from the Transaction Toolbar before you record the transaction. This will make the entry revert to its original state.

◆ ◆

The Report button lists all the times you used a memorized transaction in your register. This can be helpful if you are not sure whether to keep or delete a memorized transaction. First select the transaction line, and then click on the Report button. Quicken displays the report onscreen. This report feature can also be used to list all the transactions for a particular payee, but there are better ways to accomplish that in Quicken Reports. You will learn more about reports Sunday morning.

By default, Quicken memorizes transactions as unlocked QuickFill entries. You can at any time lock a QuickFill entry, thereby turning it into a memorized transaction. To do so, click in the Lck column for the desired transaction. To lock a group of transactions, select the rows with your mouse and then click on the Lock button at the bottom of the window. For Figure 2.14, I selected several noncontiguous rows by holding the Ctrl key down while clicking on rows. Then I clicked on the Lock button at the bottom of the window to convert these former QuickFill items to memorized transactions.

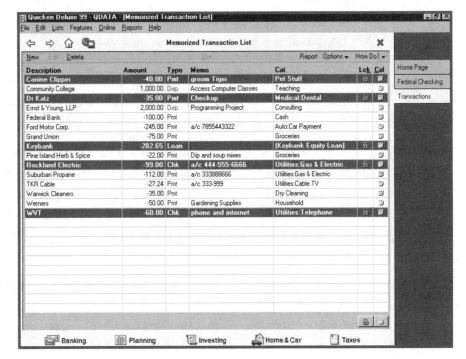

Figure 2.14

Lock in the transactions that you expect to use in the future.

The Calendar icon allows a transaction to be listed in the Financial Calendar. The Financial Calendar is covered later this morning. For now, just know that you can click in the Cal column for any transaction to display or remove the Calendar icon. To work with many rows at once, select the rows with your mouse and then click on the Calendar icon at the bottom of the window.

TIP

To view only the memorized transactions and not the QuickFills, choose Options, View Locked Items Only.

Memorizing Transactions on the Fly

Most seasoned users of Quicken memorize transactions as they work. Whether you are in a register or in the Write Checks window, the process and result is the same. Try entering one from your current checkbook now.

Click on the Register QuickTab and enter a transaction from your checkbook that recurs each month or quarter (such as rent or a car payment). Enter the transaction as usual, and then—before recording the transaction—press Ctrl+M. Quicken displays a window explaining that this transaction is about to be memorized. Click on OK to confirm memorization, or on Cancel to exit without memorizing.

NOTE If the transaction already exists as a locked transaction in the Memorized Transaction List, Quicken displays a second window asking if you want to replace that transaction with this newer one or add another memorized transaction to the same payee to the list. You can also choose Cancel at this point to exit without memorizing anything.

You can also select an entered transaction from your register or Write Checks screen, and then press Ctrl+M. For transactions with multiple category splits, Quicken asks if you want to memorize the split items as percentages. In most cases, you will not want to memorize the split items as percentages.

Using Memorized Transactions

Now that you've memorized a transaction, how do you use it? Most of the time you will simply begin entering your transaction and let Quicken fill in the rest, just as you do with any transaction in which QuickFill takes over.

NOTE For auto-completion of memorized transactions to work, the Complete Fields Using Previous Entries and Recall Memorized Transactions check boxes in the Register Options dialog box must be checked, although Auto Memorize New Transactions can be unchecked.

Remember that you can override any memorized transaction details with different information. However, the next time you recall the changed transaction, it will appear as you originally memorized it.

Removing a Memorized Transaction

There may be times when you want to remove a transaction entirely from the Memorized Transaction List. Perhaps you no longer do business with a company and that company name keeps coming up when you try to enter a similarly named company in your register. Or maybe you entered a name incorrectly and the misspelled name keeps appearing when you try to enter the name.

To remove a transaction from the Memorized Transaction List (and thus from the QuickFill feature), follow these steps:

1. Open the Memorized Transaction List (Ctrl+T).

2. Click on the transaction you want to remove.

3. Click on the Delete button at the top of the list. A dialog box will appear, telling you you are about to remove a transaction.

4. Click on OK in the dialog box. The transaction will be removed from your Memorized Transaction List.

Removing a transaction from the Memorized Transaction List doesn't affect any of the transactions already in your register.

TIP Plan to review your Memorized Transaction List once a year, lock and unlock transactions as needed, and clear out any unused items. Quicken can help you keep the list up to date if you set a special program option. To set this option, choose from the menu bar Edit, Options, Quicken Program. Click on the General tab (see Figure 2.15) and check the Remove Memorized Transactions Not Used in Last check box. Then enter a number into the Months box. I keep mine set at 13 months—this way once-a-year payments don't expire right before I need them. Note that this feature only works on unlocked QuickFill transactions. Your memorized transactions will not be affected.

Figure 2.15

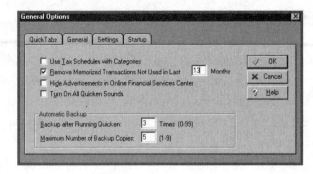

Let Quicken
maintain your
QuickFill list by
setting the Remove
option and
specifying the
number of months.

Tracking Your Paycheck

Paychecks are about the most common transactions to split out and memorize. They happen frequently, at a set time, and usually for a set amount. Intuit recognized the need to automate paycheck data entry and tracking and created the new Paycheck wizard. So get out your paystub, one of your spouse's paystubs, or a paystub from an old job and you'll work through the Paycheck wizard. Then I promise I'll give you that long-awaited break!

Setting Up a Paycheck

Your paycheck contains withholding in several categories. Thus your *gross pay*, the total amount you earn, is higher than the actual amount on the paycheck. You could enter the amount on your paycheck as salary income and not concern yourself with the gross pay or the withholding amounts, but that wouldn't present you with an accurate picture of your income and expenses.

If you need to produce a statement for a lender such as a bank, you will want your income to reflect the gross amount you earn. And if you use information from Quicken for tax planning, you will need to know your gross income and your deductions.

Quicken makes entering your paycheck easy. Using the Paycheck wizard, you can enter your gross pay and all your deductions and make sure everything is getting into the right category. And if you are salaried and your paycheck is the same each time, the process is even easier because you only have to enter your entire paycheck once.

To set up a paycheck, follow these steps:

1. From the menu bar, choose Features, Banking, Set Up Paycheck. The first Paycheck Setup dialog box will appear (see Figure 2.16).

2. Click on Next to continue. Quicken displays the EasyStep tab (see Figure 2.17).

3. Check the boxes for the deductions that you want Quicken to track for you. Click on Help for a detailed discussion of each item. Uncheck the boxes that do not apply. Click on Next to continue.

4. In the next EasyStep page (see Figure 2.18), Quicken asks you to enter a Paycheck Name (such as "JK Pay").

Figure 2.16

Paycheck Setup creates the memorized transaction for your paycheck.

Figure 2.17

By letting Quicken track your payroll deductions, you'll know how much has been contributed to pension plans, taxes, and other items.

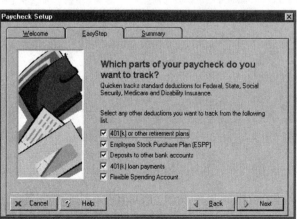

Figure 2.18

The Paycheck Name
you enter becomes
the entry in the
Payee field.

5. Click on the down arrow in the How Often text box and select the frequency that you receive paychecks (for example, Twice A Month). Click on Next to continue.

6. The next EasyStep page (see Figure 2.19) asks you to enter the date of this paycheck and the account to deposit this paycheck into. Click on Next to continue.

7. In the next EasyStep page, enter the gross amount, net amount, and category for this paycheck transaction. Click on Next to continue.

8. The next EasyStep page asks if there are any other income items on your paystub (above and beyond the gross amount) that you need to

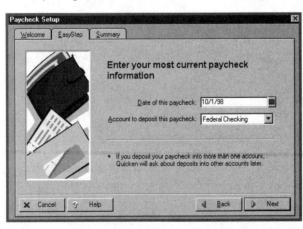

Figure 2.19

The date that you
enter will be the
date of this
transaction and the
basis for Quicken to
schedule future
transactions at the
interval you specify.

enter. Examples would be a bonus, a commission, or reimbursed expenses. If so, click on Yes and enter a category and amount for each income item (see Figure 2.20). If not, leave the default answer as No. Click on Next to continue.

> **TIP** Click on the Back button at any time to review or change your responses so far.

9. In the next EasyStep page, you need to enter the amounts for the federal and state taxes that are deducted from your paycheck. Click on Next to continue.

10. The next EasyStep page allows you to enter other types of taxes that are deducted from your paycheck. Click on Next to continue.

11. At this point, EasyStep starts to ask you about special deductions such as those for a 401(k) plan or profit-sharing plan. Follow the instructions onscreen and click on Help as needed for more explanation.

12. The last EasyStep screen (see Figure 2.21) asks if you would like Quicken to automatically remind you when it's time to record your paycheck. Click on Yes, and then on Next to continue.

Figure 2.20

If you regularly incur expenses for work that are reimbursed in your paycheck, consider setting up a Reimbursed Work Expenses category.

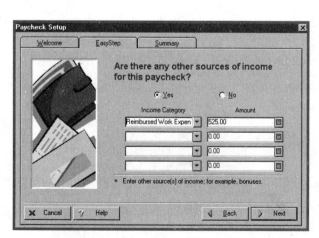

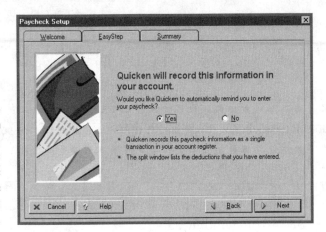

Figure 2.21

Quicken will record your paycheck in the register complete with the split to the categories you specified.

13. The Summary tab appears (see Figure 2.22). Review the details and click on the memo and amount fields as needed to adjust. Click on Done to enter your paycheck transaction.

14. Quicken displays an informational dialog box explaining that you have set up a scheduled transaction and when you will see the first reminder. Click on OK and the Paycheck Setup wizard closes. The paycheck transaction can be seen in the register. Take a moment to find and review the paycheck transaction.

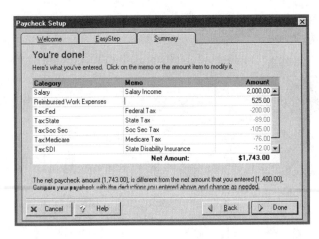

Figure 2.22

At the bottom of the Summary tab, Quicken lets you know if the net paycheck amount differs from what you initially specified.

Take a Break

Curious about how scheduled transactions work? Good. When you return from the break (this is how I made sure you would return!), I'll unmask the mystery and teach you how to save even more time each month. Go get a donut and check on the pets. See you back in a bit.

Scheduling Future Transactions

So by now you realize that the Paycheck Setup not only captured your multicategory paycheck information and memorized it, but also scheduled reminders in Quicken based on the frequency you receive paychecks. In the example I used in the figures, the paycheck is dated October 1 and I specified that paychecks occur every two weeks. Quicken will remind me to enter the next paycheck after October 15. The Reminder will appear on the Reminders tab. You will learn more about reminders later in this seciton.

Like this feature? Good, because you can schedule any recurring transactions (deposits as well as payments) using the Scheduled Transaction feature. Common examples of scheduled transactions include loans and mortgage payments, rent, and utilities. Use Quicken's Scheduled Transactions feature to make all your recurring transactions easier. When you create a scheduled transaction, you provide Quicken with all the information about your deposit or payment—as if you were entering the actual transaction in your register. You also tell Quicken how frequently this item should occur and on what day of the month.

You can ask Quicken to remind you of scheduled transactions, in which case each time you open the Quicken program you will see a reminder of any scheduled transactions that are now due. Alternatively, you can have Quicken go ahead and enter the transactions in your register. For example, if you have your paycheck directly deposited to your bank account, set this up as a scheduled transaction to be entered automatically—then, whenever a paycheck is due, Quicken will enter the deposit in your register. This way your balance will always be up to date.

Creating a Scheduled Transaction

To set up a scheduled transaction from an existing transaction, follow these steps:

1. Find a sample of the transaction you want to schedule in your register.

2. Right-click on the transaction. A shortcut menu appears.

3. Click on Schedule Transaction. The Create Scheduled Transaction dialog box appears (see Figure 2.23).

4. Verify that all parts of the transaction are correct: the account name, the type of transaction, the payee, the category (including split categories), and any memo information.

5. Indicate on what date the next payment is due by changing the date at Next Date.

6. Select the frequency of the transaction by clicking on the down arrow in the How Often box and choosing a frequency.

7. In the Record in Register box, indicate if you want Quicken to automatically record this transaction in your register or prompt you with a reminder.

8. Indicate the total Number of Payments expected on this transaction. If the payments are ongoing (as with your paycheck, which you expect to continue receiving for a long time!), leave the amount at 999. If you are entering a loan with a fixed number of payments

Figure 2.23

Use an existing transaction to set up a scheduled transaction quickly.

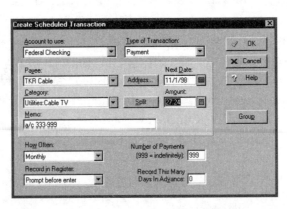

remaining, you can change this number to indicate how many payments you still have to make.

9. Indicate how many Days In Advance you want to receive the reminder about this payment. If you are requesting automatic entry in your register you will probably want to leave this at 0. If you need to write a check and get the payment in the mail, you probably want a few days' notice.

10. Click on OK and you're finished!

From now on, Quicken will remember that you have a payment or deposit due and either remind you or directly enter the amount in your register.

Getting Reminders from Quicken

Quicken goes out of its way to remind you of your financial events and tasks. You may have noticed the Home Page QuickTab, which appears by default when you open Quicken. At a glance, the Home Page brings you up to date on Scheduled Transactions, Alerts, and Reminders. You can customize the Home Page (top right corner) to show information or items pertinent to you but not specifically provided in Quicken. You can also use the Home Page as an access point to most of Quicken's features including your accounts, planning, Internet sites, and how-to help on common tasks.

Another nifty feature is the Billminder. You can ask Quicken to display the Reminder list each time you start Windows. This is handy when you haven't opened Quicken for a week or so and bills or other financial transactions need your attention.

To activate Billminder and set other Reminder options, click on Features, Reminders, Reminders from the menu bar. The Reminders QuickTab appears. Click on the Options button in the Button bar and choose Reminders to view and set reminder options (see Figure 2.24). The Days Shown option allows you to specify the number of days in advance you want to be reminded. You can also specify the time period (such as this week or this month) that you want to see Financial Calendar notes.

Billminder options can be viewed and set by choosing Options, Billminder from the Reminders Button bar. Here you can control whether Billminder

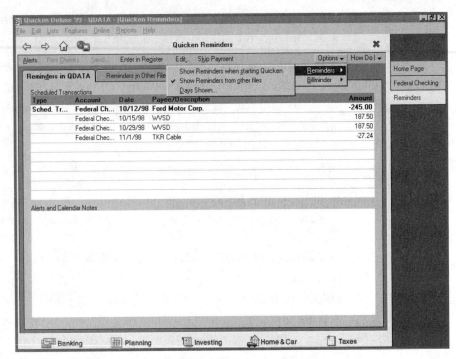

Figure 2.24

By default, Quicken displays the Reminder List when you start Quicken.

appears when you start Windows and which reminders you want Billminder to display (see Figure 2.25).

TIP In case you don't open Quicken for a week or so, it is a good idea to turn Billminder on.

As you can see in Figure 2.26, you can select the transaction you want to work with and then click on the appropriate button in the Button bar: Enter In Register, Edit, or Skip Payment. If you select Edit, the Record Scheduled Transaction dialog box appears (see Figure 2.27). From here, you can edit any aspect of the scheduled transaction, and then record or skip the payment.

TIP To work with Scheduled Transactions in the Highlights Center, right-click on the scheduled transaction and choose Create, Edit, Skip, or Enter (Record) This Scheduled Transaction from the shortcut menu. If you've written any checks but haven't printed them, you also get a "Print This Check" option.

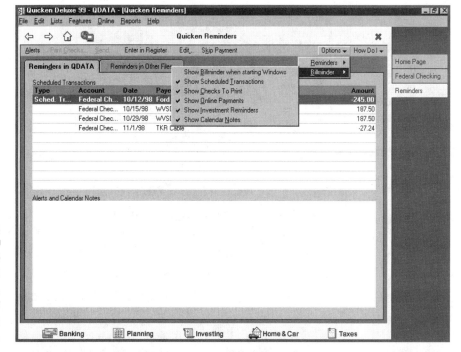

Figure 2.25

To see reminders every time you open Windows, check Show Billminder when starting Windows.

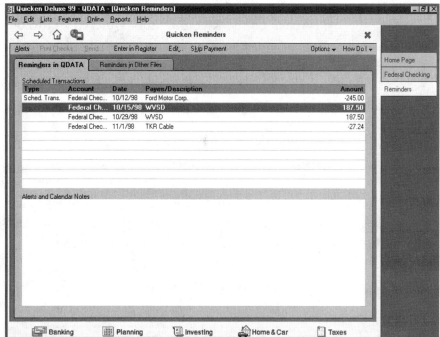

Figure 2.26

You have to select a scheduled transaction to display the new Button bar.

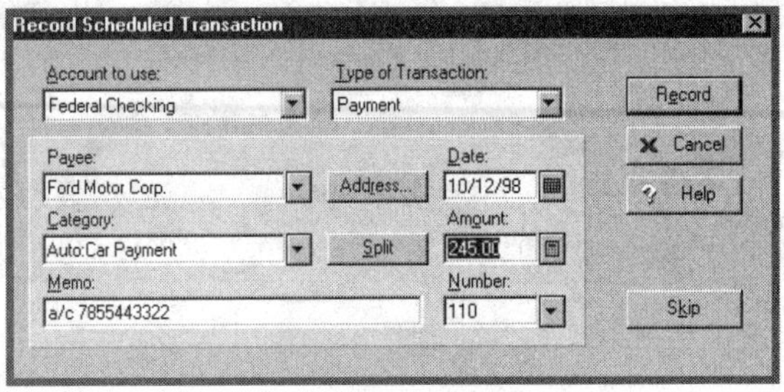

Figure 2.27

Use the Number field to enter the check number of any other valid Num field entry.

Paying Scheduled Transactions Early

You're not limited to making scheduled transaction payments at the designated time. If the transaction is not yet due, it will not appear in the Reminder box. Instead, you can find the transaction on the Scheduled Transaction List and then make the payment.

Open the Scheduled Transaction List (see Figure 2.28) by choosing Lists, Scheduled Transactions (or press Ctrl+J). Click on the transaction you want to pay, and then click on the Pay button at the top of the window. The Record Scheduled Transaction window will appear. To pay the transaction now, click on the Record button. Quicken will record the transaction in the appropriate register, just as though you'd entered it by hand, and will set up the check to be printed if you're using that feature.Because you paid the bill early, Quicken will not remind you to pay it again this period, but will instead increment the due date accordingly.

Using Quicken Alerts

Quicken Alerts can be used to notify you when an account balance is getting low, when you've hit the limit on a credit card, or when taxes are due. This is a very flexible feature. To set up Alerts, click on the Reminders QuickTab and then click on the Alerts button in the Button bar. The Set Up Alerts dialog box appears (see Figure 2.29).

The box on the left lists the areas for which you can set up an alert. The text in the box on the right will change to display the appropriate alert settings. Check boxes and fill in amounts as specified. Click on the tabs to set up Alerts for your Accounts, Investments, General, or New items.

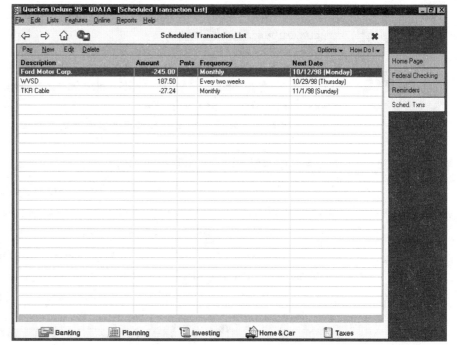

Figure 2.28

You can use the Scheduled Transaction List window to create new scheduled transactions, edit or delete existing ones, or pay a scheduled transaction.

Click on Apply to post the alerts immediately. Click on OK to close the dialog box when you finish.

Once an Alert is set, Quicken lets you know when you exceed a limit or when an important date comes up. For example, suppose you set up an alert that explains your account must have a minimum balance of $1,000. While working in the register, you enter a transaction that would bring the

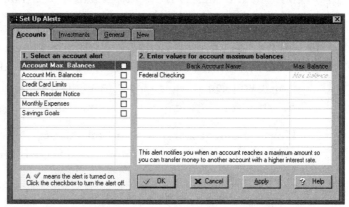

Figure 2.29

Use Alerts to set financial limits and remind yourself of important financial dates.

balance down to $900. An Alert message appears on the screen and instructs you what to do next.

TIP   To turn an Alert off, open the Set Up Alerts dialog box and deselect the desired Alert options. Click on Apply, and then on OK.

Using Quicken's Financial Calendar

Quicken's Financial Calendar lets you schedule transactions quickly, see an entire month's financial activity at a glance, visualize your spending and income with graphs, and even enter personal reminders.

Open the Financial Calendar by choosing Features, Reminders, Financial Calendar from the menu bar. Quicken's Financial Calendar appears with the current month displayed (see Figure 2.30).

Seeing Details of Items in the Financial Calendar

Click twice on any day in the Financial Calendar and a box opens showing details of all transactions for that day, as shown in Figure 2.31. Once you see the box showing the transactions for a particular day, you have the following options:

- **New.** Enter a new transaction for that date by clicking on the New button, and then entering the details of the transaction in the new Transaction dialog box that appears. Click on OK when you finish.

- **Edit.** Click on a transaction you want to change, and then click on the Edit button. An Edit Register Transaction dialog box appears in which you can make changes to the transaction. Clicking on OK transfers your changes to the designated register.

- **Delete.** Remove a transaction from the register by clicking on the transaction, and then clicking on the Delete button.

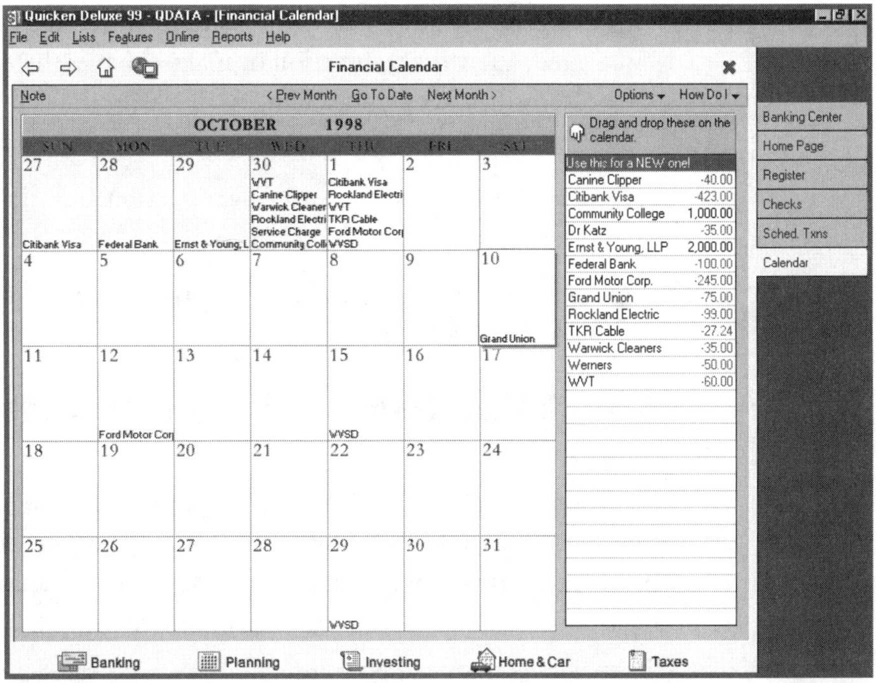

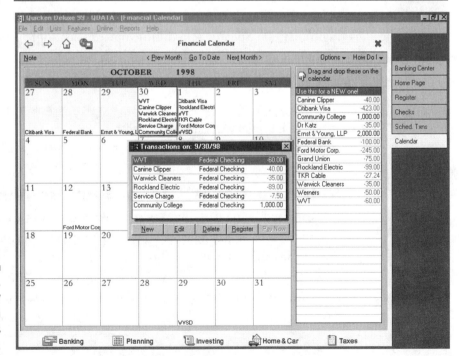

Figure 2.30

The Financial Calendar displays all the financial activity for an entire month. View a different month by clicking on the Prev Month or Next Month buttons on the Button bar.

Figure 2.31

You can add, edit, delete, or pay transactions from the Transactions dialog box.

✿ **Register.** Go right to the register in which the transaction was created. View the transaction or make changes there, and then click on Record to keep your changes. Click on the Calendar QuickTab at the right side of your screen to return to the Financial Calendar.

✿ **Pay Now.** Select a scheduled transaction and click Pay Now to enter the transaction in your register.

✿ **X.** Click on the X to close the Transactions dialog box and make no changes.

Scheduling Transactions in the Financial Calendar

To create a new scheduled transaction, drag and drop a payee listed to the right of the calendar onto the desired date. Quicken displays the familiar New Transaction dialog box. By default, the new transaction is set up as a register transaction (a one-time-only, nonrecurring transaction).

To specify as a scheduled transaction, click on the Scheduled Transaction button and the dialog box expands to show the scheduling options (see Figure 2.32). Specify scheduling options as appropriate and edit the remaining information as needed. Click on OK to post the new transaction in the Calendar.

TIP   Press Ctrl+P to print your Financial Calendar.

Getting a Visual View of Your Monthly Finances

You can see how you're doing with a quick graph of the finances for the month. Display a graph by clicking on the Options button at the top right side of the calendar. Choose Show Account Graph. The graph appears beneath the calendar (see Figure 2.33). Your daily account balance can be viewed in relation to the graph on the left side of the screen. Click on any day in the calendar to highlight that day on the graph, and then hold your

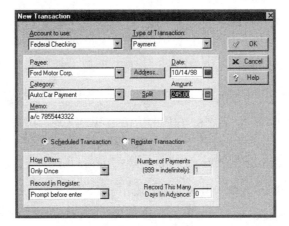

Figure 2.32

Create new transactions in the Financial Calendar by dragging and dropping payees.

mouse over the highlighted bar in the graph to see the actual account balance for that day.

Use the graph to visualize how much money you have or will have on a particular date. If you have scheduled transactions, you can quickly see where you will need more money to cover the future payments.

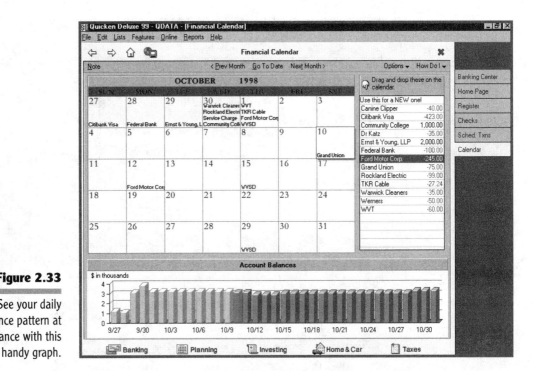

Figure 2.33

See your daily balance pattern at a glance with this handy graph.

Making Notes in Your Calendar

It's *your* calendar, after all. You can make any kind of personal or business entry that you want. To enter a note in your calendar, follow these steps:

1. Click on the day on which you want to make a note.

2. Click on the Note button at the top of the Financial Calendar window. The Note dialog box appears onscreen (see Figure 2.34).

3. Enter a note in the Note box. Change the note color, if you wish.

4. Click on Save when you finish.

The existence of a note will appear in the calendar as a colored Post-it note on the day of the note. Click on the box to read your note.

Any notes you enter in your calendar will appear in your reminder box when you see your reminders. After all, what's the use of writing yourself a note to remember your sister's birthday if you aren't reminded of it when the time comes?

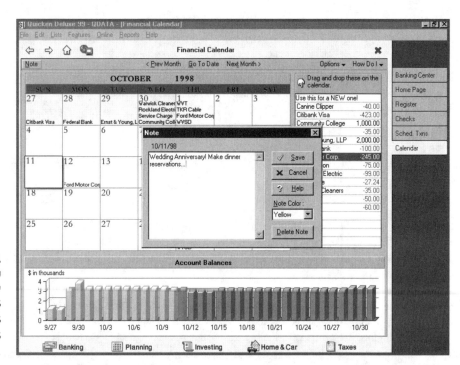

Figure 2.34

Use note colors to organize your notes better (birthdays as yellow, deadlines as blue, or whatever).

Tools You Can Use

Quicken offers several shortcuts for making the entry of items in your register easier and quicker.

Quicken's Calculator

When you get ready to enter amounts in your register, you may notice that Quicken has already entered an amount for you. This is because Quicken looks for a previous transaction with the same payee or payer, and if it finds one, it will enter the amount. You can override this amount by typing right over it, or you can press Delete to make the amount disappear completely.

But what if you need to do some calculating before you can arrive at the proper amount? Maybe you have two bills you are paying to the same company and you need to add them together, or perhaps you have the right to take a discount if you make your payment on time and you want to figure out the discount.

Use Quicken's onscreen calculator with the mouse. While in a number field, click on the little calculator icon that appears at the right side of the field. A miniature calculator will appear onscreen.

Perform any standard mathematical operation in the calculator by using your mouse to click on the numbers or using the number keys on your keyboard (or numeric keypad). Use the following mathematical symbols to perform operations:

+ addition

- subtraction

* multiplication

/ division

Press the = sign or press Enter and your calculation will be entered into your register, or press Esc to remove the calculator without entering anything in the register.

To find a calculator when you aren't in a number field, choose Edit, Use Calculator. Clicking on Paste from this calculator will place the results of your calculation in the field where your cursor rests.

Use Find to Search for Transactions in Your Register

Are you trying to find an earlier transaction involving a particular amount or payee? You can instruct Quicken to search through the register and quickly report back to you.

Click on the Find button at the top of the register. The Quicken Find dialog box appears in which you can enter the text or number for which you are searching (see Figure 2.35). Then click on Find to go to one occurrence of the item in the register, or click on Find All to produce a quick report listing all occurrences of the item.

TIP   Press Ctrl+F anytime while in the register to open the Find dialog box

Producing Quick Reports

You can instruct Quicken to produce Quick Reports of transactions in your register. Choose between a Quick Report based on transactions of a particular type, transactions with the same payee or payer, or all the transactions in your register.

Quick Reports Based on Particular Transactions

To request a Quick Report based on transactions with a particular person or company, or transactions from the same category, follow these steps:

Figure 2.35

Let Quicken search your register for previous transactions.

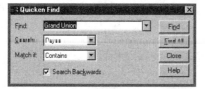

1. Click on a transaction that meets the criterion you are seeking. For example, if you want to produce a Quick Report of all payments to your power company, click on one of the power company transactions.

2. Click on the Report button in the Button bar.

3. From the drop-down menu, you can choose a report based on the payee or payer of the transaction or category you selected, or you can view a summary graph.

4. When the report appears, you can scroll through to view all the entries. You can double-click on a particular transaction to be taken directly to that transaction in the register.

● ●

NOTE If you double-click on a transaction in a report, you are taken to that transaction in the register. You can return to the report by clicking on the report QuickTab at the right side of the screen.

● ●

5. Close the report when you finish with it by clicking on the X in the upper right corner of the report.

Quick Register Reports

You can produce a Quick Report showing all the transactions in your register by clicking the Report button in the register button bar. Choose Register Report and a report appears listing every item in your register. This is essentially similar to the traditional register in your manual checkbook.

In a Register report or any report, you have control over several features:

✿ Change the dates the report covers by clicking on the down arrow at the top left side of the report and making a choice among the time period options, or enter precise dates in the spaces provided at the top of the report. Press the Update Button or press Enter after you make or enter your selection.

✿ To see more (or less) of particular columns, drag the column separators at the tops of the columns.

✿   Sort the report for any of the columns by clicking on the Sort button at the top of the report window. In the Select Sort Criteria dialog box, click on the column by which you want to sort.

Sorting Your Register

By default, your register appears sorted by date, and then sorted by transaction number within each date. You can change this sort option to any of several selections. To change the feature by which your register is sorted, click on the Options button in the Button bar. From the drop-down list that appears, choose the sort option you want to use.

Using the Financial Address Book

Another handy tool in Quicken is the Financial Address Book, which is where Quicken stores the addresses you enter when you write checks in Quicken. You can also use this address and phone book for personal and business contacts. You can enter new contacts, group contacts, print mailing labels and Rolodex cards, and export data to other programs.

To open the Financial Address Book from within Quicken, choose from the menu bar Lists, Track Important Addresses. The Financial Address Book for the current data file appears (see Figure 2.36).

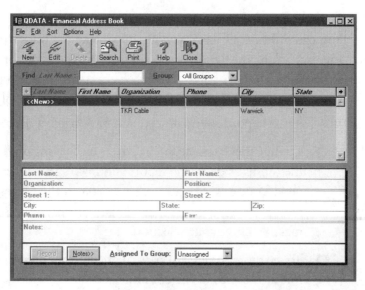

Figure 2.36

Click on any name to see the details of that person or company.

TIP You can also access the Financial Address Book without being in Quicken by clicking on
Start, Programs, Quicken, Financial Address Book.

Adding a New Record

To add a new address to the book, click on the New button or double-click on the <<New>> row in the address listing. Your cursor moves to the Last Name field in the bottom half of the screen. Type the name and press Tab. Continue filling in the fields in this manner. If you do not need a field, leave it blank. To save the new record, click on the Record button. To enter a note about the record, click on the Notes button. By default, the Address Book sorts by last name, so your newly recorded entry should be filed away alphabetically by last name.

TIP To edit or delete a record, select the entry and click on the Edit or Delete button.

Searching for a Record

Use the Find Last Name field just below the toolbar to quickly find a record when you know the last name. As you type the last name, the highlight bar moves through the records list and completes the typing for you.

If you don't know the last name, use the Search button on the toolbar. Search allows you to enter text and specify how the search should be performed. You can search all fields and groups, or just selected fields and groups.

TIP If you aren't sure of the spelling of a name, check the Find Words That Sound Like This Word option in the Search dialog box.

Using Address Groups

You can organize your address book into groups such as work, family, and financial. By default, the Financial Address Book comes with five predefined groups: Quicken, Family, Friends, Work, and Unassigned. Click on the Group down arrow just below the Toolbar to view a list of groups you already have available.

To assign individual records to a group, just select the address record, click on the Assigned To Group down arrow and select the desired group.

TIP   To create a new group, select Options, Set Up Groups and click on <<New>>. Enter the desired group name in the Add New Group text box and click on Record to save the new group name.

Printing Records

You can print a variety of useful stuff from the Financial Address Book:

- ✿   The address book itself
- ✿   A phone book
- ✿   Mailing labels (Avery 4143, 4144, 4145, 5160, and 5161 only)
- ✿   Rolodex cards (Avery 4168 and 5385 only)
- ✿   Envelopes (#10 only)

For all these outputs, you can specify to print all records or just selected records. You can also change the font type, style, and size to be used. To set print options and print, click on the Print button in the Toolbar or press Ctrl+P.

TIP   To review before you print on fancy label or Rolodex paper, choose File, Print Preview from the menu bar. You will set the same options as described above and be able to print or exit without printing after your review.

Using QuickEntry

Sometimes, less is more. Maybe not with chocolates or vacations, but when it comes to software the assortment of features, bells, and whistles can be overwhelming to the new user. You may have noticed on your desktop another icon near the Quicken Deluxe 99 icon named QuickEntry 99. This is a slimmed down version of the Quicken Register that allows you to do basic transaction processing. You can enter transactions for any of your accounts using QuickEntry (which loads faster) instead of loading Quicken Deluxe.

Another benefit of QuickEntry is that you can optionally hide all your prior transactions. In other words, only the transactions currently being entered would show up on the screen. This is handy in situations where you have someone else entering transactions for you and you want your financial history kept private.

Showing Transaction History

By default, QuickEntry hides your transaction history. If you want to see all prior transactions in QuickEntry, you need to set that option in Quicken Deluxe before you open QuickEntry. To do so, click on the Options button in the Register and select Register Options. When the Register Options dialog box appears, click on the Miscellaneous tab and check the option Show Transaction History in QuickEntry. Click on OK and the next time you go into QuickEntry, all your prior transactions will appear just like in the Quicken Deluxe Register. You can check and uncheck the Show Transaction History option as needed, at any time.

■■■

TIP Want a bit more security? You can also check the Use File Password setting in the Register Options dialog box to restrict QuickEntry access to only certain individuals. To protect Quicken Deluxe in the same way, choose File, Passwords, File and enter a password that you can easily remember, but others would not be able to guess. Note that the Quicken Deluxe file password does not protect your file from being copied, deleted, or renamed. For optimal file security, use Windows 98 file security settings. However, copied or renamed files won't open in Quicken Deluxe without the correct password.

■■■

Opening QuickEntry

To open QuickEntry, close Quicken Deluxe and double-click on the QuickEntry icon on the desktop. As you can see in Figure 2.37, you can easily work with the register for any account. The Button bar contains the familiar Delete, Find, Transfer, and Options buttons. Above the Button bar, a Start Quicken button provides you with quick access to Quicken Deluxe. QuickEntry even knows what the next check number is when you ask for the next check number in the Num field. The current ending balance appears in the bottom right corner.

At any point you can close QuickEntry and reopen it as needed. When you reopen QuickEntry, all the transactions you just entered will still appear in QuickEntry.

Transferring QuickEntry Data

Once you finish entering the batch of transactions, click on the Start Quicken button (or just open Quicken Deluxe if QuickEntry is closed), and Quicken will ask if you want to record the QuickEntry transactions to the Quicken Deluxe Register (see Figure 2.38). At this point, the transactions are transferred from QuickEntry to a holding list in Quicken Deluxe—you have to accept them before they will be entered into your

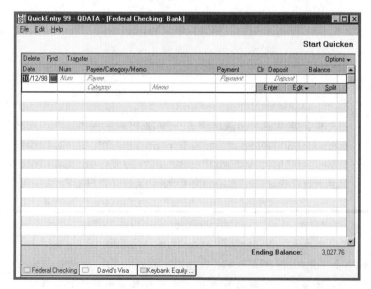

Figure 2.37

If you prefer to enter transactions in batches, you'll like using QuickEntry.

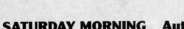

Figure 2.38

Quicken requires
you to review
QuickEntry
transactions before
it will record them.

Accept Transactions

These entries were made outside of Quicken. To place them in your register, you must accept them. A question mark means you need to edit that transaction before it can be accepted. You can edit any transaction by highlighting it and then pressing Edit.

Date	Num	Payee	Category	Account	Amount
10/12...	111	Suburban Propane	Utilities:Gas & Electric	Federal Checking	
10/12/98	111	Pine Island Herb & Spice	Groceries	Federal Checking	22.00
10/12/98	112	Warwick Cleaners	Dry Cleaning	Federal Checking	35.00

Accept All | Accept | Edit | Delete | Help | Finish Later

Quicken Deluxe registers. You can click on the Accept button to record individual transactions, or use the Accept All button to record all transactions. Quicken will flag any transactions that are incomplete or have any problems by putting a question mark to the far left. Use the Edit button to edit any transaction as needed. You can also click on the Delete button to remove a QuickEntry transaction from the list. The Finish Later button allows you to bypass the Accept Transactions window and deal with the QuickEntry transactions at a later time

Creating Other Types of Accounts

Now that you've got the hang of working with your checking account in Quicken, you're ready to expand your horizons. You can set up account registers for any other bank accounts you might have (such as a savings account). You can also set up your credit cards just as you set up your checking account. And if you're like me and you tend to wonder where all the cash in your pocket goes, you can set up a cash account to track your cash expenditures.

Setting Up Credit Card Accounts

You create a credit card account and record your credit card purchases the same way you record checks in your check register. This will help you see what types of items you are spending your money on. When you make payments on your credit card, Quicken shows the payments as a transfer between your checking and your credit card accounts.

Before setting up your credit card account, decide where you want to start. The best way to begin tracking your credit card transactions is to go back to the same starting date you used for setting up your checking account. You'll want to get each credit card statement from the starting date to the present.

NOTE   If you don't have (or don't want to bother with) any old credit card statements, you can still set up your credit card account. You will just start with a zero balance and begin recording your credit card transactions from this point forward.

To create a credit card account in Quicken, follow these steps:

1. From the menu bar, choose Features, Banking, Create New Account. The Create New Account dialog box appears (see Figure 2.39).

2. Click on Credit Card, and then click on Next to bring up the next screen.

3. Quicken next asks you to name the account. Enter the account name and an optional description, and then click on Next to bring up the next screen.

4. Quicken wants to know if you are using a credit card statement balance for your beginning balance or if you are starting with a zero balance. If you have your credit card statements handy, click on Yes;

Figure 2.39

Click on Credit Card and Next to set up your credit card account.

if you can't find any statements or you want to start with a zero balance on your credit card account, click on No. Then click on Next to bring up the next screen.

5. If you clicked on yes, enter the starting point for your credit card account. If you are going to enter your transactions for the entire year to date, your starting point should be January 1 of the current year. If you are starting with your most recent statement, your starting point will be the date on that statement. The amount you enter is the amount owing on your credit card statement as of the starting date. Click on Next after you enter this information.

6. Quicken wants to know if this account is a Quicken credit card or is set up for online banking. You will find out more about these features this afternoon. For now, you should probably answer no to this question, and then click on Next to bring up the next screen.

7. You can enter a credit limit for this account. This entry is optional. If you give Quicken this information, Quicken will display a running balance of your remaining credit limit in the credit card account register. Click on Next to advance to the next screen.

8. View the summary of the information you entered and make any changes at this time. Click on Done. Your credit card account has been added to the account list.

To view your shiny new credit card register, click on the credit card account name at your Home Page. The credit card account register will appear with your opening balance showing (see Figure 2.40).

The balance due on your credit card appears in red, as a negative balance. As you enter additional transactions, the balance due amount *increases*, to indicate that you owe more on this account. When you record payments, the balance *decreases*.

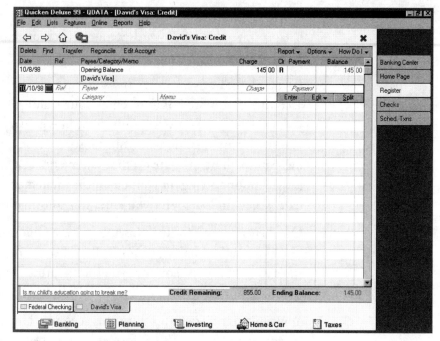

Figure 2.40

Enter transactions in your credit card register just as you would in your checking account register.

Entering Charge Transactions in Your Credit Card Account

Enter a charge purchase in your credit card account by following these steps:

1. **Date.** Enter the date on which the transaction occurred.

2. **Ref.** Skip the Num field if you wish. However, some people like to put a personal reference number in this column.

3. **Payee.** Enter the name of the place where you made the charge.

4. **Charge.** Enter the amount charged in the amount column on the left, in the same way as you would enter a check in your check register.

5. **Category.** Choose a category for your charge. This will enable Quicken to properly categorize your charge purchases in your financial reports. You can split the transaction among several categories just as you can with checks.

6. **Memo.** Enter anything or nothing here; the memo field is optional.

TIP Although the memo field in your register is small, it is a great place to record information necessary for tax-deductible business expenses. If your charge purchase is a business meal, for example, enter the names of your companions and the business purposes in the memo field. If you need more space, click on the Calendar button and record a Note in your Financial Calendar.

Making Credit Card Payments

When you make a payment on your credit card account, you will enter the payment in the register from which you are issuing the payment (probably your checking account). The category you should choose for your payment is Transfer. This category is found at the very bottom of the shortcut category list, or, if you start typing the name of your credit card (MasterCard, for example), Quicken will fill in the rest of the name. The transfer account name appears with brackets around it, indicating that it is a transfer to another Quicken account and not an actual category.

When you enter a payment in this manner, Quicken automatically updates your credit card account to reflect the payment.

TIP Click on the down arrow in the Category field and then click on the Transfer button. Quicken displays a very handy Transfer dialog box (see Figure 2.41).

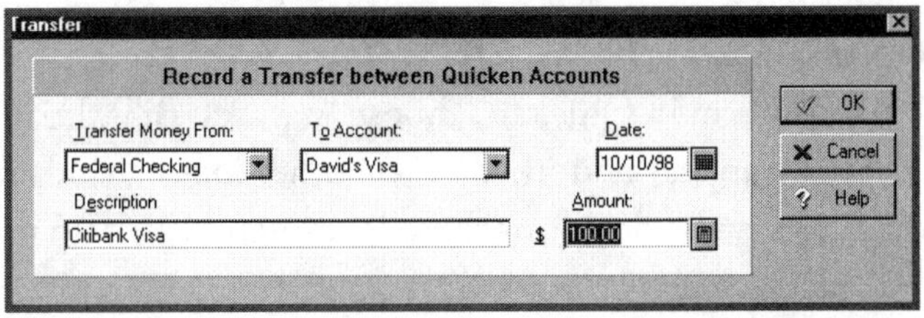

Figure 2.41

The payment entered in your checking account is automatically applied to the credit card account when you choose a transfer as your category.

Reconciling Your Credit Card Account

When you get your credit card statement, you'll want to compare the items on the statement to those you entered in your credit card account register. This process works just the same as the process for reconciling your bank account.

Setting Up Loan Accounts

To get a complete picture of your financial situation, it's important to feed Quicken as much information as possible. Not only does this enable Quicken to provide you with financial statements that reflect all aspects of your finances, but all your entries will be faster and more precise if Quicken has all the information it needs.

To this end, I recommend that you establish loan accounts in Quicken, setting up separate accounts for your car loan, business loan, mortgage, student loan, and any other type of loan you might have.

You can use Quicken to track the payment of both principal and interest on a loan, thus providing you with an up-to-date balance of exactly how much you owe on each loan.

Here's the information you will need to set up your loan in Quicken:

- ✿ **Original amount borrowed.** This is not the amount of the loan principal as of the starting date of your entries in Quicken, but the actual amount you borrowed when you first took out the loan.

- ✿ **Original date of the loan.** Your loan document should indicate the date on which you acquired the loan.

- ✿ **Terms of the loan.** This information will also appear on your loan document.

Setting Up Your Quicken Loan

To set up a loan in Quicken, choose Features, Bills, Loans. The View Loans screen will appear and, if you have other loans already set up in Quicken, you can view the details of those loans here. Click on the New button and

the Loan Setup dialog box will appear (see Figure 2.42). Click on Next in this window to proceed with your loan setup.

To set up a loan account, follow these steps and click on Next after completing each screen:

1. Indicate whether you are the borrower or the lender on the loan.

2. Enter the name for this loan account.

3. Indicate whether previous payments have been made on the loan. If this is a brand new loan, payments have probably not yet been made. If you are setting up an existing loan, payments have probably been made.

4. Enter the date the loan was created and the original amount borrowed.

5. Indicate if there is a balloon payment due at the end of the loan term.

6. Indicate the original loan term. This is not the number of years left on the loan as of today, but the total number of years (or months) for which you borrowed the money.

7. Enter the interval for your payments (monthly, quarterly, or annually, for example).

Figure 2.42

The EasyStep loan setup walks you through the process of creating a new loan account.

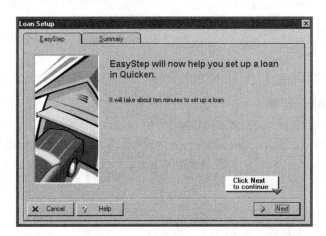

8. Enter the compounding period. This is often (but not always) the same as the payment interval. Your loan document will indicate the compounding period (or you can contact your lender to find out).

9. Enter the current loan balance. This is optional—if you know the balance, enter it; if not, Quicken will calculate your loan balance for you.

CAUTION   Quicken assumes that you are entering a loan with a fixed rate of interest. If you have an adjustable interest rate, you will not want Quicken to calculate the current loan balance for you. Quicken will not be able to provide you with an accurate balance.

10. Enter the date on which your next loan payment is due.

11. Enter the amount of your next loan payment, if you know the amount. If you are unsure of the amount, you can let Quicken calculate the payment for you.

12. Enter the current interest rate on the loan as a decimal (for example, 7.50).

13. Review the three summary screens and make any changes necessary to correct the information.

14. Click on Done when you are satisfied that all the information is entered properly. If you didn't enter a payment amount, Quicken will calculate one and display it in the Payment Amount field.

Setting Up Recurring Loan Payments in Quicken

As soon as you finish entering your loan information, the Set Up Loan Payment dialog box appears onscreen (see Figure 2.43). Verify the information in the Set Up Loan Payment box. You may need to make some changes or add information.

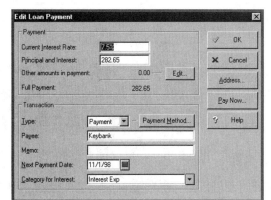

Figure 2.43

Set up your recurring loan payment information in the box provided.

Even though you see the total loan payment on this screen, Quicken will take care of splitting out your interest from your principal payment. If, however, you wish to include additional payment information, such as escrow amounts on a home mortgage, click on the Edit button. This displays a Split Transaction window. Any amounts you enter on the Splits screen will be added to your total loan payment amount.

Choose the type of payment you'll be making: a regular register entry (Payment) or a check written by Quicken (Print Check). This payment will automatically be designated a memorized transaction. If you want to make this a scheduled transaction as well, click on the Payment Method button and enter the scheduling information such as the frequency. Also verify the category chosen for interest expense. When you are satisfied that everything in the Set Up Loan Payment window is correct, click on OK.

Your loan information appears in the View Loans list (see Figure 2.44) and is always accessible by choosing Features, Bills, Loans. From this window you can make changes to the loan information (Edit Loan), the payment amount (Edit Payment), or the interest rate (Rate Changes). Click on the Payment Schedule tab to review the payment schedule by payment date (principal, interest, and balance). Click on the Payment Graph to get a picture of the loan balance, payment history, total interest, and future balance.

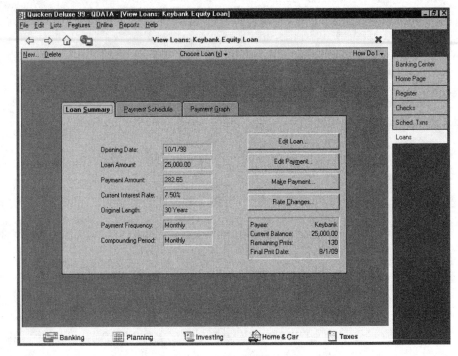

Figure 2.44

You can edit the loan or the payment or make rate changes to your Loan account here.

Recording Your Assets in Quicken

You can use Quicken to keep track of your possessions. In fact, once you've entered all your belongings in Quicken, you can make a copy of the data on a disk and tuck it away in your safe deposit box or some other safe place away from your home. You hope you'll never have to recover a list of your possessions after a casualty or theft, but should something awful happen, at least you will have detailed information about the goods that were damaged or stolen.

You can also use Quicken to keep track of the change in value of your assets. For example, if you add more coins to a coin collection, or make improvements on your house, you can enter the additional value to the asset account—you'll always have the up-to-date value of the account available to you.

In addition, and perhaps most important, by using Quicken to keep track of the things you own, you can present a more complete picture of your personal finances in your statements.

What's an Asset?

An asset is a possession of value. Your assets include your house, car, boat, collections of jewelry, coins, or stamps, investments such as stocks or mutual funds, retirement accounts, and cash accounts. I've already discussed how to set up your bank accounts, and I'll cover investments and retirement accounts later, in this evening's session.

Meanwhile, in this session, you'll learn about using Quicken to create accounts for your possessions such as your home, the contents of your home, and other tangible property you own.

Creating an Asset Account in Quicken

Each asset you intend to track in Quicken will get a separate account. The steps to creating an asset account are quite similar to the steps for setting up a cash account. You will need to enter the following types of information:

- A name for the asset
- The value of the asset
- The date on which you want to start tracking the asset

To set up an asset in Quicken, follow these steps:

1. From the menu bar, choose Features, Banking, Create New Account.

2. The Create New Account dialog box appears. Select Asset as the type of account and click on Next.

3. Enter a name for your asset (this will become the name of the account) and an optional description. Then click on Next to proceed to the next screen.

4. Click on Yes if you plan to enter a value for your asset. The value you enter can be your original cost or the current value, depending on how you want to present the asset on your financial statements. If you don't know the value, you can click on No and edit the asset later.

5. If you chose to enter a value, enter a date of valuation and the amount.

6. Click on Next to see a summary of your entries (see Figure 2.45), and then click on Done to finalize the entry of the asset. Quicken displays the new Asset account's register.

TIP

Click on the Tax button to verify or choose a tax schedule (such as Form 1040, Schedule A) to be associated with the transfers in and out of this account. For a loan account, the tax-deferred check box would not apply.

NOTE

The tax law has changed regarding the taxation of home sales. Prior to May 7, 1997, sales of homes had to be reported to the IRS and gains on such sales were subject to income tax. You could postpone the tax by *rolling over* the gain on a house to the next house, if you purchased a house of greater value than the one you sold. House sales after May 6, 1997 are tax free for the most part (as with any good IRS rule, there are exceptions to this one). Be sure to check with your accountant before assuming your sale will be completely tax free.) Also, ask your tax accountant about any limits that may apply to you. In most cases, keeping track of the basis of your house is not as important as it once was. However, if you use part of your home for business, it is still imperative that you keep track of the basis of your home.

Figure 2.45

Click on the Info button to enter any additional information about the account.

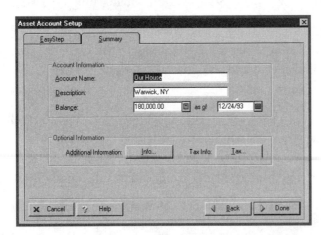

Updating Your Asset Accounts

As time goes by, the value of your asset will change. If you have a collection of coins or stamps, you may add to the collection and therefore need to increase the value of that asset. If you own a house and you are keeping track of the *basis* of the house (your cost plus the cost of improvements) as opposed to the current market value, you will want to note the additions to the basis in your asset account.

To enter changes in your asset account, you will use the account's register the same way you use your checking account register to record payments and deposits. Open the account register (click on the Accounts icon, click on the asset account, and then click on Open) and enter any changes you have made directly in the account.

Alternatively, if you have made a purchase from your checking account that affects your asset account, make the entry in your checking account and choose a Transfer to Asset category. Quicken will take care of updating your asset account for you.

Quicken's Home Inventory Feature

You can keep track of all your belongings in Quicken's Home Inventory program. Keep an inventory for insurance purposes so that you will always know exactly what you own and what it is worth.

This is a stand-alone program, which means that even though you can access the program from within Quicken if you are using Quicken at the moment, you can also use the Home Inventory program without opening the Quicken program.

To use Home Inventory from within Quicken, point to the Home & Car icon and choose Record My Home Inventory. If you are not in Quicken, choose Start, Programs, Quicken and then Quicken Home Inventory. The Home Inventory program opens (see Figure 2.46).

The Iconbar options in Home Inventory include the following:

✿ **Locations.** See a list of existing locations in your house, and change, add, or remove items from this list.

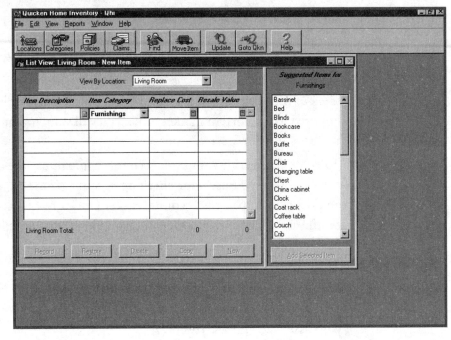

Figure 2.46

Quicken's Home Inventory program provides you with a tool for tracking all your personal possessions.

⚙ **Categories.** See a list of category items for classifying your possessions. Change, add, or remove items from this list.

⚙ **Policies.** See a list of existing insurance policies that cover you and your possessions. Enter information about these policies, add to the list, or delete items from the list.

⚙ **Claims.** Enter information about existing insurance claims.

⚙ **Find.** Search through your inventory records for a particular item.

⚙ **Move Item.** Did you list your refrigerator in the bedroom by mistake? Better move it to the proper room. (Of course, if you later decide to put your fridge in the bedroom for late-night convenience, you can always move it back there on the list as well!)

⚙ **Update.** Send your inventory values to Quicken to be included in financial reports.

⚙ **Goto Qkn.** Switch to your Quicken program. If it isn't open, your computer system will find the program and open it.

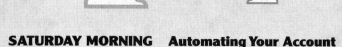

The left side of the Quicken Home Inventory screen contains an area in which you can enter your possessions and their estimated value. The right side of the screen contains a list of typical possessions.

Recording Items in the Home Inventory

To enter an item in the Home Inventory program, follow these steps:

1. Choose a location for the item by clicking on the down arrow next to the current location, and then clicking on the location of your choice. If the location you want to use is not on the list, click on the Locations button on the Iconbar and add a new location to your list.

2. Click on an item from the category list on the right, and then click on the Add Item button at the bottom of the list. The item will be added to your list at the left with a suggested value. To accept that value, do nothing. To change it, type right over the existing value, and then click on Record.

3. If you want to view items from a different category, click on the down arrow in the category field in the list view on the left side of the screen, and then choose a category. The items on the right side of the screen will change to fit the new category.

4. To add an item not on the category list, type the item description in the category Item Description field at the left. Enter a replacement cost and a resale value, and then click on Record.

5. Continue entering items until you have finished with each area of the house.

6. Click on the Update button to send your information to Quicken. Click on Yes to confirm the transfer, or on No to cancel the transfer.

Viewing Home Inventory Items in Quicken

Once you update information in Quicken from the Home Inventory, you can see the value of your home inventory on the Home & Car Center page (choose Features, Centers, Home & Car). A Home Inventory account will have been created by Quicken and the total value of your inventory items will be displayed. You cannot edit this account from within Quicken. However, you can create Quicken reports that incorporate your home inventory value. You'll get to creating reports on Sunday morning.

Customizing Quicken's Display

Would you like to have a little fun with the appearance of your Quicken screen? This section is completely optional and you may want to skip it now and return to it sometime when you find yourself in endless telephone hold limbo or waiting for the water to boil.

Changing the Screen's Appearance

Tired of the same old colors on your screen? Change things around by following these steps:

1. Click on the Options button at the top right corner of your register. A drop-down menu will appear.

2. Choose Register Options. The Register Options dialog box will appear.

3. Click on the Display tab.

4. Click on the Colors button. A Colors dialog box will appear.

5. Choose the color scheme you prefer for each type of register.

6. Click on OK, and then on OK again. Your new color scheme will be in place.

You can always return to the Colors dialog box and click on Reset to go back to your original color scheme.

Register Display Options

In the Register Options dialog box, the same place you went to play with the color scheme, there are a few other options you can choose for altering your screen display. Select Options, Register Options, and then choose from a host of screen-altering items:

- On the Display tab of the Register Options dialog box, you can switch the order of Date and Num fields in your register, and of the Memo and Category fields.

- On the Display tab you can also remove (or add) the toolbar at the top of the register.

- On the Display tab you can remove (or reinstate) the Transaction toolbar in the register.

- On the Miscellaneous tab you can specify circumstances under which you want Quicken to notify you (such as when you forget to assign a category to a transaction), and set data entry options (such as automatically entering split data).

- On the QuickFill tab you can request that Quicken automatically capitalize the first letter of the Payee or Category field in a transaction entry.

- On the QuickFill tab you can turn on or off the QuickFill options.

- On the QuickFill tab you can request that the Enter key operate like the Tab key, moving you from one field to the next in a transaction.

What's Next?

The very next thing you should do is probably eat lunch! Get yourself some nourishment to prepare for this afternoon's session. The next session covers the online features of Quicken. Not equipped to go online yet? Never fear, get comfortable and spend the afternoon reading up on what you're missing.

After lunch, you'll learn about the following:

- Ways to get online

- The benefits of Quicken's online features

- Online banking

- Paying bills online
- How to keep up to date via the Web
- The online insurance feature

Have a good lunch break!

Historians will look back upon the end of the 20th century and write praises about how the Internet transformed the business and personal lives of humanity, worldwide. If you haven't had an opportunity yet to explore this new world, read on and I'll give you a taste of what you've missed. If you are already Internet savvy, just wait until you learn how to save time (yes! even more time!) with Quicken's online features.

This afternoon, you will find out:

- What you need to get online
- The benefits of Quicken's online features
- The security issues of going online
- How to get online with Quicken
- How to get your checking account online
- How to pay bills online
- How to get your credit card account online
- Where to shop for better financial deals online
- How to update Quicken online

NOTE The dynamic nature of the Internet makes it very easy for Web sites to change, and they frequently do—even on a daily basis. Every care has been taken in this session to give you the tools and skills necessary to use Quicken's online features. However, you should be aware that the figures of the Web sites that I use in this book may differ from what you see when you go there today. If nothing else, the financial news for today will be different from what it was when I wrote this session. But the way in which you access the financial news from within Quicken Deluxe should be the same.

So grab that soda left over from lunch and get started.

Defining Online

First, let's define *online*. Technically, the word refers to the process of your computer's using a modem to dial a phone number and talk to another computer. For example, if you have ever logged onto a Bulletin Board System (BBS) or linked up to a computer network at work, you have already been online. Older versions of Quicken allowed you to dial up computers to pay bills (via the CheckFree network). The downside of going online this way was that your computer had to dial a different phone number for each target computer you wanted to work with. And sometimes the phone number you had to call was long distance, causing you to incur phone charges for every minute you were connected to that other computer.

The Internet solves this problem, while providing you with a more user-friendly interface and speedier service. Your computer dials up locally to your Internet Service Provider (ISP). The ISP is like a telephone company providing you with a phone number to call for access to the Internet and a name on the Internet so people can send you messages via *e-mail*—electronic mail. You can think of the Internet as a system of train tracks linking up computers all over the world.

Quicken Deluxe uses the Internet as the primary means of getting online. For example, you may have registered your Quicken Deluxe software when you installed it by using the online feature. In this case, Quicken found

your ISP dial-up information and instructed the modem in your computer to link up to the Quicken Web site on the Internet. Using a secure link, your registration information was sent from your computer to Intuit.

Before you delve into the details of the online features in Quicken, review what you need to get online and why you might want to go online with Quicken.

Getting Online

To use the online features of Quicken, you need the following:

- ⚙ A computer (yeah, it sounds silly, but just try to do it without one!)

- ⚙ A modem (I highly recommend a fast modem—28.8 baud or higher)

- ⚙ A phone line (to plug into the modem)

- ⚙ Microsoft Internet Explorer version 4.01 or higher

 NOTE If you do not install Microsoft Internet Explorer 4.01 or higher, some online features such as online banking, online investment tracking, and online billing will not be available. In addition, your view of the Internet will be outside of Quicken, in your browser's window instead of Quicken's internal browser window.

- ⚙ Internet access (via an Internet Service Provider, an online service such as America Online, or a local area network connected to the Internet)

You must provide the first three items on this list. Quicken can take care of the last two items for you if you don't already have Microsoft Internet Explorer and an Internet connection.

Installing Microsoft Internet Explorer

Quicken Deluxe 99 ships with Microsoft's Internet Explorer 4.01. If you didn't install Internet Explorer when you installed Quicken, you can still do so. Here is a quick overview of how to install Internet Explorer on its own.

NOTE The Quicken version 4.01 of Internet Explorer includes an enhanced encryption feature, which provides you with the best possible security for your financial transactions.

1. Exit Quicken.

2. Put the Quicken Deluxe CD or Disk 1 in the drive and run Setup.

3. When the Setup program prompts you to select the type of installation, choose Custom.

4. Remove the check marks from all items on the list except Internet Explorer.

5. Click on OK and Setup will just install Internet Explorer.

Getting Internet Access

Access to the Internet can be through a network at work or school, or more often through an account with an Internet Service Provider (ISP). If you don't have Internet access with an ISP, Quicken can help you sign up for service. To sign up for an ISP through Quicken, choose Online, Internet Connection, Setup and then select "Tell me how to sign up for an Internet account" (see Figure 3.1). Click on Next and follow the onscreen instructions. Click on Help whenever you need more of an explanation on what to do.

Figure 3.1

The Internet Connection Setup dialog box helps you set up Quicken to use online features.

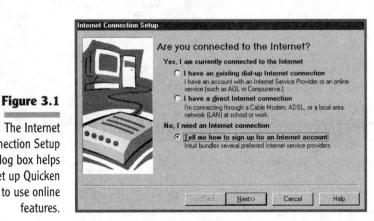

CAUTION   Quicken Deluxe 99 does not work with the Concentric free limited access account provided with older versions of Quicken Deluxe. You will need to upgrade to the full access Concentric account or another full-service ISP.

Testing Your Internet Connection

If you already have access to the Internet, Quicken's install procedure should find the ISP information automatically. To test the connection, make sure the phone cord is plugged into the modem, and choose Online, Quicken On The Web, Quicken.com (see Figure 3.2).

You should see the Quicken Web browser window open with the Connecting dialog box displayed. After your user name and password have been verified, you should see the Quicken Web site (see Figure 3.3).

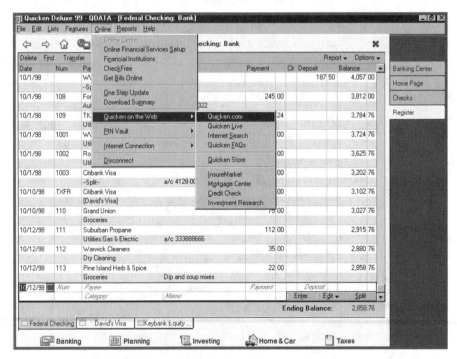

Figure 3.2

The Online menu gives you easy access to Quicken.com.

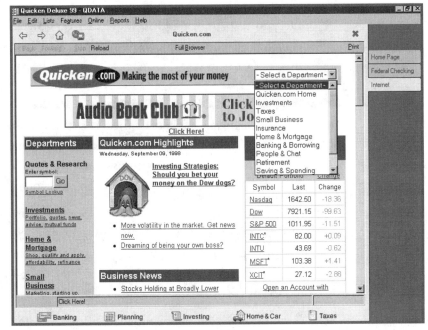

Figure 3.3

Click on the Select A Department button at the top of the Quicken Web site Home Page for a good overview of Quicken.com.

Troubleshooting Internet Access

If Quicken was unable to connect, search the Help system's Find tab for the topic "Troubleshooting/Internet." This is a long Help topic, so I recommend that you print it out. Here is a brief listing of the major troubleshooting steps:

- Does the phone line have a dial tone? If not, you may need to contact your phone company or see if someone is using that line somewhere else in the house or office.

- Can you connect to your ISP outside of Quicken through your normal browser or e-mail application? If not, you need to contact your ISP to determine what is wrong.

- Do you use Pacific Bell, MCI, or GTE as your ISP? Quicken is unable to detect the connection with these ISPs. You need to run the Internet Connection Setup again, so choose "Direct Connection

Setup" and leave the proxy setting blank. You will need to start your Internet connection before you start Quicken to do online tasks.

✿ Do you use America Online (AOL) version 2.5? If so, you need to upgrade to a more recent version. Contact AOL support for instructions.

Setting Quicken Internet Options

You can control how Quicken connects to the Internet as well as what browser to use (Quicken's or yours). To set the connection options, choose Online, Internet Connection, Options. The Internet Connection Options dialog box appears (see Figure 3.4). You can determine:

✿ Whether to stay connected or disconnect from the Internet after updating Quicken data. If you must pay your ISP by the minute, or have a limit on the number of hours you can surf, you might want to disconnect after getting data, or use the prompt feature discussed next.

✿ How information is downloaded from the Internet. The default is to download data in the background, which allows you to do other work while a file is downloading. This feature is similar to back-

Figure 3.4

Let Quicken help you manage your finances better with automatic update reminders.

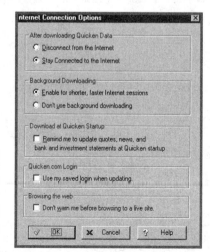

ground printing. If you opt to disable background downloading, your Internet sessions may seem slower.

 Whether you would like Quicken to remind you to update Quicken software, news, or quotes every time you start Quicken. You can always get this information from within Quicken via the Online menu.

 Whether you want Quicken to use your saved login ID when updating or require you to type it in each time. If your computer is used by several people, or if you are concerned about security, it is best not to enable this option.

 Whether Quicken should warn you before browsing a live site (unsecured) or not. By default, this option is not checked.

To change the browser or ISP you use with Quicken, you need to run the Internet Connection Setup program again. As you click on Next, you will see your current ISP selection appear (see Figure 3.5), along with any other ISP accounts that Quicken found on your computer. To change the ISP you use, select another existing account. To set up a new ISP, select Other.

TIP

If you travel frequently, you will like the fact that you can change the access phone number (in the Windows Connect To dialog) or ISP (in the Quicken Internet Connection Setup dialog) as needed to get connected while on the road.

Figure 3.5

You can switch between ISPs at any time by rerunning the Internet Connection Setup program.

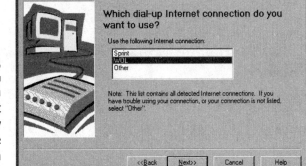

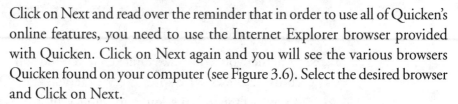

Click on Next and read over the reminder that in order to use all of Quicken's online features, you need to use the Internet Explorer browser provided with Quicken. Click on Next again and you will see the various browsers Quicken found on your computer (see Figure 3.6). Select the desired browser and Click on Next.

The next Internet Connection Setup screens ask you if you want to send Intuit (the maker of Quicken) diagnostic information. The default setting is Yes. The diagnostic information that would be sent to Intuit includes the name of your ISP, the ISP access phone number you used, the modem name and model number, the actual connection speed (baud rate), the version numbers of Quicken and your operating system, and call failure data. This information would be sent to Intuit periodically during your online sessions to help the company better maintain the online service. No financial or personal (name, address, and so on) information is sent. Select Yes or No and Click on Next.

The last screen displays your current settings. At this point, you can click on Finish to complete setup, Back to change any settings, or Cancel to exit without changing anything.

Reviewing Quicken's Online Features

To whet your appetite (I know, you're still full from lunch), here is a brief overview of the online features in Quicken. If you're not sure whether you want to use the online features, this is the section to read before skipping

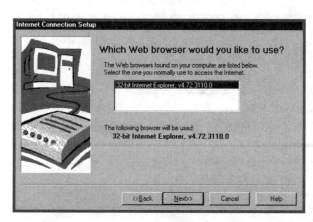

Figure 3.6

To use all of Quicken's online features, select the Internet Explorer browser.

over this entire session and taking the afternoon off! Even if you're not online yet, you might want to read through this stuff and rely on the figures to provide you with a "virtual" online experience.

- **Online Banking.** Gives you 24-hour access to your checking, savings, money market, and other bank accounts. You can see cleared transactions, transfer funds, download transaction history, and send e-mail to your financial institution.

- **Online Bill Payment.** Allows you to pay bills electronically without printing a check, using an envelope, or buying a stamp. You can schedule recurring bill payments, schedule payment while you are away on vacation, and edit payments as needed, 24 hours a day.

- **Online Billing.** A new feature—not many companies support it yet, but it should catch on quickly. Vendors post bills electronically through Quicken, which you can access 24 hours a day to review them and pay as needed from anywhere in the country.

- **Online Credit Card.** Allows you to download credit card statements for review and payment. Quicken automatically splits the individual transactions and assigns categories based on prior use.

- **Online Investment Support.** Allows you to track investment account information, get stock quotes, monitor market news and activity, and manage your portfolio 24 hours a day. These features are covered in this evening's session, "Automating Investments."

- **Online Financial Decision Making Support.** Allows you to search the World Wide Web for the best prices on insurance, mortgages, interest rates, credit card rates, and much more. You can apply online to refinance a mortgage or get a better credit card or cheaper car insurance.

- **Software Updates.** Allows you to update your Quicken software for bug fixes and new features throughout the year, 24 hours a day.

NOTE All these online banking features are integrated with Quicken to minimize your data entry time. For example, if you download your bank reconciliation information, Quicken automatically fills in the Clr field with a C if the transaction has cleared the bank. With credit card data, your transactions are automatically split into the categories you taught Quicken to use (for example, a charge from Bill's Sunoco goes to Auto Fuel). Of course, Quicken allows you to review and change this information as needed. As always, Quicken knows you're the boss! Now, if only the kids could learn!

So, without further ado, let's get down to the nitty gritty.

Online Banking

Online banking gives you access to your bank accounts (checking, savings, money market, or whatever) via the Internet. With online banking, you have 24-hour around-the-clock access that lets you:

- Review your account status (transactions, balance, and so on).

- Transfer money between accounts at the same financial institution.

- Download transactions and automatically reconcile the bank's information to your register.

- Get in touch with your bank's customer service department.

Does My Bank Support Online Banking with Quicken?

You can only use this feature of Quicken if your bank or other financial institution supports the Quicken online service. To determine if your bank does provide online services, point to the Banking icon in the Activity Bar and select Get Started With Online Financial Services. In the dialog box that appears, click on Financial Institutions. Quicken will connect to the Internet and display the Financial Institution Directory.

TIP

Register in advance! It takes 7 to 15 business days, depending on the financial institution, to process your request and issue a personal identification number (PIN).

FIND IT ▶
ONLINE

If you don't have access to the Internet, use the Quicken Fax-Back service to get a current list of Financial Institutions (Help, Product Support). At the time of this writing, I found a handy list of participating financial institutions at **http://classic.quicken.com/banking/participating.html**. The nice part about this list is that it covers Quicken for Windows, Quicken for Macs, and QuickBooks for online banking and electronic bill payments (described in the next section).

CAUTION

FIND IT ▶
ONLINE

Most banks charge for online banking (also called PC Banking). Some have free trial periods, others offer free service provided you maintain a minimum balance. The Quicken Financial Network provides a list of fees charged by banks as a guideline (**http://www.bankrate.com/brm/publ/onlifees.asp**).

Of course, contacting your bank directly would be the best source of current information for your collection of accounts. At the time of this writing, my bank charged $7.50/month for online banking and a $.40 charge for each payment over 20 per month.

TIP

Check to see if your financial institution supports Quicken's Online Banking, Online Bill Paying, and Credit Cards Online features. If so, and you think you might want all three within the next year, you might want to apply now. Frequently banks will discount the price for all three if you sign up for them at the same time.

Applying for Online Banking

To apply for online banking with Quicken, follow these steps:

1. Choose Online, Online Financial Services Setup from the menu bar. The Get Started With Online Financial Services dialog box appears (see Figure 3.7).

Figure 3.7

Use the Get Started
with Online
Financial Services
dialog box to set
up Internet access,
apply for online
banking,
and enable
your accounts.

2. Click on the Apply Now button. Quicken explains that you need to have an Internet connection to use the Online Banking Features. Click on Next to continue.

3. If you haven't registered your copy of Quicken, Quicken prompts you to do so now. Next, Quicken displays the Internet Connection Options dialog box so you can adjust the settings if needed before connecting.

4. Click on OK and Quicken displays a message that it is about to connect to the Internet. If you don't want Quicken to display this alert every time before connecting, check the Skip This Message In The Future box. Click on OK and Quicken displays the Apply For Online Financial Services Web page (see Figure 3.8).

5. In the Online Financial Services frame, select Banking Account Access. The Financial Institution Directory changes to list only those offering online banking.

6. Select your financial institution. For most financial institutions, you can apply right over the Web. Some list phone numbers to call, or provide a link to their own Web site for application. Figure 3.9 shows you one example. If your financial institution does not provide online banking with Quicken, consider applying for an account with one that does. Some even allow you to open an account online!

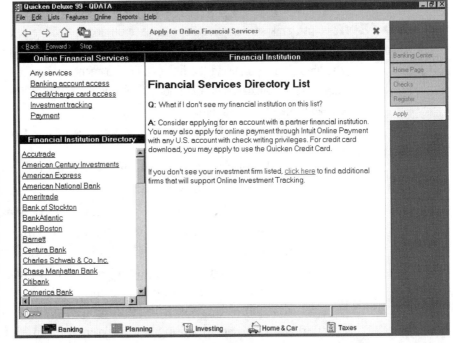

Figure 3.8

The key in the bottom left corner of your screen indicates that your link to the Internet is secure. A broken key indicates an unsecured connection.

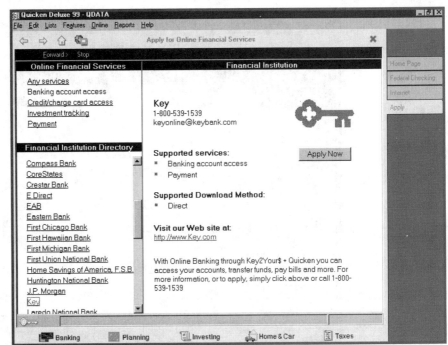

Figure 3.9

Some banks support both online banking account access and online bill paying.

● ●

NOTE For most bank services, you need to have an account with a financial institution that supports online banking with Quicken. However, you can do Online Bill Payment with any checking account by using the Intuit Online Payment service (covered in the next section), and for Online Credit Card download, you can apply for the Quicken Credit Card (covered later in this session).

● ●

7. If applicable, click on the Apply Now button. The Online Services Application appears (see Figure 3.10).

8. Complete the Online Services Application, pressing Tab and using the scroll bar as needed to move through the long page. Click on the Print button to print yourself a copy of the application so you can review your data before you submit the application. When you finish, click on the Submit button (usually at the bottom of the Web page). After submitting the application, you should see a confirmation message thanking you for your application (see Figure 3.11).

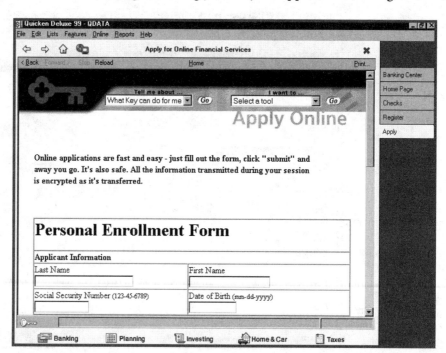

Figure 3.10

The Online Services Application

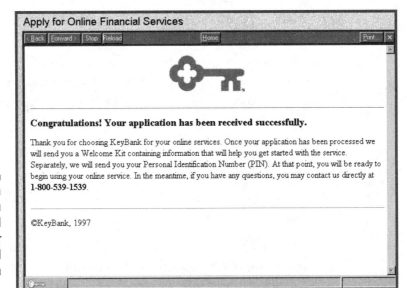

Apply for Online Financial Services

< Back | Forward > | Stop | Reload | Home | Print | X

Congratulations! Your application has been received successfully.

Thank you for choosing KeyBank for your online services. Once your application has been processed we will send you a Welcome Kit containing information that will help you get started with the service. Separately, we will send you your Personal Identification Number (PIN). At that point, you will be ready to begin using your online service. In the meantime, if you have any questions, you may contact us directly at **1-800-539-1539.**

©KeyBank, 1997

Figure 3.11

The confirmation page should let you know when you will receive your Personal Identification Number (PIN).

TIP

Write down the customer service phone number given on the confirmation page! In most cases, it will let you reach the only people working for your bank who know about the online service and when your service begins. Call them the next day to confirm they got your application and ask when you will receive your PIN. If it doesn't come on time, call again!

9. To end your Internet session, click on the X in the top right corner of the Apply QuickTab page. Depending on your connection setup, Quicken should ask you if you want to disconnect. If it doesn't, press Alt+Tab to switch to the Connection dialog box and click on Disconnect.

NOTE

Keep in mind that you can also sign up at your local bank, over the phone, or by mail in most cases. Signing up in person or over the phone is good since you can ask questions (provided the bank employee is well-versed in the service).

Enabling Your Quicken Account

After you receive your PIN from the financial institution, you need to enable your Quicken account for online banking. If you haven't created the Quicken account yet, you can create the account during the enabling process. More to the point, if you're working through this session while waiting for your PIN to arrive, you can create the account ahead of time.

1. Choose Online, Online Financial Services, Setup. The Welcome dialog box appears.

2. Click on the Enable Accounts button. The Select Financial Institution dialog box appears.

3. In the Financial Institution drop-down text box, click on the down arrow and select your financial institution (see Figure 3.12). If your financial institution is not listed, click on the Add Financial Institution button. Quicken will connect to the Internet and get the necessary information to add your financial institution.

4. Click on Next. The Online Account Setup dialog box appears (see Figure 3.13).

5. If you don't have a Quicken account set up for this bank account yet, click on Create New Quicken Account. When you click on Next, Quicken launches the Create New Account wizard (see the Saturday Morning session for step-by-step instructions). After the basic setup screens, go to Step 7.

Figure 3.12

Quicken lists the financial institutions you previously accessed when you applied for online banking service.

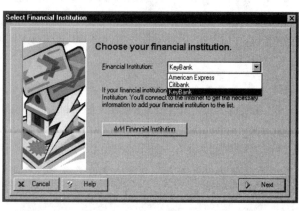

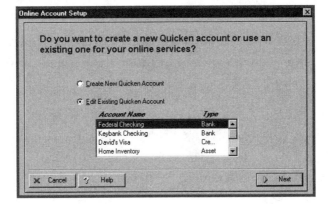

Figure 3.13

Set up one account at a time for online services.

6. If your account is already set up in Quicken, click on Edit Existing Quicken Account and select the Account Name in the list box. Click on Next to continue. The EasyStep tab appears asking you to choose the online services for this account (see Figure 3.14).

7. Click on Yes for online account access. If you want the online payment service too, you can go ahead and select that now as well. Click on Next to continue.

8. On the next screen, Quicken asks for the bank's routing number. Type in the number at the lower left corner of your check—the one in magnetic ink to the left of the check number. (It will also be in the package with your PIN, but why wait a week or so to finish the entry?)

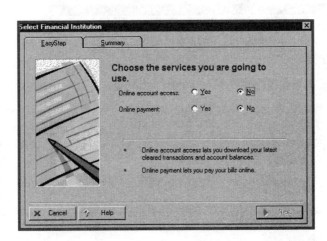

Figure 3.14

You can set up your account for online banking and bill paying at the same time.

9. Click on Next and enter your account number and account type.

10. Click on Next and enter the Customer ID number you received from your financial institution (some banks just use your social security number).

11. Click on Next and you will see the first page of the Summary tab for your account (see Figure 3.15).

12. Click on Next and you will see the new second page of the Summary tab for your account (see Figure 3.16).

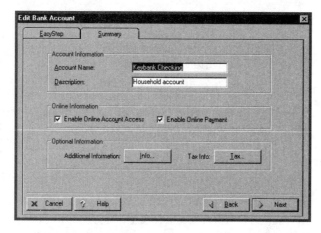

Figure 3.15

Notice that your selections of online services appear in the Online Information box.

Figure 3.16

You can change any settings in the Summary tab by just clicking on a field.

> **NOTE** Take a moment to double-check the routing, account, and customer ID (social security) numbers before you continue.

13. Click on Done to enable the account for online banking. Quicken displays the Service Agreement Information dialog box (see Figure 3.17). Read it over and click on OK.

14. Quicken asks if you have other accounts to be set up for online services. Click on Yes to set up another account, or No to exit Online Account Setup. Click on Next. Quicken returns to the Welcome dialog box.

15. If you are done, click on Cancel to close the Get Started dialog box.

Reviewing Your Account Online

Now that you're all set up for online banking, take a look at your account online. Choose Online, Online Center from the menu bar. The Online Financial Services Center QuickTab window appears (see Figure 3.18). Take some time now to explore the parts of this window.

Button bar:

> **Delete.** Deletes the selected transaction.

> **Payees.** Displays the online payee list.

Figure 3.17

Quicken explains that the online banking service agreement is between you and your bank, not between you and Intuit.

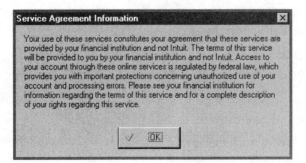

Service Agreement Information

Your use of these services constitutes your agreement that these services are provided by your financial institution and not Intuit. The terms of this service will be provided to you by your financial institution and not Intuit. Access to your account through these online services is regulated by federal law, which provides you with important protections concerning unauthorized use of your account and processing errors. Please see your financial institution for information regarding the terms of this service and for a complete description of your rights regarding this service.

✓ OK

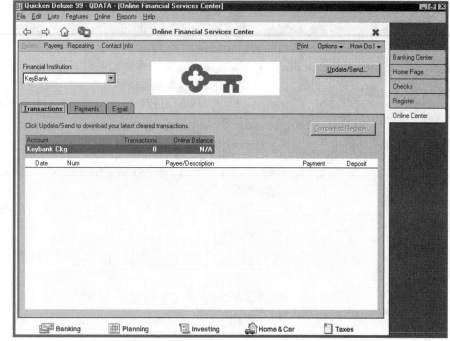

Figure 3.18

Use the Online Financial Services Center to review account transactions, make payments, or send e-mail.

Repeating. Displays the repeating online payments list and a new tab in the Scheduled Transaction List window.

Contact Info. Displays contact information for your financial institution (customer and technical service phone numbers, as well as the e-mail address for online banking support).

Print. Allows you to print the current online transactions, or transaction history for a range of dates.

Options. Provides quick access to online banking options such as using the PIN Vault, downloading, and Web connection settings.

Financial Institution. A drop-down list of financial institutions you have set up for online banking or other online services.

Update/Send. Initiates an Internet connection with the financial institution to update your Quicken window and send any payment or account transfer instructions.

Tabs:

Transactions. A listing of transactions from your bank.

Payments. Similar to the Quicken Write Checks window, this is where you enter online payments (covered in the next section).

E-mail. A listing of e-mail messages to and from your financial institution and their status (sent and unsent as well as read and unread).

Downloading Transactions

The first time you enter the Online Financial Service Center, your Transactions tab will be blank. You need to download your current account transactions from your bank. To do this, follow these steps:

1. Choose Online, Online Center from the menu bar.

2. Select your Financial Institution from the drop-down list. Click on the Update/Send button. The Instructions To Send dialog box appears (see Figure 3.19).

3. Click to check or uncheck (toggle on or off) the download transactions, payment update option, and individual payments.

4. Click on Send when ready. The first time you use the online feature, a Change Assigned PIN dialog box appears (see Figure 3.20).

Figure 3.19

You can download bank transactions while getting updates on confirmations and status reports.

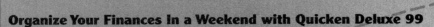

Figure 3.20

Most banks require that you enter the PIN they sent you and change it to a new PIN immediately, as an extra security precaution.

CAUTION

Some banks require you to change your PIN just once when you first access your account online, while others ask you to change the PIN periodically. In addition, some financial institutions will require you to have a different PIN for each account or service. Regardless of the frequency, you need to be careful in two very important areas.

First, always reread your bank's rules on PINs—how many characters, uppercase and lowercase sensitivity, and characters allowed (alphabet, numbers, and so on).

Second, how are you going to remember the new PIN? Write it down exactly as you typed it (note any spaces and be careful about uppercase and lowercase letters) and store it in a safe place that you will remember. I can't tell you how many times my clients have called in a panic because they hid it so well, they can't even find it themselves!

5. If you get the Change Assigned PIN dialog box, enter the PIN your bank sent you, enter a new PIN (see caution for important information), and enter the new PIN a second time to confirm. Click on OK.

    Otherwise, just enter your PIN at the bottom of the Instructions To Send dialog box.

6. Quicken connects to the Internet and accesses your bank account (see Figure 3.21).

7. When the download completes, Quicken displays the Online Transmission Summary dialog box (see Figure 3.22). Read over the summary, and then click on OK to close the dialog box.

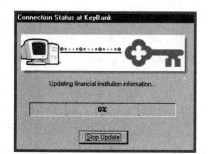

Figure 3.21

Quicken reports the status of updating your online account.

Figure 3.22

Quicken summarizes what was accomplished during the online session.

8. On the Transactions tab of the Online Financial Services Center, you can see the newly downloaded transactions (see Figure 3.23).

Comparing Downloaded Transactions

After you have downloaded transactions, the next step is to compare them to what you have recorded in your register. When you choose Compare To Register from the Transaction page of the Online Financial Services Center, Quicken displays the register with a listing of online transactions to be reviewed (see Figure 3.24). Quicken tries to match as many of the downloaded transactions as it can. The matched transactions appear with the status word "Match." When you click on a downloaded transaction, Quicken skips to the matching transaction in your register. You can then

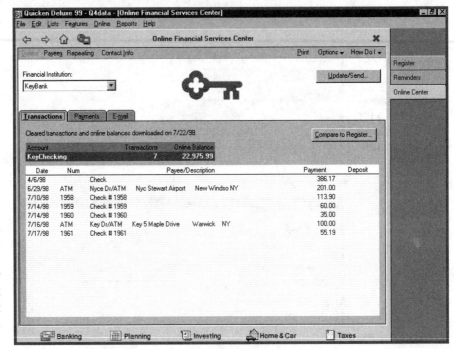

Figure 3.23

Every transaction which would normally appear on your bank statement downloads to Quicken.

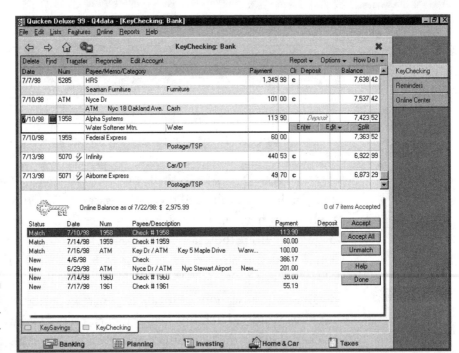

Figure 3.24

Downloaded transactions appear below the register for easy comparing.

click on Accept to clear the transaction (no need to wait for your paper bank statement anymore!) or click Unmatch if the transaction does not match. As you get used to how Quicken matches transactions, you might trust the matching process enough to use the Accept All button. In any event, you can always recompare the transactions and change the cleared status in the register as needed. If Quicken could find no match for the transaction, the status is labeled "New." When you select a New transaction, Quicken adds the transaction to your register. You can then edit the transaction as needed to add a memo or assign a category. When you finish, click on Accept to record and clear the new transaction. If you use automated teller machines, you will love this auto-entry feature.

To compare and accept downloaded transactions, follow these steps:

1. In the Online Financial Services Center Transaction page, click on the Compare to Register button. The register appears with the unaccepted downloaded transactions listed.

2. Click on the first downloaded transaction.

3. If the status is Match, review the matched register transaction. If you agree that the transaction in your register matches the downloaded transaction, click on Accept. If you don't agree that they match, click on Unmatch.

TIP You can edit a register transaction if needed before accepting it.

4. Repeat Step 3 until all of the Match transactions have been Accepted or Unmatched.

5. For downloaded transactions that have the status New (see Figure 3.25), select the New transaction and edit as needed to assign a category or enter a memo.

6. Click on Accept. Repeat Steps 5 and 6 for the remaining New downloaded transactions.

Figure 3.25

Once a transaction has been accepted, the status changes to Accepted and the letter "C" appears in the Clr column.

7. Click on Done. Quicken will give you the option to finish now or finish later.

Sending E-mail to Your Bank

Why play phone tag with your bank's voice mail system when you can send an e-mail message directly to the right person? You can use the E-mail feature in the Online Financial Services Center to check on payments you ordered, ask questions about your account, or get information on other bank services.

1. Choose Online, Online Center from the menu bar.

2. Click on the E-mail tab (see Figure 3.26).

3. Click on the Create button. The Create dialog box appears.

4. Select the radio button for E-mail About An Online Account (see Figure 3.27) or E-mail About An Online Payment (grayed out unless you have the online payments in process). If your message is about online payment, specify the account and payments involved.

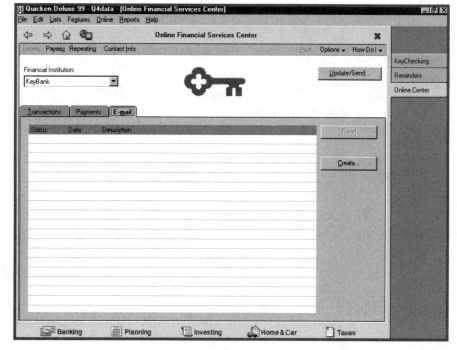

Figure 3.26

Quicken neatly organizes your e-mail messages regarding online accounts and indicates the status of each.

5. Click on OK. The Message window appears with the To field completed.

6. Enter your name in the From field.

7. Enter a topic in the Subject field.

8. Select the account name for the Regarding Account field.

9. Enter your question or comment in the Message box (see Figure 3.28).

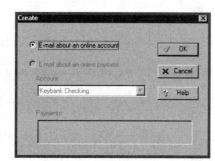

Figure 3.27

By default, the E-mail about an online account is selected.

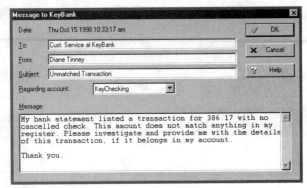

Figure 3.28

The e-mail dialog
box follows
a familiar e-mail
user-interface
design.

10. When you finish, click on OK. To exit without saving the message, click on Cancel. No e-mail is sent at this time. The message will be sent the next time you click on the Update/Send button.

TIP To print a copy of the message, select the E-mail tab, select the message, click on Read, and then click on Print. To delete a message without sending, select the E-mail tab, select the message, click on Delete, and then click on Yes to confirm the deletion.

Disabling Online Service

If you later decide that you no longer want an online banking service, you can disable an account within Quicken. However, disabling the online service within Quicken does not cancel the service (and—more importantly—the service fees). You need to contact the financial institution directly to cancel the service (usually over the phone, as opposed to via e-mail).

To disable the online feature of an account within Quicken, follow these steps:

1. Open the register for the account.

2. Click on the Edit Account button on the Button bar.

3. Uncheck the Enable Online Account Access option, if desired.

4. Uncheck the Enable Online Payment option, if desired.

5. Click on Done.

6. Click on OK when Quicken prompts you to confirm your action.

Take a Break

Finally! It's break time! Go check on the mail, get a snack (maybe something nutritious like some cheese and fruit), and stretch your legs a bit. When you return, you'll learn how to get your bills online, and how to save money by shopping around the Web for better prices on insurance and interest rates.

Paying Bills Online

Having fun yet? Well the good news is that you now know the basics of paying bills online because the process is very similar to the online banking process just covered.

Getting Set Up

As with online banking, you need to find out if your financial institution provides online bill payment service via Quicken. Refer back to the earlier section, "Does My Bank Support Online Banking with Quicken," for more information.

After you have determined that your financial institution does offer online payment services, you need to apply for that service and wait for a PIN to come in the regular mail from your bank. Refer to the earlier section, "Applying for Online Banking," for more information.

After you receive your PIN in the mail, you need to enable your account in Quicken. Here too, the process is the same as that discussed in the section "Enabling Your Quicken Account."

• •

 If your bank doesn't support online payments, you can apply for an account with Intuit's Online Payment service and use it with your existing checking account. Choose Online, Online Financial Services Setup and click on Apply Now. From the Financial Institutions list, choose Intuit Online Payment. Click on Apply Now and fill in the application. Intuit will request that you send in a voided check from the account you will be using for payments, and they will need your signature on file as well. A welcome kit should arrive within a week or two.

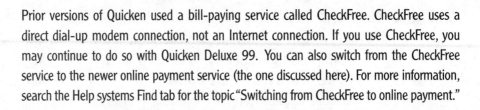

Prior versions of Quicken used a bill-paying service called CheckFree. CheckFree uses a direct dial-up modem connection, not an Internet connection. If you use CheckFree, you may continue to do so with Quicken Deluxe 99. You can also switch from the CheckFree service to the newer online payment service (the one discussed here). For more information, search the Help systems Find tab for the topic "Switching from CheckFree to online payment."

Setting Up Payees

Next, you need to set up your online payees. The bank relies on this information to properly process your payment. In the event of a computer breakdown, or if the payee is not set up to receive electronic payments, the financial institution will create and mail a regular paper check.

NOTE In this section, you'll continue to work in and learn about the Online Center. However, I would be remiss if I didn't mention that all you do here can be done from the Write Checks window. I find it easier to do all my bill paying in the Write Checks window since some of my bills must be paid with old-fashioned paper checks. Just check the Online Payment box in the Write Checks window (appears next to the memo line for accounts that have online payments enabled) to convert any payment to an online payment. If the payee is not set up for online payments, Quicken will display the Set Up Online Payee dialog box to prompt you for the necessary information.

You can set up payees as you enter transactions to be paid, or use the Payee List dialog box to enter payees in advance. To add payees using the Payee List dialog box, follow these steps.

1. Choose Online, Online Center.

2. Click on the Payees button on the Button bar. The Online Payee List window appears (see Figure 3.29).

3. Click on the New button in the Button bar. The Set Up Online Payee dialog box shown in Figure 3.30 appears.

4. Start typing the name of the online payee, or use the drop-down arrow to browse the QuickFill/Memorized transaction list. Press Tab.

Figure 3.29

The Online Payee List shows the payee name, lead time needed by the payee, and account number.

5. If you use the QuickFill or Memorized Transaction features, any address information you may have entered for Write Checks will appear. If not, enter the address information. Note that the address to send a payment is the one on the envelope, not necessarily the address of the company on the invoice. Press Tab.

 NOTE The implementation of QuickFill and Memorized transaction features in the Set Up Online Payee dialog box is less than desirable. Although the payee name appears in the Name field's drop-down list and QuickFill completes your typing in this field and pulls in any address information you have previously used for check writing, the amount, category and split, and memo fields are not completed automatically.

You will need to rememorize a transaction (that is, add a new one) with the transaction type Online Pmt—or edit the existing memorized transaction to change the transaction type to Online Pmt.

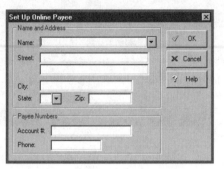

Figure 3.30

For each online payee, you need to enter an account number and phone number the bank can use in case of problems.

TIP

Make your first online payment a check to yourself. That way, you can see the entire process from start to finish, gauge how long it takes, and see what an online payment check looks like.

NOTE

Note that online payments arrive at their destination without the stub portion of the statement or invoice. There is sufficient information on the check (your name and account number) or in the electronic payment to identify whom the payment is from. But still, some large-volume payment processing facilities have trouble handling payments without their own bill stub. As a result, your payment might not be credited to your account for several days (it could be delayed for a couple of weeks or more). In those cases, you may need to send your payment to a separate address where it will receive special handling. Call your vendor and ask if you should use another address when submitting payments without the stub.

6. Enter the number of your account with this payee. The number is usually on the invoice you received. It might be labeled "Customer ID." Use your last name if no account number appears. Press Tab.

7. Enter the area code and phone number (Quicken fills in the punctuation) for the payee's customer service billing department. Banks will use this number to contact the payee if any problems occur with paying this bill.

■ ■

TIP

As time goes on, periodically verify that you are using the correct billing address. Payees will often change the billing address on the return envelope without any notice to you!

■ ■

8. Click on OK when you finish. Quicken displays the Confirm Online Payee Information dialog box (see Figure 3.31). To add your new online payee, click on the Accept button. To return to the Add Online Payee dialog box, click on Cancel.

After a payee has been entered, it appears in the Online Payee List window (see Figure 3.32) and the remaining buttons on the Button bar become active. You can modify the payee information by selecting the payee and clicking on the Edit button. Or remove a payee from the list by selecting the payee and clicking on the Delete button. The Report button lists all online transactions for the selected payee. The Use button pastes the selected payee information into the Payments tab of the Online Financial Services Center.

Preparing Payments Offline

All your work in the Online Financial Services Center is offline until you click on the Update/Send button. If you have entered your payee information, you can select the payee from the Online Payee List and click on the Use button. Quicken displays the Payee information in the Payments tab as shown in Figure 3.33. All you need to do at that point is enter the amount and category information (including splits) and a memo. Then click on the

Figure 3.31

Review your online payee information before accepting it.

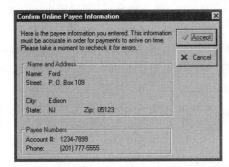

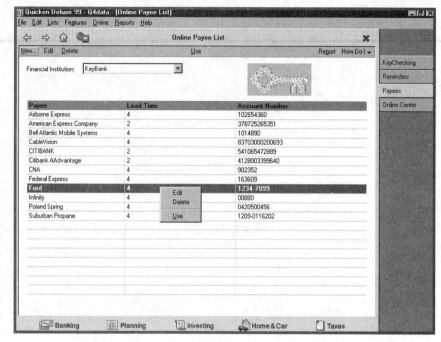

Figure 3.32

Right-click on a payee to view a shortcut menu of commands—no need to use the Button bar.

Enter button to record the transaction. Recorded transactions appear in the Payment Status List box with the status marked as Not Sent.

TIP To recall a memorized online transaction, press Ctrl+T to display the Memorized Transaction list, select the online type transaction, and click on the Use button.

TIP If you accidentally select a printed check type of transaction instead of an online type of transaction in the Memorized Transaction List to use, Quicken records it in the register as a Print check transaction, not in the Online Center. To correct this situation, select the transaction in the register and click on the Num field. Click on the arrow button, select Send instead of Print, and then press Enter to make the change in your transaction.

To enter a payment in the Online Center Payments tab, follow these steps:

1. Choose Online, Online Center.

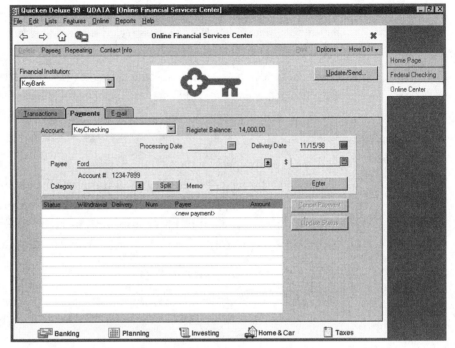

Figure 3.33

The Payments
screen closely
resembles
the Check
Writing screen.

2. Select the financial institution from the drop-down list and then click on the Payments tab. Select the appropriate account.

3. In the Delivery Date field, ASAP (as soon as possible) appears by default. If you are not sure of how much lead time your financial institution needs, leave this field set to ASAP and Quicken will calculate the earliest possible delivery date. If you want to enter a delivery date, use a date that is within the next 12 months and about four days before the due date on your bill.

NOTE *Lead time* is the number of business days (not including weekends or holidays) needed between when you send the bank your online payment instruction to when the payee is expected to receive the payment.

Payees who are set up to receive wire transfers of money, called Electronic Funds Transfers (EFTs), usually have a lead time of one or two business days.

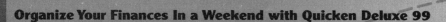

For payees that aren't set up to receive EFTs, the bank must print a paper check and send the payment through the U.S. mail. This means the lead time is greater, usually four or five business days.

When you click on the Update/Send button, Quicken communicates with your financial institution and updates the lead time required. You should review this information periodically to learn of changes in your financial institution's EFT status.

4. Enter the payee's name, or select it from the drop-down list. Press Tab. If you haven't set up the online payee yet, the Set Up Online Payee dialog box appears (as discussed in the preceding section). Complete the online payee information, click on OK, and then Click on Accept. You will be returned to the Payments screen.

5. Enter the amount and press Tab.

6. Select a category or click on Split to spread the amount over several categories. Press Tab.

7. Enter a memo (optional).

NOTE   The Category and Memo fields will not appear on the check or EFT. The account number that you entered in the Set Up Online Payee dialog box will always appear in the EFT or on the check sent to the payee.

8. Click on the Enter button to record the transaction.

TIP   To view a recorded online payment, click on the desired transaction in the Payment Status List. To get a blank payment screen, click on the <new payment> row in the Payment Status List.

NOTE Where you decide to enter online payments is up to you. You now have experience in the Online Center's Payments tab, the Write Checks window, and the register. To enter online payments in the Write Checks window, just be sure to check the Online Payment box (appears next to the Memo field for accounts with online payment set up). To enter online payments in the register, just select the Type as Send. Personally, I use the Write Checks window for both paper and online bill paying. As you work with Quicken, you'll find the combination that works best for you.

Uploading Your Payments

At this point, all you've done is enter instructions for your financial institution on what bills to pay and when to pay them. Now you need to send these instructions to your financial institution by clicking on the Update/Send button. You will be prompted to enter your PIN (see Figure 3.34). Click on the Send button to connect to the Internet and communicate with your financial institution.

Quicken sends all your e-mail messages and payments, receives any e-mail for you, updates payment lead times, and downloads cleared transactions. At the end of your transmission, Quicken displays a summary of what information was sent and received (see Figure 3.35).

The status of individual transactions changes to reflect payments as Sent, and a check number appears in the register transaction. Notice the lightning bolt symbol that appears next to an electronic payment in the Num field (see Figure 3.36).

NOTE You can cancel and inquire about online payments from the account register. Just right-click on the online payment transactions (marked with a lightning bolt) and choose Cancel Payment or Payment Inquiry from the shortcut menu.

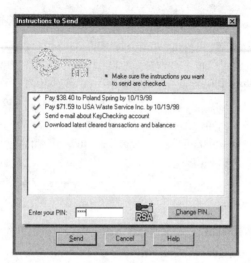

Figure 3.34

Quicken displays the instructions to be sent.

NOTE

Want to know when the cash leaves your account? Your best bet is to call your financial institution. Each bank processes EFTs differently, and if a paper check was generated, it may be a week before the transaction clears your bank. If you have online banking, you can monitor the cash drain by using the Transactions tab of the Online Financial Services Center.

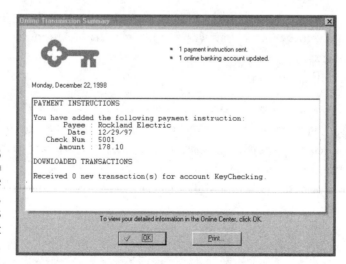

Figure 3.35

At the end of the transmission, Quicken lets you know what was done.

Figure 3.36

The lightning bolt makes it easy to spot electronic payments in the register.

Checking On and Changing Payment Status

After you've sent a payment, Quicken enables the Cancel Payment and Update Status buttons (see Figure 3.37). You can cancel an online payment at any time up to the processing day. The processing day is the delivery date minus the lead time. For example, if the delivery date is November 15 and the lead time is four days, you can cancel payment any time up to midnight on November 10 (the processing day is November 11).

CAUTION ◆

Don't void an online payment transaction in the register! If you do, Quicken cannot get the confirmation number it needs to stop the payment. Use the Cancel Payment button in the Online Services Payments window instead.

◆ ◆

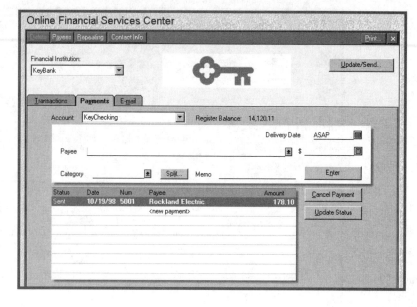

Figure 3.37

Click on a Sent
payment to
get access to the
Cancel Payment
and Update
Status buttons.

If you need to cancel a single repeating transaction, select the transaction and use the Cancel Payment button. If this payment is a loan payment, Quicken will automatically adjust your loan information to reflect the skipped payment.

If you need to cancel all pending transactions in a series of repeating online payments, delete the repeating online payment instruction. To do so, open the Scheduled Transaction List and select the Repeating Online tab. Select the repeating online payment instruction and click on the Delete button in the Button bar.

Once a payment has been cancelled, the status changes to Cancel (see Figure 3.38).

Use the Update Status button to check on the status of a particular payment. The next time you click on Update/Send, the financial institution's computer will check on the status of that payment. A Transmission Summary dialog box will appear and you will be able to see the current status.

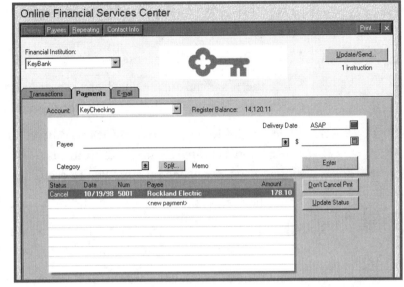

Figure 3.38

For cancelled payments, Quicken provides a Don't Cancel Payment button.

NOTE To see the Payment Inquiry status information, select the transaction in the register, click on Edit, and then choose Payment Inquiry. The status of the payment from your last online connection appears. If you want a confirmation that the payment was actually processed as scheduled, request a status update.

Repeating Online Bill Payments

The online payment service allows you to send instructions ahead of time for both single and multiple payments. A nice side benefit of this feature is that you can also send a single instruction to make an online payment according to a payment schedule that you specify. For example, suppose you had a car loan that was due every month on the 5th of the month. You could send a single instruction to your bank saying to process a payment every month for the next year for a bill due on the 5th. That's all you need to do! One less bill to do each month! And you don't even need to write a reminder or enter data. Quicken and your financial institution do all the work. You have all the fun. Isn't technology grand?

Quicken calls these ongoing scheduled payments *repeating online payments*. To set up a repeating payment, follow these steps:

1. Choose Online, Online Center.

2. Select the Financial Institution from the drop-down list and then click on the Payments tab. Select the appropriate account.

3. Click on the Repeating button in the Button bar. The Scheduled Transaction List opens and Quicken displays the Create Repeating Online Payment dialog box (see Figure 3.39).

4. Enter the date of the first payment and press Tab.

5. Fill in the Payee, Memo, Category, and Amount fields. If the transaction needs to be split into multiple categories, click on Splits.

6. In the Schedule box, enter values for frequency and duration.

7. In the Register Entry box, enter the number of days before the due date that you want Quicken to remind you to connect.

● ●

NOTE Note that the payment will proceed as scheduled even if you don't go online with Quicken a few days before the scheduled payment. The purpose of this connection is to get confirmation of the payment and the check number and record them in your register.

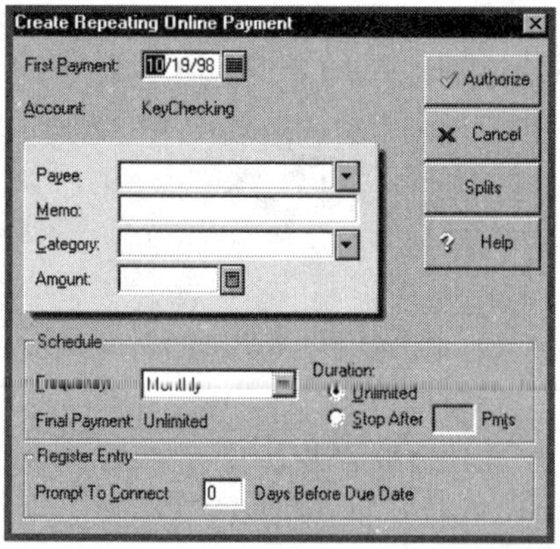

● ●

Figure 3.39

You can instruct
your bank to
generate repeating
online payments
based on
the schedule
you specify.

8. Click on Authorize to add the repeating online payment or on Cancel to exit without creating a repeating instruction.

NOTE If you already have a scheduled transaction set up, you cannot use that information to set up a repeating online payment instruction. You will need to enter the information (again) into the Create Repeating Online Payment dialog box.

Online Billing and Credit Card Accounts

If you travel a lot, you may worry about the bills piling up at home. Why spend your weekend doing the bills when you can do them in that lonely hotel room in Des Moines, Iowa?

And if you don't travel, you're bound to like getting those bills earlier so that you can plan your payment better. Nothing better than knowing that you're on top of the bills as opposed to buried beneath!

Getting Bills Online

The Bills Online feature of Quicken is so new that not many vendors are set up to send bills electronically. More and more vendors come online each day, however. Especially as consumers begin to switch to vendors that offer online billing as a customer service.

NOTE At the time this book was written, the Bills Online feature was being beta tested in certain regions of the country. The list of participating billers only had a few entries, but there are bound to be more by the time you read this. Therefore, this session is set up to have you first update the Participating Biller list before proceeding.

To get your bills online, follow these steps:

1. Point to the Banking icon on the Activity Bar and choose Get My Bills Online. The Online Billing window appears (see Figure 3.40).

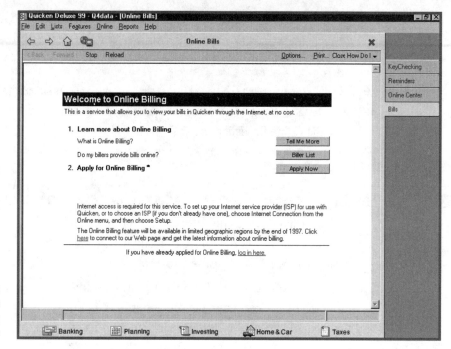

Figure 3.40

The Online Billing window

2. Click on the Biller List button.

3. Click on the phrase "click here" in the last sentence to connect to the Internet and see an updated list of billers.

4. Select your biller and follow the instructions on the screen. Applying for online billing is very similar to applying for online banking (see the section, "Applying for Online Banking," earlier in this session for help).

After you receive your bill online, you can pay the bill with a handwritten check, a Quicken check, or an online payment instruction.

Setting Up Credit Card Accounts Online

Possibly the most convenient bill to receive online is your credit card statement. I always save credit card bills for the end because they take the longest to enter (each charge must be analyzed and split into categories). If you use your credit cards to pay for daily needs such as food, gas, and dry-cleaning, you're going to love this feature.

NOTE You may decide to set up a credit card account and enter charges as each transaction occurs. In this case, you would already have the "splits" and not go through this agonizing credit card analysis at bill payment time.

The process of getting your credit card statement online is similar to getting your bank account online. First, you need to determine if your credit card company provides an online service that works with Quicken. Then you need to apply for the service and wait for your PIN to arrive. After the PIN arrives, you need to enable your credit card account within Quicken. If you skipped the online banking section earlier in this session, read over the section for a detailed explanation of getting an account online.

The steps to apply for online service with a credit card company are the same as applying for online banking and enabling the account in Quicken. Choose Online, Online Financial Services Setup. After you click on the Apply Now button, Quicken connects to the Internet and displays the Apply for Online Financial Services Web page. In the Online Financial Services list box, select Credit/Charge Card access. The Financial Institution Directory changes to list only those offering online credit card accounts.

Select your credit card company. For most credit card companies, you can apply right over the Web. Some list phone numbers or provide a link to their own Web site for an application.

TIP If your credit card company does not provide online account access with Quicken, consider applying for an account with one that does. Some even allow you to open an account online!

If applicable, click on the Apply Now button (see Figure 3.41). An online service application appears. Complete the online service application, pressing Tab and using the scroll bar as needed to move through the long page. When completed, click on the Submit button (usually at the bottom of the Web page).

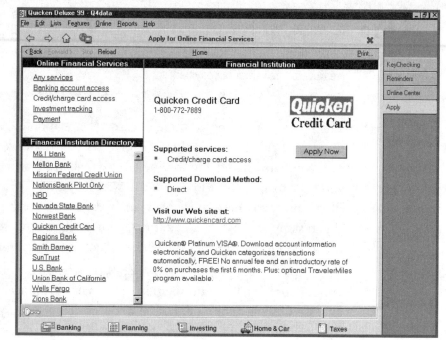

Figure 3.41

The Quicken Credit Card boasts no annual fee and 0 percent interest on all purchases in the first six months.

After submitting the application, you should see a confirmation message thanking you for your application.

After you receive your PIN from the credit card company, you need to enable your Quicken account for online credit card transactions. If you haven't created the Quicken account yet, you can create the account during the enabling process (to see how to enable an online account, refer to the earlier section). The Quicken EasyStep dialog box will walk you through the process (see Figure 3.42).

Reviewing Your Account Online

Use the Online Services Center to review your account online. The process is the same as the bank account review.

1. Choose Online, Online Center.

2. Choose the credit card company from the Financial Institution drop-down list. The Transactions and E-mail tabs appear for that credit card company (see Figure 3.43).

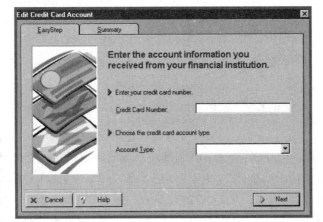

Figure 3.42

Quicken's EasyStep prompts you to enter the credit card number and account type.

3. Click on the Update/Send button. The Instructions to Send dialog box appears. Click to check or uncheck (toggle on or off) the download transactions option.

4. Click on Send when ready. The first time you use the online feature, a Change Assigned PIN dialog box appears.

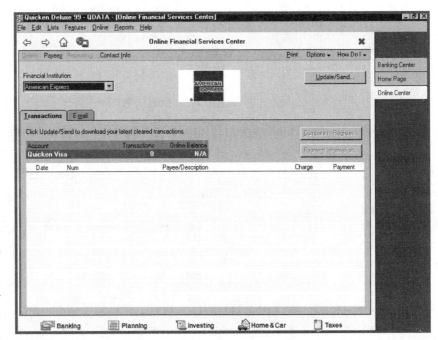

Figure 3.43

Quicken uses the same online service center for your credit card transactions.

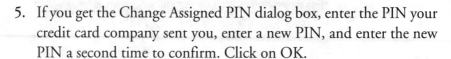

5. If you get the Change Assigned PIN dialog box, enter the PIN your credit card company sent you, enter a new PIN, and enter the new PIN a second time to confirm. Click on OK.

6. Quicken connects to the Internet and accesses your credit card account. Current transactions download to your Transactions tab.

• •

Each downloaded credit card transaction contains a merchant code that Quicken translates into a Quicken category. Before adding a transaction to your credit card register, Quicken searches the register for a matching payee, and if if finds one, uses the category you used last time. If not found, Quicken uses the default category for that merchant code.

• •

Accepting and Paying Credit Card Transactions

Just as when you reconcile a bank account, you need to review the downloaded credit card statement transactions and compare them to the entries in your register (provided that you have been entering credit card transactions from your receipts during the past month). All cleared transactions (called Accepted in credit-card-land) will be marked with the letter "C" in the Clr field.

To review downloaded transactions and accept those that meet your approval, follow these steps:

1. Open the Online Financial Services Center.

2. Select your credit card company in the Financial Institution drop-down list and then select an account.

3. Click on Update/Send to get the latest transactions and enter your PIN when prompted.

4. Click on the Compare To Register button. The Compare To Register window opens.

5. Select a matched transaction and compare it to the one in your register.

6. Click on Edit if you need to add a memo or specify the category.

7. Click on Accept to accept the transaction.

8. Repeat this process for each matched transaction.

9. For the first unmatched transaction (one you haven't entered into your credit card register yet), select the transaction. Quicken adds it to the register.

10. Click on Edit to add a memo or specify the category.

11. Click on Accept to accept the transaction.

12. Repeat Steps 9 to 11 for each unmatched transaction.

13. Click on Done.

TIP To update your credit card register in one step, click on the Accept All button in the Compare To Register window. If you set up a credit card account in Quicken and entered your charges, each one should automatically match up. If not, Quicken might guess wrong for a few. But every one it guesses right is one less you have to enter!

When the credit card company sends you your monthly statement online, the Payment Information button is enabled. You can use this to process a payment with the splits to various categories automated by Quicken!

Shopping for Better Financial Deals

The Quicken Web sites contain so much financial information that they can be a bit overwhelming, even for this tax accountant writer! To help you focus on specific financial areas to improve, the Quicken program provides several online launch pads in the Activity Bar. I know you're getting hungry for dinner, but bear with me for just a bit longer. You may even save enough to take the family out for dinner tonight!

Better Insurance Rates

To research insurance rates, follow these steps:

1. Point to the Home & Car icon on the Activity Bar and choose Research Insurance Rates. The Quicken InsureMarket window opens (see Figure 3.44).

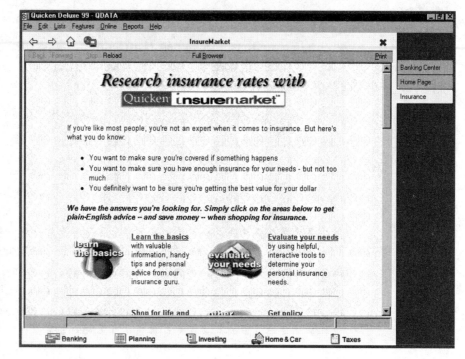

Figure 3.44

Unsure of insurance
terms and what to
do? Quicken
provides expert
advice on many
areas, including
insurance.

2. Click on Learn The Basics to get expert advice and learn the basic
   terminology and issues.

TIP   Use the Back and Forward buttons on the Button bar to move between Web pages.

3. Click on Evaluate Your Needs to determine your life and auto insurance needs.

4. Scroll down as needed to see the other choices. Click on Shop For
   Life And Auto Insurance to go online and get the latest rates for the
   nation's top insurance companies.

5. Click on Get Policy Information to go online and get policy information and contact local agents on annuities, disability insurance,
   and long-term care.

6. Scroll down further to see icons with links to Web sites for many
   popular insurance companies.

7. At the very bottom of the Web page, click on the Visit Quicken InsureMarket Online to visit the home page for this feature (**www.insuremarket.com**).

FIND IT ▶
ONLINE

Better Mortgage Rates

The same type of service and expert advice is available for mortgage rates. To research mortgage rates, follow these steps:

1. Point to the Home & Car icon on the Activity Bar and choose Research Mortgage Rates. The QuickenMortgage window opens (see Figure 3.45).

2. Click on Start Here. Quicken connects to the Internet and displays the Mortgage Web site (**www.mortgage.quicken.com**).

FIND IT ▶
ONLINE

3. As shown in Figure 3.46, the site offers you assistance on comparing loans, applying online, refinancing, rates, mortgage advice, and even real estate news!

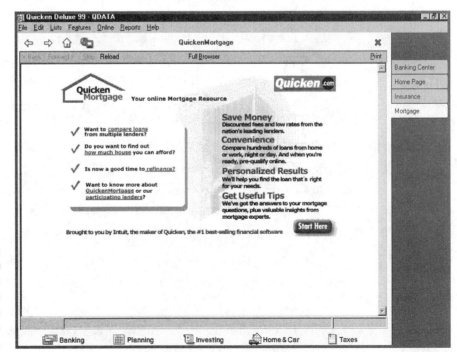

Figure 3.45

QuickenMortgage helps you compare loans and decide whether to refinance or not.

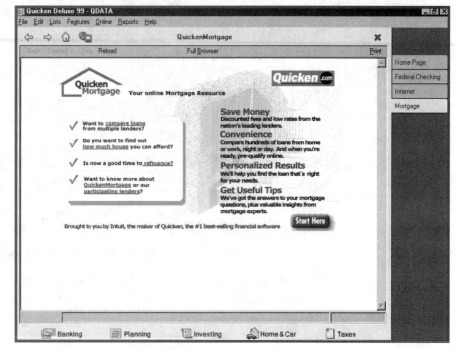

Figure 3.46

Click on How much house can you afford? for advice on how big a mortgage you can comfortably handle.

4. Click on What Are Today's Rates. Select your state and type of mortgage (fixed, balloon, or whatever) and then click on Show Today's Rates. Quicken displays a list of average mortgage rates.

5. Click on Let's Get Started! to get help in obtaining a mortgage.

Software Updates

I've left the best for last. You can update Quicken online any time of the day or night. No need to order diskettes or download from unknown sites; Quicken gives you direct access to the latest bug fixes and enhancements.

To update your copy of Quicken, follow these steps:

1. Choose Online, One Step Update. The Quicken 99 Download Selection dialog box appears (see Figure 3.37).

2. Check or uncheck as desired the online features you want to let Quicken update. If you only want software updates, uncheck all the Internet features.

Figure 3.47

Quicken always checks for software updates, but you can control what other types of online features you want updated at the same time.

> **Quicken 99 Download Selection**
>
> Select the items you want to update:
>
> ✓ **Online Quotes**
> ✓ **Portfolio Export**
> ✓ **Web Transaction Download**
> ✓ **Quicken Reminder Export**
> ✓ **Security News**
> ✓ **Download American Express statement**   PIN: [   ]
> ✓ **Download KeyBank statement**   PIN: [   ]
>
> 7 out of 7 items selected
>
> Get the latest prices for your portfolio holdings
>
> ✕ Cancel   ? Help   Customize...   ▶ Update Now

3. Click on Customize to set investment download instructions (covered in this evening's session).

4. Click on Update Now to connect to the Internet and start downloading software updates. The Update status dialog box appears and lets you see how the process is going.

5. When your download is complete, an Update Summary box appears, listing any new features or fixes downloaded. You can double-click on a new feature to learn how to use it.

6. Click on Done when you finish.

What's Next?

Dinner! I'm starved! Take your time and enjoy the break. When you return tonight you'll learn how to automate your investments, track and analyze investments, and use Quicken's online investment features. Don't forget to bring a friend with a lot of money to invest.

SATURDAY EVENING

Automating Investments

✪ Exploring the Investment Types in Quicken

✪ Setting Up an Investment Account

✪ Entering Transactions

✪ Viewing Your Portfolio

✪ Tracking Retirement Accounts

t slices, it dices, and yes, it even helps you manage your investments! Whether you own a lot of stocks and bonds or just have a small retirement plan, Quicken can help you get a handle on your current investments and plan for future investments. And, if you have access to the Internet, Quicken can keep you up to date on the news and value of each of your investments. An informed investor is always a good investor.

This evening, you will:

- Learn about types of investment accounts
- Set up investment accounts
- Record investment transactions
- View your portfolio
- View security details and news
- View market indexes
- Track your 401(k) or other retirement account
- Use online investment features

Before you begin, take a look at the financial terms that will be used in this session:

A **bond** is a certificate of ownership of a specified portion of a debt due to be paid by a government or corporation to an individual

holder. It usually bears a fixed rate of interest. Organizations sell bonds (they promise to pay you back plus interest) to raise funds to finance their work at hand.

A **stock** is a certificate of ownership of a portion of a company's capital (assets minus liabilities) usually measured in shares.

A **mutual fund** is a group of investments (stocks, bonds, and money market accounts) that is managed by an investment company. The investment company sells shares (portions) of the fund to investors such as you.

A **portfolio** is a group of investments. Your personal investments are called your portfolio. A mutual fund has its own portfolio for its investments. When you buy from a mutual fund, you wind up with shares of its portfolio instead of shares in the companies in which it has invested.

Securities is a generic term for stocks and bonds, as well as things like options and subscription rights that are too technical to get into this weekend. One security is literally one thing in that category— say, one bond. Quicken uses the word "security" to mean any investment with a value and (usually) a share price.

Send the family out to the movies—it's time to get started.

Exploring the Investment Types in Quicken

You may have noticed—back when you used the Create New Account dialog box to create your bank account—that Quicken lists several investment account types:

- **Money Market.** Similar to a checking or savings account but specifically designed for money market accounts with check writing privileges. In Quicken, money market accounts work just like checking accounts. Consult the Friday Evening and Saturday Morning sessions for guidance on how to set up and use a money market account. If you need to track the rate of return on a money market account, you can use an investment account set up as a mutual fund (as discussed later in this session).

 Investment. Used to track stocks, bonds, and mutual funds. Also used to track retirement plans such as IRA, IRA-SEP, and Keogh. Updates to investment accounts are transaction based. You enter data every time you buy, sell, earn dividends, or reinvest dividends. As a general rule of thumb, you should set up a separate account for each mutual fund you own, and then use the brokerage type of account to track all the other stocks and bonds. Furthermore, the investment account can be set up to track a single investment (such as a specific mutual fund), or track multiple investments like a real brokerage account.

401(k). Used to track retirement plans, such as 401(k), 403(b), and 457, in which you make regularly scheduled pretax contributions. Updates to 401(k) accounts are statement based. You enter data every time you get a new statement, not when you make contributions, earn interest, or reinvest dividends.

NOTE If you use the Quicken Paycheck wizard and have 401(k) contributions deducted from your paycheck, Quicken will post these to your 401(k) register. When you get your 401(k) statement, you will be able to reconcile the contributions on the statement to your register. Then, you will proceed with updating your 401(k) investment account with gains or losses and movements between investments within your 401(k) plan. This is covered later in the chapter in "Setting Up a 401(k)."

Setting Up an Investment Account

You can set up an investment account by choosing Features, Banking, Create a New Account.

How Many Investments Per Account?

You need to decide how many investments you want to track within an account. You can use one investment account to track multiple stocks, bonds, or mutual funds, while using another investment account to track a single investment such as a mutual fund. In general, most investors prefer to set up a single mutual fund account for each of their mutual fund investments. However, you should keep in mind the differences outlined in Table 4.1 and weigh the pros and cons against your individual needs.

TABLE 4.1   SINGLE VS. MULTIPLE INVESTMENT ACCOUNTS

Feature	Single Investment Account	Multiple Investment Account
Number of securities tracked	One	Many
In register, market value and balance total shown	Market value and share balance	Market value and cash balance
Transactions tracked	Income, capital gains, and this mutual fund's performance	Income, capital gains, and overall performance of *all* securities in the account
		Also tracks interest, miscellaneous income and expense (not applicable for most mutual funds)
Ability to change account type later	Yes, a mutual fund account can later be changed into a multiple investment account	No, once a multiple investment account, always a multiple investment account

TIP When in doubt, see if your mutual fund has a cash balance. If it does, you may be better off using the multiple investment type of account because it tracks the cash balance.

Setting Up an Investment Account

To set up an investment account, follow these steps:

1. Choose Features, Banking, Create New Account.

2. Select Investment and click on Next to continue. The Investment Account Setup dialog box appears (see Figure 4.1).

TIP If you are familiar with investment account setup, you can click on the Summary tab and enter your settings directly rather than use the EasyStep interview method.

3. Fill in the Account Name and (optionally) the Description box. Click on Next.

4. If you have applied for online service for this account, click on Yes; otherwise leave the selection set to No. I will cover online services later in this session. Click on Next.

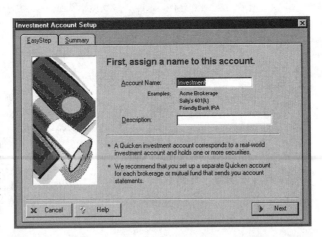

Figure 4.1

Name your investments account in a way that distinguishes it from your other accounts.

5. If the account allows you to write checks or use a debit card, click on Yes, otherwise click on No. Click on Next to continue.

6. If your account does allow you to write checks or use a debit card, the screen in Figure 4.2 appears. To set up a new checking account, click on New Quicken Account and fill in the balance and as of date. Or if you want to use an existing checking account, click on Existing Quicken Account and select the account from the drop-down list. Click on Next to continue.

7. Now you are at the important screen where you can decide if you want a multi-investment account or a single investment account (see Figure 4.3). For a multi-investment account, choose Stocks, Bonds,

Figure 4.2

If needed, Quicken creates a link between the investment account and a check writing account for you.

Figure 4.3

You can always convert a mutual fund account into a multi-investment account, but not vice versa.

Or Several Mutual Funds. For a single investment account, choose One Mutual Fund. Click on Next to continue.

8. If the account is tax-deferred (amount invested and earnings are not currently subject to income tax), click on Yes, otherwise leave the default option set to No. Examples of tax-deferred investments include pension plans and retirement plans. Click on Next to continue.

9. The Summary tab appears (see Figure 4.4). Review and edit any information as needed. When you finish, click on Done. Quicken automatically proceeds to the next process, which is to set up securities to go into the investment account.

Setting Up Mutual Fund Securities

1. Next, the Set Up Mutual Fund Security dialog box appears (see Figure 4.5). This is where you define the mutual fund.

2. Enter the security's ticker symbol (usually listed in the fund's prospectus) or click on Look Up to find the symbol on the Internet (requires Internet access). Quicken uses the security name you entered to search for the symbol and displays a list of search results (see Figure 4.6). When you finish, click on the Go back To Quicken button. Later, you will see how Quicken uses the ticker symbol to track the investment's performance online and retrieve online investment news.

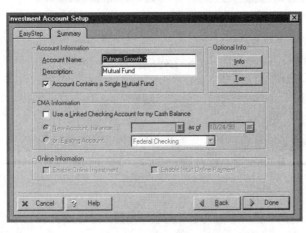

Figure 4.4

You can uncheck the Single Mutual Fund setting or link to a checking account at any time by editing your account.

Figure 4.5

By telling Quicken about the mutual fund, you enable Quicken to help you track and analyze the investment over time.

3. Select the type of security (defaults to Mutual Fund).

4. Optionally, select something from the Goal drop-down list (choices are High Risk, Low Risk, Income, College Fund, Growth, and none).

Figure 4.6

Quicken's Internet site helps you find the ticker symbol for your mutual fund or other security.

■ ■

TIP   You can create your own investment goal words by choosing Lists, Investment, Investment Goal, and clicking on New.

■ ■

5. In the Asset Class section of the Set Up Mutual Fund Security dialog box, you can specify a single asset type (such as large cap stocks or global bonds) or specify a mixture of asset types in the investment account. If you select Mixture, an Asset Class Mixture dialog box appears (see Figure 4.7) allowing you to assign percentages to the various asset classes. If you prefer, you can check the Download Asset Class Information item on the Set Up Mutual Fund Security dialog box to have Quicken pick up the exact percentages and mixture, if any, from the Web site.

6. Optionally, enter a High End Price and a Low End Price for the mutual fund.

7. If you would like Quicken to monitor this investment, check the Show In Watch List check box. The check mark will make Quicken put the investment in the Watch List (covered later in this session).

8. If you want to use the average cost basis for tracking this investment account, check the Use Average Cost box. Note that the Average Cost method should only be used for mutual funds.

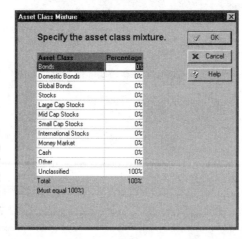

Figure 4.7

Tracking your investment by asset class helps you manage your investments.

9. Click on Other Info to enter other information such as the broker's name and phone number or the security's rating, maturity date, or estimated annual income per share. You can also enter comments or change the tax-free nature of the security (see Figure 4.8). Click on OK.

10. When you finish setting up the mutual fund, click on OK.

TIP You can always go back and edit the security settings and other information by choosing Lists, Investment, Security, to open the Security List window. Select a security and then click on the Edit button on the Button bar.

11. The Create Opening Share Balance dialog box appears (see Figure 4.9). If this is a new security you just purchased, you can fill in the Opening Balance as of date, Number of Shares, and Price per Share text boxes. If it's an existing security, you're better off leaving the screen blank.

12. Click on OK when you finish and you will (finally!) see the Investment register for your mutual fund (see Figure 4.10).

Entering Transactions

Before you start entering investment transactions, take a good look at the new buttons on the Button bar.

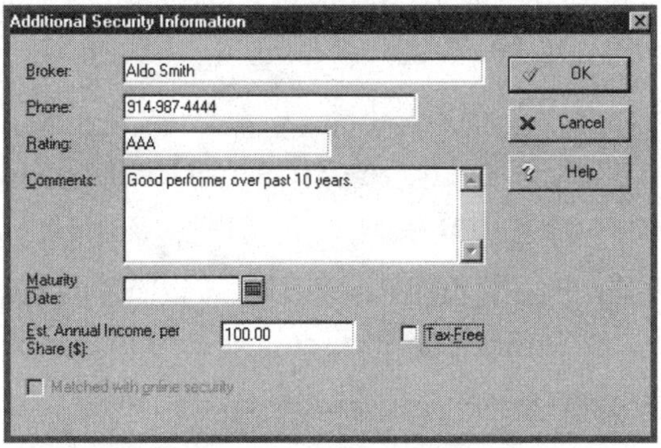

Figure 4.8

If you use a broker, keep the broker's name and phone number handy, right next to the comments about what led you to invest in this security.

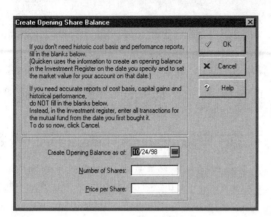

Figure 4.9

If you've had this
security for a while
and you need an
accurate historic
cost basis, do
not create an
opening share
balance. Leave this
screen blank.

CAUTION It's possible to use the Create Opening Share Balance dialog box as a shortcut if you don't need a historic cost basis—but people subject to U.S. taxes will almost certainly need the information, and others may find it useful.

If you do need an accurate historic cost basis for capital gains calculations (or another purpose), ***do not enter anything!*** In this case, you will need to pull out all your statements since you opened the fund and enter all transactions to date. It may seem painful, but it is the only way to arrive at an accurate historic cost basis (usually needed for tax purposes).

○ **Easy Actions.** Displays a drop-down list of investment transaction types. The Advanced command on this list opens another menu of choices for transfers, fund name changes, stock dividends, and setting reminders. Easy Actions opens an EasyStep dialog box that walks you through the process of entering the transaction by using an interview methodology.

○ **Detail View.** Displays the Security Detail View window (discussed later in this session).

○ **Portfolio.** Opens the Portfolio View listing all your investments and their value information (discussed later in this session).

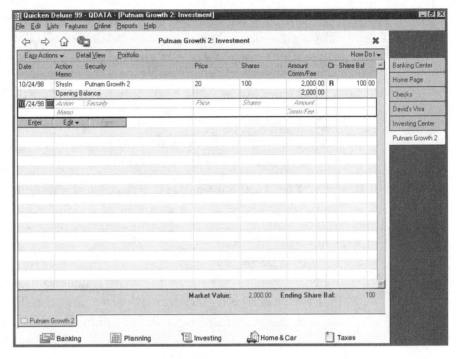

Figure 4.10

Throughout Quicken you can use the register skills that you learned Friday night!

You will also notice that the register's field names and column headings are different. The new fields are:

⚙ **Action.** The transaction type, which you can select from the Easy Actions button or from the drop-down list that appears when you arrive on that field. If you use Easy Actions, the EasyStep dialog box helps you fill in the remaining fields for this transaction.

⚙ **Security.** The name of the security, which you can either select from the drop-down list or type in yourself.

⚙ **Price.** The price of a single share, which you type in.

⚙ **Shares.** The number of shares in the transaction, which you type in.

⚙ **Amount.** The total, which Quicken computes as the price multiplied by the number of shares.

■■
Enter any two—price, share, or amount—and Quicken will calculate the third value.
■■

- ⚙ **Memo.** An optional field for notes describing the transaction.

- ⚙ **Xfer Acct.** For transfer transactions, the account name to transfer to or from (select from the drop-down list when you arrive on that field). Appears only for transfer actions.

- ⚙ **Xfer Amt.** For transfer transactions, the amount being transferred, which you type in. Appears only for transfer actions.

- ⚙ **Comm/Fee.** The commission or fee on the transaction, if any, which you type in.

Whenever you need to record security transactions, it is very important that you open the register for the correct account. The quickest way to open all the investment registers is to point to the Investing icon on the Activity Bar and choose Use My Investment Register. Then you can click on the appropriate Account Name tab to switch to the proper account.

■■
If you repeat investment transactions during the year (say, maybe buying the same stock each month, or reinvesting a CD every quarter), you can memorize the investment transaction. Click on the transaction you want to memorize, press Ctrl+M, and then click on OK. You can view, edit, and use memorized investment transactions by choosing Lists, Investment, Memorized Investment Trans.
■■

Recording a Purchase

To record a purchase of additional stock, a new bond, or more shares in a mutual fund by using the EasyStep method, follow these steps:

1. Open the register for that transaction.

2. Click on Easy Actions.

3. Choose Buy/Add Shares. The Buy/Add Shares EasyStep dialog box appears (see Figure 4.11). If you have multiple securities, Quicken will prompt you to select the specific security for which you want to add shares.

4. If you paid for or will pay for the purchase from an existing Quicken Account, click on Yes and select the account name. If not, click on No. Click on Next to continue.

5. Enter the number of shares acquired and the cost in dollars per share. Enter the date and any commission or fee. Click on Next to continue. Quicken displays the Summary tab (see Figure 4.12). Review and edit the information as needed. Click on Done to record.

6. Quicken records the transaction in your investment account (see Figure 4.13), and at the same time (if applicable) records the payment transaction in your checking account.

Figure 4.11

If you know how to record a purchase, you can click on the Summary tab and enter your information directly.

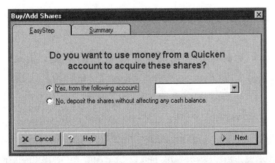

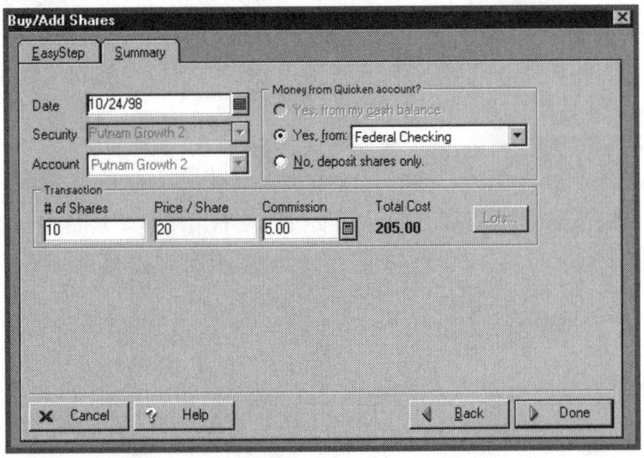

Figure 4.12

The Summary tab shows the details of the transaction.

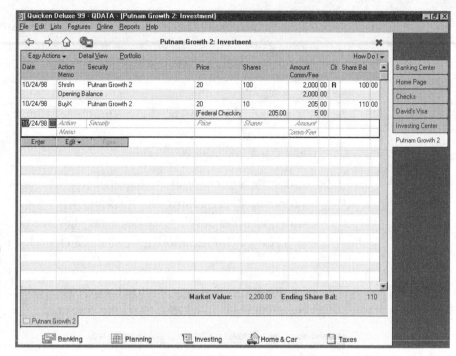

Figure 4.13

To quickly move between the investment registers and the checking account registers, use their QuickTabs.

NOTE   If you had Quicken record the payment transaction in your checking account, your work is not done yet. Switch over to the checking account to review the payment transaction. If you want Quicken to print a check for you, select Print Check in the Num field. If you already wrote the check manually, enter the check number. If you need Quicken to effect an electronic funds transfer for you, select EFT and remember to go online to send your payment instructions!

TIP   Click on the Edit button on the Transaction toolbar to get easy access to transaction tools such as the Restore, New, Delete, Memorize, Edit, Copy, Paste, and Go To functions.

Recording a Sale

The process of recording a sale is similar to the process of recording a purchase. Even the EasyStep screens are the same, for the most part. To record a sale of stocks, bonds, or shares in a mutual fund by using the EasyStep method, follow these steps:

1. Open the register for that transaction.

2. Click on Easy Actions.

3. Choose Sell/Remove Shares. The Sell/Remove Shares dialog box appears. If you have multiple securities, Quicken will prompt you to select the specific security for which you want to sell or otherwise remove shares.

4. If you want the money you receive from the sale to be recorded in an existing Quicken Account, click on Yes and select the account name. If not, click on No. Click on Next to continue.

5. Enter the number of shares being sold and the price per share. Enter the date and any commission or fee. Click on Next to continue. Quicken displays the Summary tab (see Figure 4.14).

6. Review and edit the information as needed. If you need to specify which set of shares you are selling, click on the Specify Lots button. The Specify Lots dialog box appears (see Figure 4.15).

Figure 4.14

The Summary tab shows the Specify Lots button enabled for security sales.

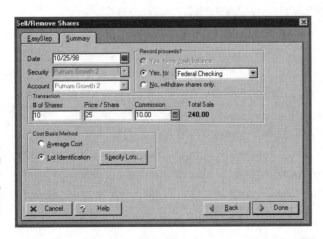

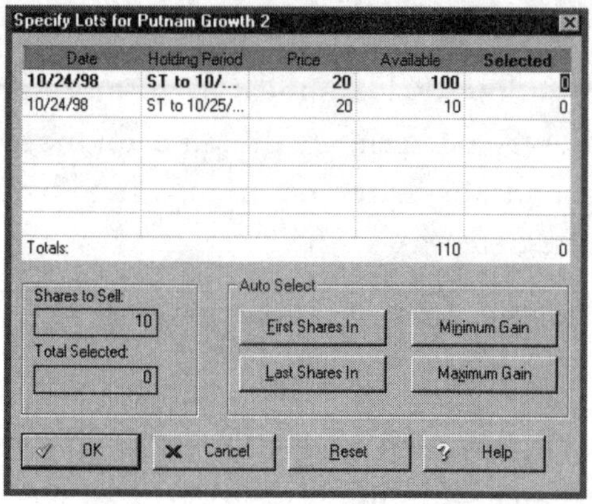

Figure 4.15

You can specify exactly which shares you are selling by purchase date, or tell Quicken to use the first or last shares purchased.

7. Instead of selecting Lots, you can click on First Shares In, Last Shares In, Maximum Gain, or Minimum Gain to have Quicken select the specific shares for you to meet that goal or requirement.

   If you make a mistake, click on the Reset button to start over. Click on OK to close the Specify Lots dialog box, or on Cancel to exit without specifying lots.

8. Click on Done to record.

Quicken records the transaction in your investment account, and at the same time (if applicable) records the deposit transaction in the checking, savings, or money market account you specified.

Recording Investment Income

And now the most fun thing to do: record the income your investment has earned for you! Income events include receiving dividends from a stock investment, earning interest on a bond, or receiving a stock split. Quicken displays a different data entry form for you to fill out for each type of income.

Interest, Dividends, and Capital Gains

To record an income event such as interest, dividend, or capital gain distribution (money paid to shareholders from a mutual fund) that isn't reinvested automatically, click on the Easy Actions button and choose Record An Income Event. The Record Income dialog box appears (see Figure 4.16).

Figure 4.16

When you record
income from
your securities,
Quicken will deposit
the funds into
a Quicken account
for you.

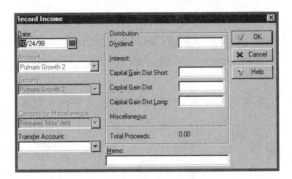

Select the account and the security and fill in the date and distribution amount by type (Dividend, Interest, Capital Gain Dist Short, Capital Gain Dist Long, or Miscellaneous). If you want the amount deposited into a Quicken account for you, select the account under Transfer Account and enter an optional Memo. When you finish, click on OK. Quicken records the transaction in the investment register.

Reinvesting Income

To record an income event in which you are reinvesting the income that you receive, click on the Easy Actions button and choose Reinvest Income. The Reinvest Income dialog box appears (see Figure 4.17). Select the security and then fill in the date and distribution amount (dollars and shares) by type (Dividend, Interest, Capital Gain Short, or Capital Gain Long). Fill in the optional Memo field, if desired. When you finish, click on OK. Quicken records the transaction in the investment register.

Figure 4.17

If you are
reinvesting a CD,
use the Reinvest
Income dialog box.

NOTE Quicken grays out distribution boxes and other security items that do not apply to your particular security. For example, stocks earn dividends, not interest, so the interest field is grayed out.

Stock Splits

To record a stock split, click on the Easy Actions button and choose Stock Split. The Stock Split dialog box appears (see Figure 4.18). Select the security and fill in the date and split ratio of New Shares to Old Shares and the Price after the split. For example, if the stock split ratio is 2:1, enter the number 2 in the New Shares field, and the number 1 in the Old Shares field. Fill in the optional Memo field, if desired. When you finish, click on OK. Quicken records the transaction in the investment register.

NOTE Sometimes companies will issue a stock split rather than pay dividends. As an investor, you receive additional shares, which change the average cost of the total shares you own. Quicken will recalculate your average cost per share. However, the market price probably changes as well, and Quicken doesn't recalculate that for you. If you need to correct the market price, enter the new price as of the date of the split. Quicken won't change previously recorded transactions as a result of the stock split entry.

Also, splits don't increase your investment. The value of your investment stays the same. However, the hope of the splitter is that the public will forget or never hear of the split and say, "Ooh, what a bargain!" and buy more of that stock. The more people buy, the higher the price of the stock, which increases the value of your investment.

Figure 4.18

Stock splits and stock dividends usually change the market price of the overall stock.

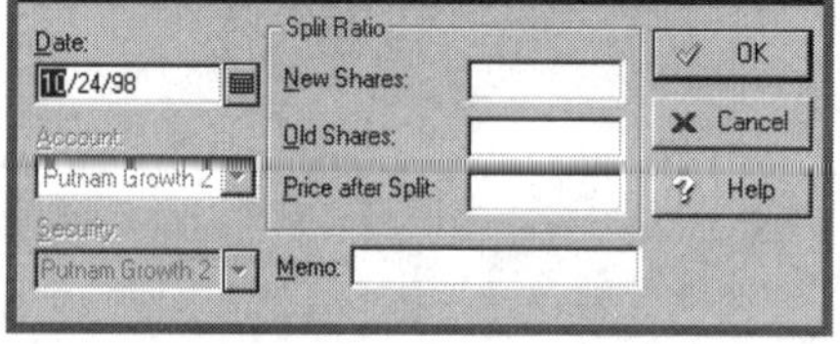

Return of Capital

A return of capital is money returned to the investor that represents a portion or all of the investor's original investment (it is not taxable income earned on investing, as interest or dividends are). For example, if you invest in a fund that sells mortgages and the borrowers pay back the mortgages, you as an investor get a portion of the returned principal (returned capital).

To record a return of capital, click on the Easy Actions button and choose Return of Capital. The Return of Capital dialog box appears (see Figure 4.19). Select the security and fill in the date and Return of Capital amount. If you want Quicken to record the cash received into an account, select the Transfer Account. If the market value differs from the cost basis, enter the market value. If desired, enter a Memo. When you finish, click on OK. Quicken records the transaction in the investment register.

NOTE Consult your statement to learn more about the new market value. Usually when there is a Return of Capital, the statement will list a factor that you can use to update the price of the security. You must update the price to arrive at a new cost basis for purposes of valuing the security and for tax purposes. Returns of capital reduce your cost basis.

Stock Dividend

When you receive a stock dividend (instead of a cash dividend), you need to record the transaction in a slightly different way. To record a stock dividend, click on the Easy Actions button, choose Advanced, and then choose Stock Dividend (non-cash dividend). The Stock Dividend dialog box appears (see Figure 4.20). Fill in the date and select the security from the drop-down list. Enter the New shares issued per share (a proportion—

Figure 4.19

Use the Memo area to describe what prompted the return of capital.

Return of Capital	
Date: 10/24/98	Return of Capital — Amount:
Account: Putnam Growth 2	Transfer Acct:
Security: Putnam Growth 2	Market Value: (If different from Cost Basis - Optional) Memo:

Figure 4.20

Stock dividends are
similar to
reinvesting in a
company.

for example, if you received a 5 percent stock dividend, enter .05). Click
on OK to record. Notice that the transaction type is Stock Split, but the
memo says Stock Dividend.

■ ■

Want to set up a Quicken Reminder for an investment? Click on the Easy Actions button,
choose Advanced, and then choose Reminder Transaction. Enter the date, description,
and memo, and then click on OK. Quicken will display the reminder in the Billminder and
Reminder windows.

■ ■

Take a Break

Want some popcorn? Me too. Take a break here and stretch your legs a bit.
When you come back, you'll learn more about viewing your accounts, the
online investment features in Quicken, and how to track your retirement
accounts. Not much more to go through tonight, so don't play hooky by
the TV!

Viewing Your Portfolio

To get the big picture of all your investments, use Portfolio View. For each
security, you'll be able to see the name, the market price, shares owned,
market value, your cost basis, and the current gain or loss. To enter Portfolio View from any open investment register, click on the Portfolio button
on the Button bar. You can also point to the Investing icon on the Activity
Bar and choose View My Portfolio. The Portfolio View window opens (see
Figure 4.21).

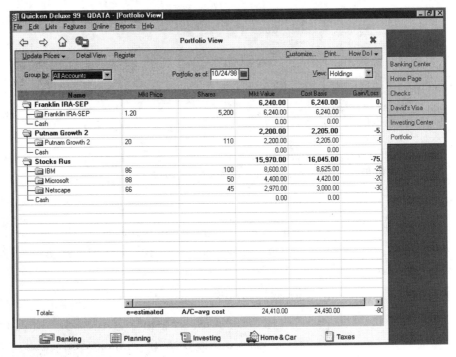

Figure 4.21

Use Portfolio View to view your holdings, portfolio performance, valuation, and price updates.

Now examine the new Button bar and other elements of Portfolio View.

Button bar:

- **Update Prices.** Displays a shortcut menu allowing you to get online quotes and news, edit price history, or get investor insight prices (what the experts think the prices will be.) To take advantage of this option, you must have access to the Internet. If you select Get Online Quotes & News, Quicken displays the Update Quicken 99 download selection Internet features dialog box, as shown in Figure 4.22.

- **Detail View.** Displays the Security Detail View for the selected security (discussed in the next session).

- **Register.** Displays the register for the selected security.

- **Customize.** Allows you to change the default view for Portfolio, specifying the columns displayed and their order as well as providing a date range. You can also rename a view or create your own custom view.

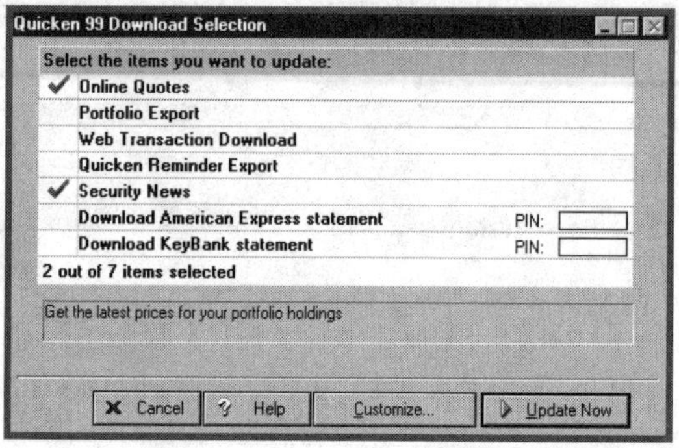

Figure 4.22

Figure 4.22

Not sure of the market value for your investment shares? Let Quicken do the work for you, using Online Quotes, and Security News!

- ⚙ **Print.** Displays the Print dialog box so that you can print the Portfolio View to paper or to a file (ASCII text, tab-delimited, and Lotus 1-2-3 .PRN files supported).

Drop-down list tools:

- ⚙ **Group by.** Allows you to sort the portfolio listing by selected accounts, security type, investment goal, asset class, or watch list. Default setting is All Accounts.

- ⚙ **Portfolio as of.** Allows you to specify a beginning date. Defaults to the current date.

- ⚙ **View.** Allows you to select the type of view as Holdings, Performance, Valuation, Price Update, Quotes, or a custom view. Defaults to Holdings View.

Viewing Portfolio Performance

Interested in how your investments are performing? Click on the View down arrow and switch to Performance on the Portfolio View screen. As shown in Figure 4.23, Performance shows you the market price, shares, money invested, and money returned. Perhaps the best information in this view is the ROI column, which shows the return on investment ratio.

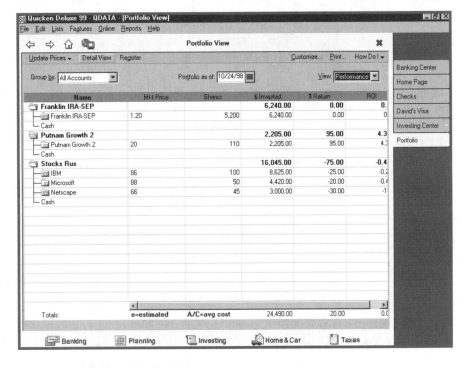

Figure 4.23

Use the Return On Investment (ROI) percentage as a guide to good or not-so-good security performance.

Viewing Portfolio Valuation

The Valuation View (see Figure 4.24) shows you the money you have invested, the return on your investment, and the current market value. Use this view to see how a security is performing in the marketplace.

Viewing Portfolio Price Update

The Price Update View lets you see how the change in market price affects your investment. As you can see in Figure 4.25, Quicken shows you the current market price and the last price.

Viewing Portfolio Quotes

The Quotes View (see Figure 4.26) shows you the high and low and trading volume, similar to the listings found in financial newspapers such as the *Wall Street Journal*.

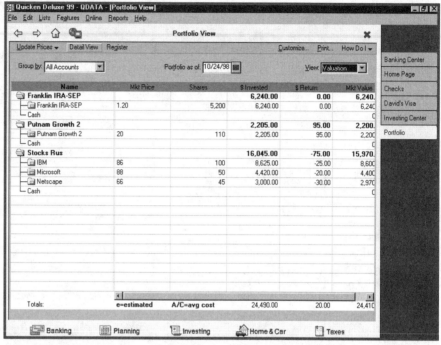

Figure 4.24

If you are considering selling or buying more shares, review the Portfolio Valuation screen.

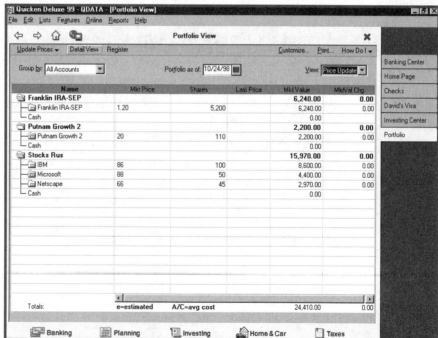

Figure 4.25

The Price Update section of Portfolio View reports the market prices from your last download.

Figure 4.26

If the quote data does not download from the Internet, check to make sure the security symbol is correct and that the security is publicly traded.

Viewing Security Details and News

Where the Portfolio View gives you the big picture on your investment activity, Security Detail View gives you a complete history of transactions for a specific security and a graph of the security's price over a specified time period.

To get to the Security Detail View, you can select a security and click on the Detail View button in the investment register, or point to the Investing icon on the Activity Bar and choose View Security Detail & News. As you can see in Figure 4.27, by default Security Detail View shows you a price history graph for the period you specify (adjusted for splits), a listing of your last five transactions, and a summary of the shares held, market value, cost basis, and the percentage of gains or losses, as well as the last price update.

Review the new commands on the Button bar and other settings in the Security Detail View window.

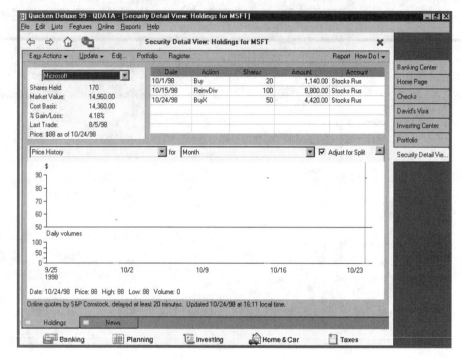

Figure 4.27

Just below the Price
History graph,
Quicken gives you
the last price
update with high,
low, and volume.

Button bar:

- **Easy Actions.** Provides quick access to investment transaction commands such as Buy/Add Shares, Sell/Remove Shares, and Stock Split, as well as Advanced actions such as securities spin-offs, stock for stock acquisitions, and corporate name changes. The last option on Easy Actions is Create New Security.

- **Update.** Use to get online price quote updates, online news, asset classes, historical prices, and to edit the price history.

- **Edit.** Displays the Edit Security dialog box.

- **Portfolio.** Displays Portfolio View.

- **Register.** Displays the Register View for the selected security.

NOTE If you have the same security in more than one investment account, Quicken will show all transactions for that security in the Security Detail View. In the Transaction List grid, you will see all transactions listed with their respective account names noted. When you click on Register, Quicken prompts you to select an investment account. For example, if you buy shares in AT&T in your Growth Fund and also invest in AT&T in your retirement account, the Security Details View will show transactions from both accounts.

✿ **Report.** Displays the default Security Report for the selected date range and security. You will learn more about reports tomorrow.

Changing the Security Detail View

By default, the Security Detail View displays information for the currently selected security and price history for the past month, adjusted for any stock split transactions. You can customize this view by following these steps.

1. In the Security list box in the upper left corner of the window, select a different security for which to view details.

2. In the View Type list box directly below the security details, select either Price History or Market Value.

3. In the Date Range list box to the right of the View Type, select the time frame you want the graph to cover (week, month, quarter, year to date, year, two years, five years, or a custom date range).

4. If you do not want Quicken to adjust the prices for a stock split, uncheck the Adjust For Split check box.

Reviewing Security Detail News

If you have access to the Internet, Quicken can give you market news for each security that you own. You must have the ticker tape symbol entered in the Edit dialog box of your security (see the "Setting Up Mutual Fund Securities" section earlier in this session where you used the Look Up button to find the ticker tape symbol online).

To get security detail news (Internet access is required), follow these steps.

1. Open the Security Detail View for the desired security. (Click in the list box in the upper left corner to find the name.)

2. Click on the Update button and choose Get Online Quotes & News. The Quicken 99 update dialog box appears.

3. Check the Security News option. You can also check the Online Quotes option if you'd like.

4. Click on Update Now. Quicken connects to the Internet and downloads the News and the other items you requested.

5. Select the News tab at the bottom of the Security Detail View window. The Security Detail View: News page appears (see Figure 4.28).

6. To view a story, click on the story title. In most cases, the story comes from the Quicken Web site (see Figure 4.29).

7. When you finish, click on the X to close the Internet window.

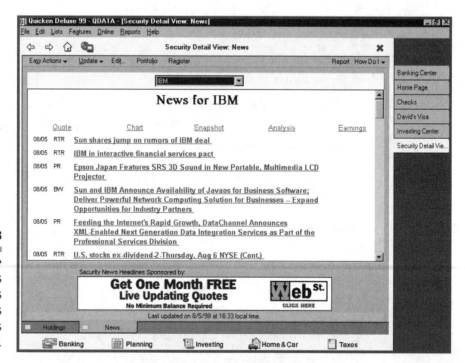

Figure 4.28

News stories are labeled as Business Wires (BW), Reuters News Releases (RTR), and Press Releases (PR).

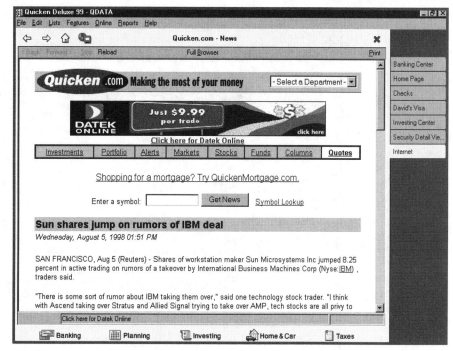

Figure 4.29

The Investment section of the Quicken Web site.

8. To view news for another security, click on the security name list box at the top of the page and select another security.

9. To view the latest stock quote, click on the hypertext "Quote" in the page header shown in Figure 4.28.

10. To view a chart of stock performance, click on the hypertext "Chart" in the page header. A sample chart appears in Figure 4.30.

11. To view a snapshot overview of a company and its critical disclosure information, click on the hypertext "Snapshot" in the page header.

● ●

NOTE Instead of Snapshots, Analysis, and Earnings for a mutual fund, you will have the option to view Morningstar (provides performance analysis information) and ValueLine (provides earnings information).

● ●

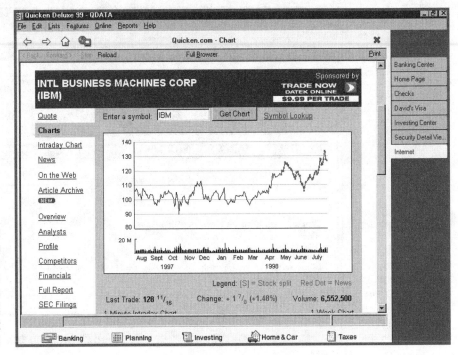

Figure 4.30

The Intuit/Excite Charts Page gives you easy access to numerous financial analysis tools, not just the chart!

12. To view ratings of a security by brokers and projected performance, click on the hypertext "Analysis" in the page header.

13. To see an online set of income statements (including earnings per share) for a company over the past five years, click on the hypertext "Earnings" in the page header.

Exploring the Investing Center

The Investing Center (see Figure 4.31) provides you with an overview of your investments and quick access to the investment features in Quicken. As with the Home Page and Banking Center QuickTabs, the page has the look and feel of an Internet Web page, making it easy to navigate. As you scroll down the page, you get a summary of your portfolio balances, asset allocations, current performance of stocks you asked Quicken to monitor for you, and a graph of your return on investment. Within each section, you can click on certain actions (hypertext—shown as underlined words just like on a Web page) such as adding an investment to your portfolio,

getting the latest quotes and news, or researching a stock or fund. The column on the right provides you with access to Quicken functions, Internet links, help text, and investment advice. To open the Investing Center, choose Investing Center from the Investing icon on the Activity Bar.

Setting Up a Watch List

Open the Investing Center by choosing Investing Center from the Investing icon on the Activity Bar. In the section titled "Watch List," click on Change My Watch List. The familiar Security List appears. The last column on the right is the Watch column. Check the securities that you want Quicken to monitor for you. Close the Security List tab when you finish.

Back in the Investing Center, click on Get Quotes And News in the Actions section under the Watch List. The Quicken 99 Download dialog box appears. Make sure that Online Quotes and Security News are checked. Click on Update Now and Quicken will connect to the Internet and update your Watch List, quotes, and news.

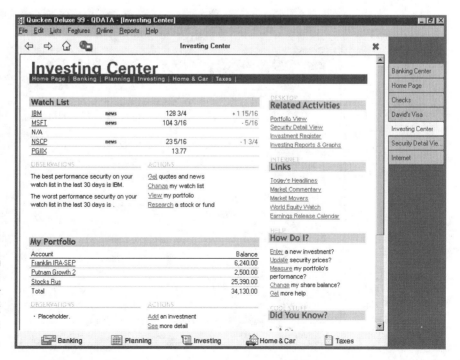

Figure 4.31

Use the Investing Center as your launch pad to set up and manage investments.

If Quicken finds any news on your Watch List items, a News icon appears to the right of the stock name. You can then click on the News icon to read more about your investment.

Researching a Stock or Fund

Sometimes you just want to find out about a specific stock or fund that someone has recommended before you start investing. Quicken provides an online research service to help you get the facts and compare investments. To research a stock or fund, you will need to know the ticker symbol. If you don't know the ticker symbol, choose from the menu bar Online, Quicken On The Web, Quicken.com. The first column on the left is Departments. The first item under Departments is Quotes & Research. Click on the Symbol Lookup link to use the Ticker Symbol Search feature.

Once you know the ticker symbol, click on Research A Stock Or Fund in the Actions section under the Watch List. The Research QuickTab shown in Figure 4.32 appears. Enter the ticker symbol for the stock or mutual fund.

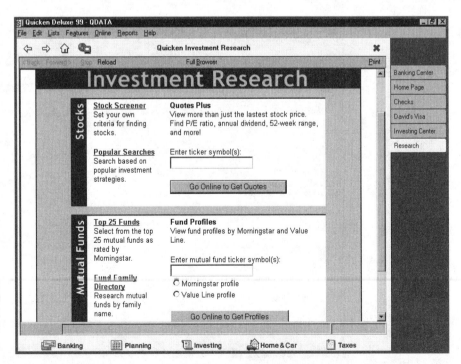

Figure 4.32

Researching stocks and funds is easy with Quicken.

You can also use the Research QuickTab to find investments based on your own criteria (click on Stock Screener), based on investment strategies (click on Popular Searches), the top-performing funds (click on Top 25 Funds), or by fund group brand name (click on Fund Family Directory).

Exploring Internet Links

No need to drive to the library or call your broker to find out what is going on in the investment world. Quicken provides you with investment resources on the Web. From Quicken.com you can use the Select A Department drop-down list to access the Investment sections, or select any news item to gain investment knowledge. In the Investing Center, click on any of the Links listed in the right column, such as Today's Headlines, Market Commentary, Market Movers, World Equity Watch, or Earnings Release Calendar. Take some time now to click on each of these links and read over the information provided. Depending on how serious you are about managing your own investments, you may want to review these links on a weekly or daily basis.

Tracking Retirement Accounts

So you plan to retire tonight? Well, not until I cover how to track your retirement plans in Quicken. Whether you already have several different types of retirement accounts or are considering opening your first retirement account, this section will serve you well.

Retirement accounts come in many different forms. The most popular kinds are 401(k), 403(b), and 457 plans, where you make regularly scheduled pretax contributions (usually deducted from your paycheck for you by your employer). For these accounts, you should use Quicken's 401(k) account type. For other retirement accounts, such as an IRA, IRA-SEP, or Keogh plan, use a single mutual fund investment account (not a multiple investment brokerage account). Because I've already covered mutual fund investment accounts, you'll spend this section exploring the 401(k) account type.

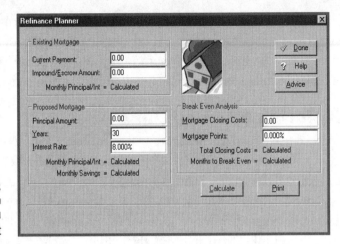

Figure 4.33

Quicken helps you
plan for retirement

Quicken also provides a retirement planning calculator (see Figure 4.33) that you can use to analyze your current Retirement savings and plan for the future. You will learn how to use the Retirement Planning Calculator tomorrow night.

Setting Up a 401(k) Account

Quicken provides an EasyStep for the 401(k) type of account that leads you through the steps of creating your 401(k) account. Before you begin, you will need to find your most recent statement for each 401(k) type of account.

To get started quickly, use your most recent statement. Later on, you can enter the historical information (needed to analyze overall performance). You should plan on spending about five minutes per statement to enter the historical data.

1. Point to the Investing icon on the Activity Bar and choose Track My 401(k). The 401(k) set up dialog box appears.

2. Choose "I want to set up a new account" and click on OK. The 401(k) Setup EasyStep tab appears (see Figure 4.34).

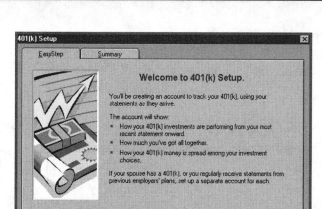

Figure 4.34

You should set up a separate 401(k) account for each 401(k) type of retirement plan.

3. Click on Next.

4. Enter the account name and description. Click on Next.

5. Enter the ending date from the statement.

6. Enter the number of securities in the 401(k) into which you invest your money. Then click on Next.

7. Click on Yes or No to indicate whether your employer contributes to your 401(k) and whether the statement lists the number of shares you own. If the statement doesn't list the number of shares, Quicken will just track the value and earnings (not the per share information). Click on Next.

8. Enter the name, number of shares (if applicable) and value of a 401(k) security. Click on Next and repeat for each of the securities in your 401(k) plan. Click on Next to continue.

9. Quicken displays the Summary tab (see Figure 4.35). Review and edit information as needed. Click on Done to create the account.

10. Quicken displays the 401(k) View for your account, including charts and graphs that illustrate the account's value (see Figure 4.36).

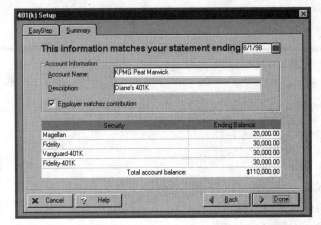

Figure 4.35

You can edit any field by clicking in the field.

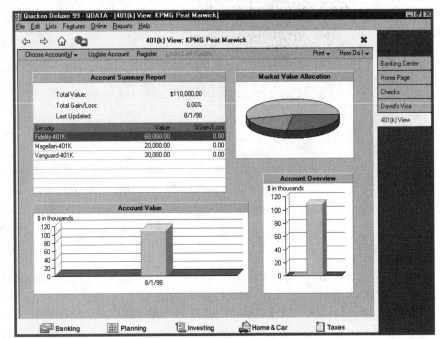

Figure 4.36

The Market Value Allocation pie chart shows which security you have most of your money in.

Recording 401(k) Statements

Unlike checking and investment accounts, 401(k) accounts are statement based, not transaction based. You only update your 401(k) account when

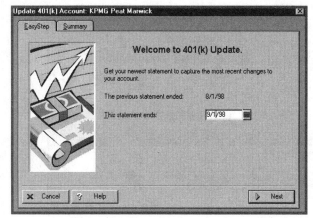

Figure 4.37

An EasyStep walks
you through the
process of updating
your 401(k).

you receive the statement from your plan administrator. To update an
account, follow these steps.

1. If your 401(k) account isn't open, switch back to the Investing Center page and click on the 401(k) plan you wish to work on (listed in the My Portfolio Section).

2. Click on the Update Account button. The Update 401(k) Account dialog box appears (see Figure 4.37).

3. Enter the new statement ending date and click on Next.

4. Check the securities still in your 401(k). Uncheck those no longer being used. Click on the Add New Security button to add a new security.

5. Click on Next. For the security name that appears at the top, enter your contribution for this period, the employer contribution (if applicable), the dividends or interest earned, and the ending balance. Click on Next and repeat for each security.

6. If you moved money from one security to another, click on Yes and enter the number of transfers. Otherwise, click on No. Click on Next.

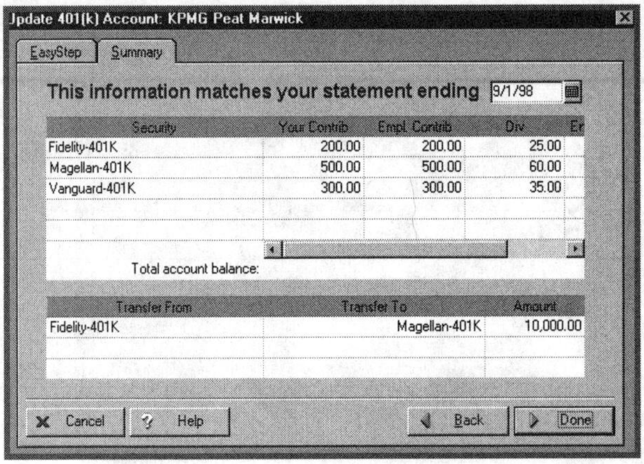

Figure 4.38

Click on the Register button in the 401(k) View window to see your 401(k) transactions in detail.

7. If there are transfers, enter the amount for each transfer and indicate the security transferred from and to. Click on Next and repeat as needed for each transfer.

8. Quicken displays the Summary tab for the 401(k) update (see Figure 4.38). Review and edit as needed. Click on Done when you finish. Quicken returns you to the 401(k) View window.

What's Next?

Sleep! Oh, but what sweet dreams. Just like a skilled carpenter, you can accomplish anything with the right tools. So far you've learned how to use Quicken as a tool to automate, track, and analyze your bank accounts and investment accounts. Tomorrow you will learn how to use the reporting and budgeting tools, the tax preparation and reduction tools, and the financial planning tools. So sleep tight, more good stuff is yet to come your way!

Reports and Graphs

- ✿ Viewing and Printing Reports
- ✿ Exploring the Other Quicken Reports
- ✿ Graphs: Getting the Financial Picture
- ✿ Creating Reports and Graphs That Fit Your Needs
- ✿ Viewing Snapshots

ood morning, so how was Sunday brunch? Hopefully you didn't have too many Mimosas! So far you've spent a lot of time this weekend setting Quicken up and entering financial data—and you've done a fine job of that. But what good is storing all that stuff in a computer if you don't know how to extract the data in the format you need when you need it? That is what you'll get a chance to concentrate on this morning.

In this chapter, you'll learn about:

- ✿ Using the reporting features in Quicken
- ✿ Getting quick answers to common questions
- ✿ Creating custom reports
- ✿ Viewing, printing, and exporting report data
- ✿ Graphing your Quicken data
- ✿ Memorizing reports and graphs for reuse

What Reports Can I Create?

Reports are very important to new users of Quicken. Seeing your data onscreen is OK, but being able to print a checkbook register or listing of upcoming bills gives you a warm, fuzzy feeling. As you saw on Saturday morning, you can print any account register by pressing Ctrl+P or choosing File, Print Register from the menu bar. Quicken allows you to enter a report title, specify the date range to include, and optionally include split transaction details. You can also print your Register report to a file (ASCII, tab-delimited, or Lotus 1-2-3 .PRN format). Figure 5.1 shows you a preview of a sample Register report.

TIP

You can also use Ctrl+P in any list window (such as Accounts, Categories, Scheduled Transactions, and Securities) to print the list. A paperless office is all very well, but a printout gives you a handy way to manage your categories or check on scheduled transactions without having to turn the PC on.

NOTE

Although you can't customize the Print Register report, you can use the Report button on the Register Button bar (choose Register Report from the drop-down menu) to view and print a fully customizable report. As you'll learn in this chapter, you can then change the column widths, add or remove columns, and set other report parameters.

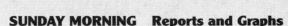

Print Preview -- Page 1 of 2							
Print	Prev Page	Next Page	Zoom Out	Help	Close		

Sample Register Report

Federal Checking   Page 1
8/7/1998

Date	Num	Transaction	Payment	C	Deposit	Balance
9/11/1998		Opening Balance cat: [Federal Checking		R	1,500.00	1,500.00
9/25/1998	101	Werners cat: Household memo Gardening Supplie	50.00	R		1,450.00
9/25/1998	102	Dr Katz cat: Medical:Dental memo Checkup	35.00	R		1,415.00
9/27/1998	103	Citibank Visa SPLIT Clothing memo a/c 4128-00-0000	214.00	R		1,201.00
		Clothing New sui	79.95			
		Books Work books	39.76			
		Software Quicker	52.00			
		Auto:Fuel car gas for month	42.29			
9/28/1998	ATM	Federal Bank cat: Cash	100.00	R		1,101.00
9/29/1998	DEP	Ernst & Young, LLP cat: Consulting memo Programming Project		R	2,000.00	3,101.00
9/30/1998	DEP	Community College cat: Teaching memo Access Computer Class			1,000.00	4,101.00
9/30/1998		Service Charge	7.50	R		4,093.50

Figure 5.1

Register reports take the place of your manual checkbook register.

As you become more familiar with (and more trusting of) Quicken, you will find that you seldom print Register reports. You'll begin to rely on the screen version and use the Find feature (Ctrl+F) to quickly locate specific transactions. You will become a more discerning user and require smarter, more refined reports.

Quicken's reports and graphs enable you to summarize, scrutinize, and visualize your financial data quickly and easily. This is where all your hard work entering transactions pays off with tangible rewards. In just a few seconds, you can locate a lost payment, analyze your spending habits, or evaluate the performance of your retirement investments. Having all these different views of your financial data at your fingertips makes it easy to see patterns and develop insight into your financial situation, which would be much more difficult and time-consuming without a product like Quicken.

Quicken provides reports for almost any conceivable situation, for home finances, business, and investments. I'll get into the details in a moment, but first here is a brief list of the main types of reports Quicken provides:

- **QuickReports.** Summaries of the current register, list, or currently selected transaction. So far this weekend, this is the only Report feature you have used (QuickReports appears as a Report or Print button on the Button bar when you're viewing a list or register).

- **EasyAnswer.** Answers to common financial questions such as "Where did I spend my money?"

- **Snapshots.** A collection of up to six mini-reports and graphs that give you the "big picture" on a financial issue.

- **Cash Flow.** Summary of your income and expenses by category in an accountant's cash flow format (inflows and outflows).

- **Monthly Budget.** Comparison of actual to budgeted income and expense by category. You will learn about budgeting and budget reports in tonight's Planning chapter.

- **Itemized Categories.** My personal favorite. A list of transactions from all your accounts grouped and subtotaled by category in an income statement (income followed by expenses) format.

- ✪ **Tax Summary.** A list of transactions from all your accounts (except nontaxable IRA and 401(k) accounts) grouped and subtotaled by tax-related category in an income statement format.

- ✪ **Net Worth.** A statement of your net worth as of a specific date. The format is assets (detailed out by accounts) less liabilities (detailed out by unprinted checks and amounts you owe such as credit card and loan accounts). The difference (assets minus liabilities) equals net worth.

- ✪ **Tax Schedule.** A list of transactions from all accounts that have tax-related categories assigned to tax schedule line items. You will learn about how to use Quicken to prepare and plan for tax payments this afternoon.

- ✪ **Missing Checks.** Another favorite of mine—this one lists missing check numbers as well as duplicate check numbers.

- ✪ **Comparison.** A side-by-side report showing the cash flow for two time periods (such as this month and last month).

NOTE All of the reports listed so far are already set up within Quicken. That means that you can create a report just by selecting a report name and clicking on Create. The report quickly appears onscreen complete with a button named Print in case you need a hard copy for your records.

But that doesn't mean that you can't create and save your own custom reports. Quicken allows you to change and specify every aspect of a report—the time period, the level of transaction detail, the accounts, categories, or classes to include, and even the text to match (great for when you can't think of that payee's exact name)! The flexibility of Quicken's report feature makes it very powerful yet very easy to use.

In addition to the home type of reports in the preceding list, Quicken provides several business and investment reports that you may or may not need to use. Those are covered later in this chapter as well as the numerous graphs Quicken can give you.

All reports appear first on your screen. When you see a report, you can further customize it by changing any settings. Once you have what you need onscreen, you can print to a printer or to a file (again, ASCII, tab-delimited, and Lotus 1-2-3 .PRN file formats are supported).

Now it's time to start working with the main report features.

CAUTION

Reports and graphs (unlike Register reports) rely on the category you assigned to each transaction to group similar transactions together. Anything you didn't classify will show up as "uncategorized," which may result in less meaningful reports. Whenever possible, try to investigate uncategorized amounts and assign categories that are more meaningful to you.

Got a Question? Use EasyAnswer Reports!

Who has time to sift through Cash Flow Reports and Balance Sheets? In most cases, all you need is an answer to a basic financial question such as:

- How much did I spend on groceries so far this year?

- How have my spending habits changed this year compared to last year?

- Am I making money on my investments?

- Do I owe taxes on any transactions?

The EasyAnswer report feature enables you to create a report by selecting a question you want answered instead of specifying the report by name. In the background, Quicken is actually using one of the basic reports listed earlier. As a new user, you will probably appreciate the EasyAnswer approach. EasyAnswer reports are a great way to get started using Quicken's reports—at least, until you become acquainted with the various report formats and learn to customize them to meet your needs. Even after you learn to use Quicken's custom reports, you'll probably find that it's faster and easier to create some frequently used reports using the EasyAnswer report feature—I know I do.

The steps for creating an EasyAnswer report are as follows:

1. Choose Reports, EasyAnswer Reports from the menu bar. The EasyAnswer Reports & Graphs dialog box appears (see Figure 5.2).

2. Pick a question from the Select A Question That Interests You list on the left.

3. In the Add Details To Your Question area on the right, specify the date range, account, or category as needed. Your choices in the Add Details section vary depending on which question you selected.

4. Click on the Show Report button—or the Show Graph button, if it's available and you'd rather see a picture—to view the answer to your question.

Quicken generates one of its standard reports to answer the question you posed in the EasyAnswer Reports & Graphs dialog box. For example, say you click on "Where did I spend my money?" Quicken uses the basic Cash Flow Report for the date range you specified. The report appears onscreen in its own Quicken window, as shown in Figure 5.3.

Now try a variety of different EasyAnswer reports. Just repeat the same four steps to create each report. Select different questions and note the different reports Quicken generates. Change the detailed settings to get reports on separate accounts, different transaction categories, and various date ranges.

Figure 5.2

EasyAnswer Reports and Graphs provide you with quick answers to your financial questions.

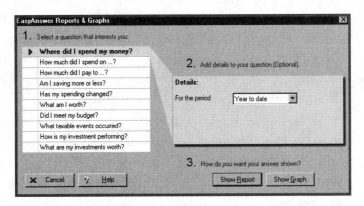

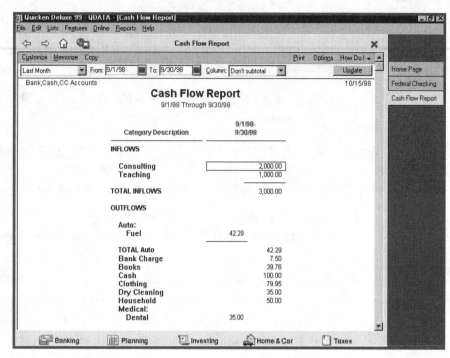

Figure 5.3

EasyAnswer
automatically
selects the
appropriate report
to answer your
question.

Each report appears in its own window. You can have several reports open at one time so they are available for easy comparison. Just use the QuickTabs to switch between reports. Table 5.1 lists the standard report generated in response to each question in the EasyAnswer Reports dialog box.

Creating a Report

EasyAnswer reports are great if you are looking for an answer to one of the questions listed in the EasyAnswer Reports & Graphs dialog box. They're quick and easy to use. You just pose a question and let Quicken select the report that will show you the answer. But when your interests go beyond the scope of these ten questions, you will need to learn how to work directly with Quicken's reports and graphs.

The Reports menu provides you with a list of reports by financial area: Banking, Planning, Investment, Taxes, and Business. Choose an area, and any report name. Regardless of which area you select, the Create Report QuickTab shown in Figure 5.4 appears. Notice that the file tabs

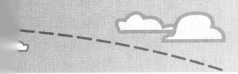

TABLE 5.1 REPORTS GENERATED IN RESPONSE TO EASYANSWER REPORT QUESTIONS	
EasyAnswer Report Question	**Generates This Report**
Where did I spend my money?	Cash Flow
How much did I spend on . . . ?	Itemized Categories
How much did I pay to . . . ?	Itemized Categories
Am I saving more or less?	Comparison
Has my spending changed?	Comparison
What am I worth?	Net Worth
Did I meet my budget?	Budget
What taxable events occurred?	Tax Summary
How is my investment performing?	Investment Performance
What are my investments worth?	Portfolio Value

correspond to the financial areas and that the report type you chose from the menu is preselected.

At this point, you can specify a date range and click on the Create button to view your report. Or, you can click on the Customize button to specify report parameters (something you can also do while viewing a report), or select another tab and report to be created.

The next few sections list the various standard reports available for each financial area. Don't be shy. The best way to learn about these reports is to

Figure 5.4

The Create Report QuickTab allows you to select a report type and set date parameters.

create them. Feel free to create the corresponding report as you go through the list. This exercise will give you the "big picture" on what Quicken reports have to offer you.

Banking Reports

Account Balances. Lists your account names by type (Asset or Liability) and the balance for the period selected.

Transaction. Lists transactions in all (or specific) accounts for the period selected. Similar to a Register report.

Missing Checks. A Transaction report that indicates missing or duplicate check numbers.

Summary. An income and expense statement organized by category name.

Comparison. A Summary report that allows you to compare your financial data for two time periods.

NOTE If you need to print the Reconciliation report, open the account and choose Reports, Banking, Reconciliation from the menu bar. The Reconciliation report lists all transactions cleared in the latest reconciliation for a given account and any uncleared items. To view this report onscreen before printing, use the Preview button in the Print dialog box.

Planning Reports

Net Worth. Same as Banking's Account Balances report.

Monthly Budget. A monthly Summary report that compares actual to budget amounts. You must first set up a budget before you can create a monthly budget report. Budgeting is covered in tonight's planning section.

Budget. A Summary report that compares actual to budget amounts for the period specified. You must first set up a budget before you can create a Budget report. Budgeting is covered in tonight's planning section.

Itemized Categories. A Transaction report organized and subtotaled by category name. The most valuable and most used report in Quicken.

Cash Flow. A Summary report that uses the titles Inflows and Outflows instead of Income and Expense. Helpful for reporting on nonprofit or other cash basis activities.

Comparison. A Summary report that allows you to compare your financial data for two time periods.

Investment Reports

Portfolio Value. A summary list of securities in all accounts. The report has columns for Shares, Price, Cost, Gain/Loss, and Balance.

Investment Performance. A detailed list of investment transactions with columns for Investment, Return, and Average Annual Return.

Investment Income. A Summary report showing income and expenses for investments.

Capital Gains. A list of securities sold, including calculations of the capital gains on those sales.

Investment Transactions. A detailed list of investment transactions by date.

Tax Reports

Tax Summary. An Itemized Transaction report that lists transactions only for tax-related categories. You can control which categories are tax-related in the Category List window (Ctrl+C). You'll learn about taxes this afternoon.

Capital Gains. A list of securities sold, including calculations of the capital gains on those sales.

Tax Schedule. A Tax Summary report organized by IRS tax form name and line number. Very helpful when it's time to prepare your tax return.

Business Reports

P&L Statement. This is the traditional Profit and Loss Statement that your bank or CPA expects to see. It's similar to a Cash Flow report but slightly different in scope, and it organizes categories into Income and Expenses instead of Inflows and Outflows.

P&L Comparison. The Profit and Loss Comparison report adds columns for previous period amounts and a difference calculation to the basic P&L Statement.

NOTE

If you keep business and personal accounts in the same Quicken file, you'll probably need to customize the business reports to report only on the business accounts and categories and ignore your personal accounts. A quick and easy way to do this is to code your transactions using the Class feature. Create a Class for each business or activity that you want to track. For example, I run my business out of the family checkbook. All business transactions are categorized with the class prefix of TSP. I also track medical expenses by family member classes (JK, DZ, and DT) so I can print reports to verify that health insurance coverage is actually being paid. To learn more about classes, search the Help index for the topic "classes, about." To customize a report (any report) for classes to include or exclude, choose Customize, click on the Include tab, and then click on the Classes radio button.

Cash Flow. A Summary report that uses the titles Inflows and Outflows instead of Income and Expense. Helpful for reporting on nonprofit or other cash basis activities.

> ■■■■■■■■■■■■■■■■■■■■■■■■■■■■■■■■■■■■■
>
> **TIP** Viewing your family finances in the context of traditional business reports can be an interesting exercise, even if you don't run a small business. Managing your family finances as if it were a business may give you a new insight or a money-saving idea!
>
> ■■■■■■■■■■■■■■■■■■■■■■■■■■■■■■■■■■■■■

A/P by Vendor. Lists outstanding bills to pay, grouped and subtotaled by vendor.

A/R by Customer. Lists outstanding customer invoices, grouped and subtotaled by customer.

Job/Project. An income and expense report grouped and subtotaled by class. If you use classes to track different jobs or projects, you can use this report to see the income and expenses associated with each project.

Payroll. A detailed listing of income and expenses related to payroll, grouped and subtotaled by employee.

Balance Sheet. A Summary report listing assets and liabilities for the business by account (same as the Net Worth report).

Missing Checks. A transaction report that indicates missing or duplicate check numbers.

Comparison. A Summary report that allows you to compare two time periods.

Working with Reports

If you haven't yet created a report, follow these steps to create an Itemized Category report as a sample:

1. Choose Reports, Planning, Itemized Categories from the menu bar. The Create Report QuickTab appears.

2. Select a Report Date range name from the drop-down box or enter specific From and To dates.

3. Click on the Create button. Quicken creates and displays your report (see Figure 5.5). Notice that the Create Report QuickTab is still open, ready for you to use again if needed.

It's worthwhile to stop and take a good look at what changed on your screen once you started working with a report, from the top down. The menu bar and Navigation Bar are the same. The Button bar now lists some new buttons:

* **Customize.** Opens the Customize Report dialog box for the currently viewed report, which you can use to control every aspect of the report.

* **Memorize.** Allows you to make Quicken memorize your report complete with report date ranges and title. Very handy.

* **Copy.** Copies the current report view to the Windows Clipboard so you can paste it into other applications.

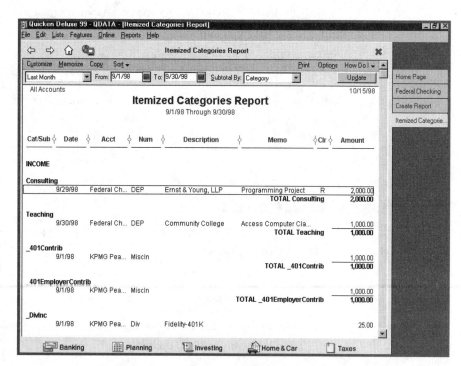

Figure 5.5

Use the Itemized Categories report to view your transactions by category.

- ⚙ **Sort.** Allows you to change the sort order for the current report.

- ⚙ **Print.** Opens the Print dialog box so you can print to paper or a file, or set font and other print features.

- ⚙ **Options.** Opens the Report Options dialog box, which allows you to control various report functions and parameters.

Beneath the Button bar you will find the date range parameter list boxes, a Subtotal By drop-down list box, and an Update button. You may also notice that your pointer has turned into a magnifying glass with the letter "Z" on it. This is called the Zoom feature.

CAUTION

After you change any report setting such as the date range, sort, or subtotal grouping, you must click on the Update button to update the report you are viewing. If you don't, the report won't reflect your new settings.

After the report header (which by default lists the accounts included, report name, date generated, and period covered), the column headings and data appear. Use the scroll bar or press Page Down and Page Up to navigate and view the entire report as needed. As you scroll through a report, you'll notice that the report title and column headings remain fixed in their position onscreen—only the body text and numbers under the column heads move as you navigate through your report. This means you won't get confused about which report you're viewing or the meaning of a column of numbers.

TIP

You can adjust the column widths by dragging the diamond symbol that appears between the column headings.

Drilling Down with QuickZoom

Nearly every item in a report is, by its nature, a summary or consolidation of data from several individual transactions. Normally, that's exactly what you want to see—a summary—not all the detail that went into it. On the other hand, there will be times when you need to check the details behind a report item. For instance, if you notice a report item that seems higher or lower than you expected, you'll want to make sure all the contributing transactions are indeed supposed to be categorized as part of that report item.

Quicken's QuickZoom feature will allow you to check on those report items to make sure they are correct. You can use QuickZoom to instantly create a report that lists in detail the items that make up a number that interests you on a report. QuickZoom enables you to dig deeper and deeper into the detail of a report item until you reach an individual transaction in an account register. Now that's something you can't do with a printed report!

QuickZoom is most beneficial in summarized reports where the detail may go down several levels. (For the next example, I've switched to a Summary report so you can see how QuickZoom uncovers the mysteries.) When you move the mouse pointer across a report you're viewing, you'll notice that as the pointer passes over a transaction, it changes from an arrow to a magnifying glass with the letter "Z" in it (see Figure 5.6). The QuickZoom feature is available to show the details of any item under the magnifying glass pointer.

TIP Another way to display the Customize Report dialog box is to point the QuickZoom magnifying glass at the report header. When the magnifying glass displays the letter "C", double-click on the header and the Customize Report dialog box will appear.

To use the QuickZoom feature, follow these steps:

1. Point to a report item for which you want to see more detailed information. (The item can be a whole line or an individual number, depending on the report you're viewing.) The mouse pointer will assume the magnifying glass shape if the QuickZoom feature is available for this item.

2. Double-click on the report item. If the report item you click on comprises more than one transaction, Quicken will create a

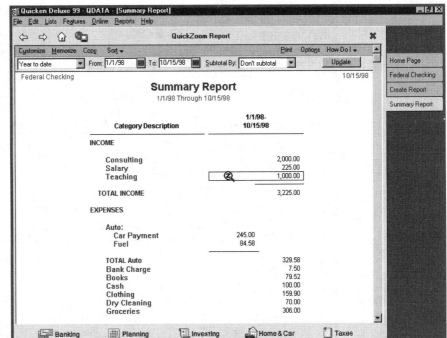

Figure 5.6

The QuickZoom feature is available wherever you see the magnifying glass pointer with a "Z" in a report window.

QuickZoom report listing the transactions (or summaries of transactions) that make up the report item in question. The QuickZoom report appears in its own window, as shown in Figure 5.7.

3. QuickZoom is available even within QuickZoom reports, so you can continue to drill down to the finest levels of detail. If you double-click with the QuickZoom pointer on an item in a QuickZoom report that is a summary of other transactions, Quicken will create yet another QuickZoom report listing the components of the item you clicked on. If, on the other hand, you double-click with the QuickZoom pointer on a report item that represents a single transaction, Quicken will open the account register in which that transaction appears and select the transaction, as shown in Figure 5.8.

4. After you reach the lowest level of detail—the transaction entry in its account register—you can simply view the transaction in context or, if necessary, you can edit the transaction.

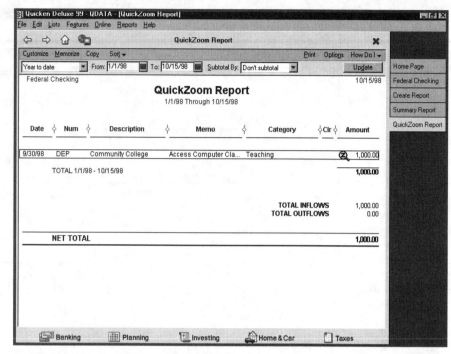

Figure 5.7

Each QuickZoom report appears in its own window.

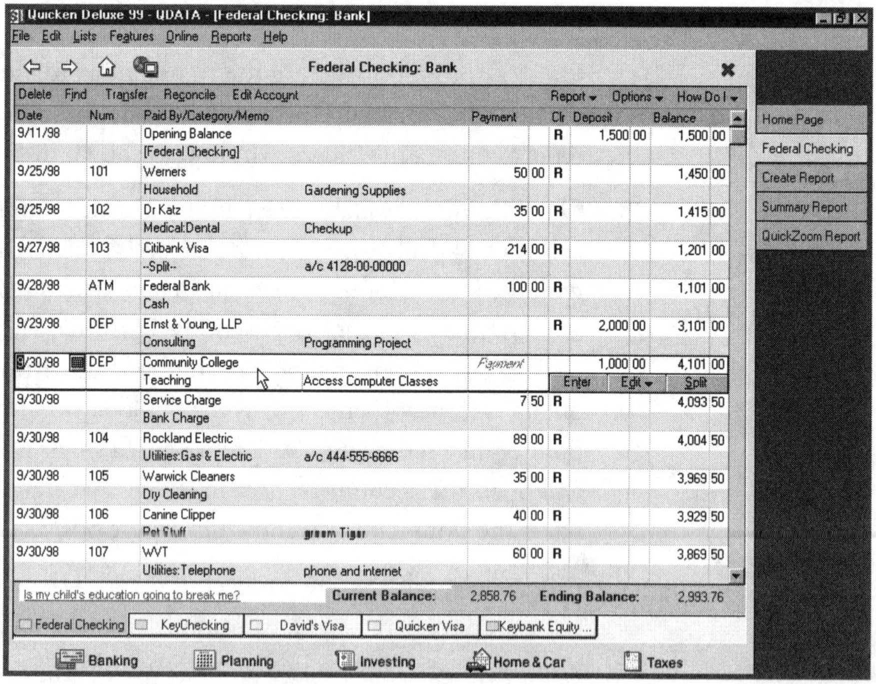

Figure 5.8

QuickZoom can ultimately lead you to an individual transaction in an account register.

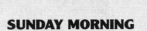

CAUTION

♦ ♦

If you use QuickZoom to locate and edit a transaction that contributes to a report, don't forget to click on Update when you return to the report window so the report will be updated with your recent changes. Otherwise, your report will be incorrect and not reflect your changes.

♦ ♦

The QuickZoom feature allows you to quickly and easily discover where Quicken got the numbers it shows in a report. Maybe you really did spend that much last month dining out! On the other hand, maybe all your books and movies crept into that item as well. Sometimes some of the transactions that make up a report item don't belong there at all. Usually, the problem occurred because you clicked on the wrong category when you originally entered the transaction in Quicken.

QuickZoom's ability to drill all the way down to the transaction entry in the account register means that you can locate and correct those errors when you discover them. (You'd be surprised how many miscategorized transactions you can find and correct by reviewing a Cash Flow or Itemized Categories report and using QuickZoom to track down the offenders.) Furthermore, the QuickZoom feature enables you to check a report and correct it if necessary before printing it out and sending it to someone else.

TIP

■ ■

Periodically, it's a good idea to run an Itemized Category report and scrutinize it for uncategorized transactions. Then you can use the QuickZoom feature to zoom in on those transactions and edit them to assign the appropriate categories.

■ ■

Keeping a Report

An on-screen report is temporary—it disappears as soon as you close the report window. And sooner or later, you will need a permanent copy of a report for your records or those of your accountant or banker. So, of course, Quicken enables you to print your reports.

The report printing process is relatively simple if you want to accept the default printing options. After you create a report, you can send it to the printer with just a couple of clicks of your mouse.

However, like most programs that produce printed output, Quicken offers several options that enable you to exert some control over the appearance of your printed reports. The report printing process gets a little more involved when you exercise those options.

TIP When you right-click on a report, Quicken displays a shortcut menu that includes the Print command and some others you're likely to want. All these commands also appear on the Button bar, but right-clicking where you are is sometimes faster than moving your mouse up to a specific button.

Setting Up Your Printer for Reports

Before you start printing reports for the first time, you should check Quicken's printer setup settings by following these steps:

1. Choose File, Printer Setup, For Reports/Graphs. This will open the Printer Setup for Reports and Graphs dialog box, as shown in Figure 5.9.

2. In the Printer drop-down list box, select the Windows system printer you want to use to print reports and graphs. (If the desired printer doesn't appear on the list, you'll need to go to the Windows Control Panel and install the printer in Windows before attempting to select the printer in Quicken.)

Figure 5.9

This is where you can select which printer to use for printing reports and graphs.

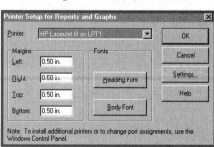

3. If you want to change the page margins for your reports and graphs, you can type new values in the text boxes—Left, Right, Top, and Bottom—in the Margins area.

4. You can change the font and type size of the text and numbers Quicken will use to print the body and column heads in your reports. To change the font for the body of your report, click on the Body Font button in the Fonts area of the dialog box.

● ●

NOTE You can ignore the Settings button in the Printer Setup for Reports and Graphs dialog box. It's just there to give you easy access to the Properties dialog box for your selected printer.

● ●

5. When you are satisfied with your selections, click on OK to close the Printer Setup for Reports and Graphs dialog box and record your settings. Quicken will use these settings when you print reports and graphs.

Printing a Report

After you've completed the printer setup for reports and graphs, you can print individual reports without much further ado. Simply follow these steps:

1. First, create a report.

2. Click on the Print button in the Button bar at the top of the report window. This will open the Print dialog box, as shown in Figure 5.10.

3. If you want to print your report to a file, select the radio button for the file type from the Print To list. When you click on OK to close the Print dialog box, Quicken will open a Create Disk File dialog box where you can specify the filename and the location where you want to save the report file.

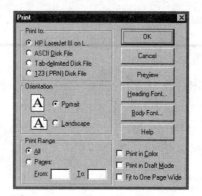

Figure 5.10

The Print dialog box allows you to manage how your report will print.

TIP

Use the ASCII Disk File option to create your report as a plain text document. The Tab-delimited Disk File option is often the best choice for reports that you intend to import into a database. The 123 (.PRN) Disk File option produces a file in the same format as Lotus 1-2-3 print files; it's useful for importing a report into some spreadsheets and other programs.

CAUTION

Before you save your Quicken report as a file, consider where you will use the file. Most programs have specific file formats that they read. For example, Excel reads all of the Quicken file formats whereas dBaseIII only reads the tab-delimited file format. The process of importing might also require additional steps. For instance, when you open a Quicken print file in Excel, Excel automatically launches an Import Wizard to walk you through the process of importing the data. Some programs are more user-friendly than others on importing data. Plan ahead and you'll be a happy financial camper.

4. Check the page orientation option in the middle of the dialog box and click on Portrait or Landscape according to your preference.

5. Specify a print range by page number, or select All to print all pages.

6. Click on the Heading Font and the Body Font buttons to specify the font type and size to be used in your printout.

7. If you have a color printer and want to print in color, check the Print In Color box.

8. If you are low on ink, or just want to save on ink costs, check the Print In Draft Mode box.

9. For multicolumn reports, if you want the report to be squeezed onto one page width (the type will become very small), check the Fit To One Page Width box.

10. Review your settings one last time, and then click on OK to close the Print dialog box and begin printing your report—or on Preview to view your report onscreen before printing (see Figure 5.11).

Modifying a Report

Having ready-to-use reports is a great time saver. But sometimes you need more control over the contents of your report—say, to change a date range or narrow your report down to just one category or payee. Quicken allows you to modify a report during the creation process or while viewing a report.

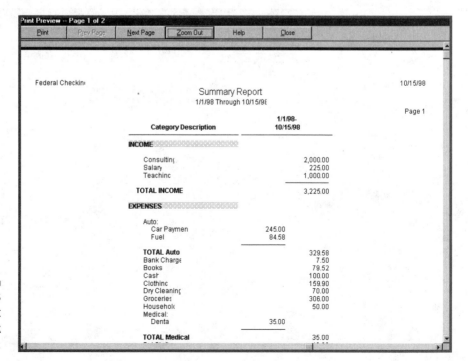

Figure 5.11

Print Preview allows you to see what your report will look like before it prints.

Updating a Report View

Near the top of each report window (just below the Button bar), you'll find the Customize Bar—a set of list boxes displaying the date range the report covers (see Figure 5.12). You can use the Customize Bar to change the date range of the report without recreating the report from scratch. Once you change the date range, click on the Update button to see your revised report.

TIP   If the Customize Bar doesn't appear in your report window, click on the Options button in the upper right corner of the window, beside the Close button. This will open the Report Options dialog box. Click on the Show The Customize Bar check box in the lower left corner of the dialog box to enable the option. Click on OK to close the dialog box and add the Customize Bar to the report window.

Customize Bar

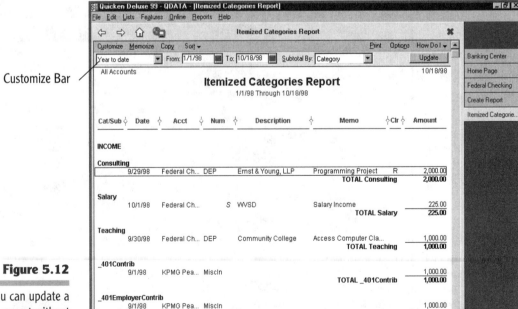

Figure 5.12

You can update a report without recreating it.

To modify a report's date range and subtotal setting, follow these steps:

1. Select a new date or date range in one or more of the drop-down list boxes to define a new date range for the report.

2. In the Subtotal By drop-down list box, select the desired item on which to subtotal.

NOTE With some reports (such as the Budget report), the Subtotal By drop-down list box is not provided.

3. Click on the Update button (located just beneath the Close button for the report window). Quicken will immediately update the report to display information from the newly defined date range.

Similarly, you can make changes to your Quicken data and then update a report you are viewing in an open window without needing to recreate the report. To do so, simply follow these steps:

1. Without closing the report window, open the account register or other Quicken window where you need to make a change. You can open a new window or use a QuickTab to bring a window that is already open to the foreground where you can work on it.

2. Enter or edit transactions or make other changes in your financial data as needed.

3. After completing the changes in your financial data, bring the report window back to the foreground by clicking on its QuickTab.

4. Click on the Update button in the upper right corner of the report window. Quicken immediately updates the report to reflect the latest changes in your financial data.

Customizing a Report

You can customize a standard report when you first create the report by clicking on the Customize button in the Create Report window (bottom right corner). Or while viewing a report by clicking on the Customize button in the Button bar. Either way, the same Customize dialog box appears (see Figure 5.13).

NOTE The contents of each tab vary slightly to present only settings that apply to the report type you have selected.

Display Tab

The first tab is the Display tab, which allows you to adjust the report dates, layout, sort settings, and column settings.

- ⚙ **Report Dates.** These list boxes should be familiar by now, since they are the same ones you've seen in the Create Report dialog box and the Customize Bar at the top of the report window. For most reports, you'll have the option of selecting a predefined date range or specifying from and to dates. If the report involves a comparison, you'll have the option of defining another set of dates to compare to. Some reports need (and have space to define) only a single date.

- ⚙ **Title.** You can edit or replace the title text for the report by typing in the text box.

Figure 5.13

The Customize Report dialog box gives you complete control over the contents and parameters of your report.

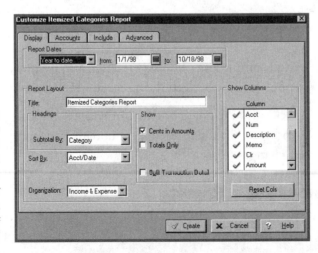

✿ **Headings.** If applicable, the Row and Column drop-down list boxes enable you to define what the rows and columns of your report will represent. For example, each row of a Cash Flow report could represent a separate category, class, payee, or account. Similarly, you could specify separate columns for each week, month, quarter, and so on. (Selecting Don't Subtotal dispenses with the separate columns for detailed breakdown and shows only a total amount.)

✿ **Sort By.** Allows you to specify the field to sort on such as the Payee, Category, or date fields.

✿ **Organization.** This option controls the overall layout of the report.

✿ **Show.** The choices in the Show area differ, according to the report type. Cents in Amounts allows you to control whether your reports display exact amounts including dollars and cents ($224.13) or not ($224). Check the Difference as % box if you want to add a column beside each amount showing that amount calculated as a percentage of the whole. Or check the Difference as $ to add a column that shows the dollar amount difference in comparison reports. The Totals Only check box can be used to summarize information into totals. Or you may want to check the Split Transaction Detail box to see all split categories and amounts.

✿ **Show Columns.** A check mark beside an item in the Column list instructs Quicken to display that column (or group of columns) in the report. Click on an item in the Column list to toggle the check mark on or off. Click on the Reset Cols button to revert back to the preset column selections.

Accounts Tab

The Accounts tab (see Figure 5.14) is where you specify the accounts to be included in the report. A check mark beside an account name in the list indicates that transactions from that account will be included in the report. Click on an account name in the Selected Accounts list to toggle the check mark on or off. You can manually scroll through the Selected Accounts list to locate specific accounts or you can click on one of the Account

Type buttons to automatically scroll the list to accounts of the corresponding type. The Mark All and Clear All buttons do just what their names imply—they automatically mark or unmark all the accounts in the Selected Accounts list.

NOTE Note that Quicken repeats the Report Dates fields at the top of each Customize tab to make it easy for you to modify dates as you create.

Include Tab

The Include tab allows you to filter your report by parameters such as a payee's name or a category (see Figure 5.15). You can define what transactions will be included in the report by specifying categories, classes, or by matching criteria. The Select To Include list works just like the Selected Accounts list on the Accounts tab—a check mark beside an item in the list indicates the transactions associated with that item will be included in the report. Use the Categories and Classes radio buttons beside the list to control what kind of items appear in the Select To Include list.

You can also use the settings in the Matching area to define very specific criteria for the transactions to be included in your report. You can use any combination of the Payee Contains, Category Contains, Class Contains,

Figure 5.14

Narrow down your report to a specific account type as needed.

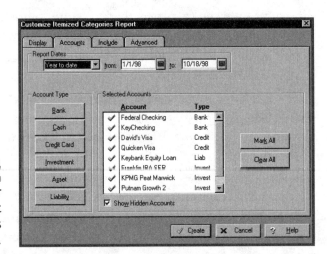

and Memo Contains settings to define the matching criteria. Transactions must match all the criteria to be included. For example, if you select Warwick Drycleaners from the Payee Contains drop-down list box and leave the other settings blank, your report will include all your transactions with that payee. On the other hand, if you also type **Jim** in the Class Contains box, your report will include only those transactions with Warwick Drycleaners that have been earmarked as Jim's.

Advanced Tab

The Advanced tab contains all other report parameters (see Figure 5.16). Adjust these settings to fine-tune your transaction selections for the re-

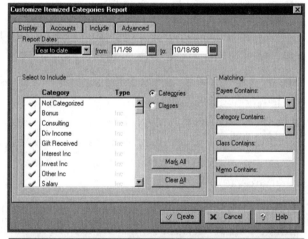

Figure 5.15

Continue your report definition by defining categories, classes, and other criteria for data to be included.

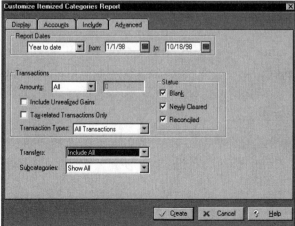

Figure 5.16

Make more precise transaction selections here.

port, and also to determine how Quicken should handle transfers and subcategories.

- **Amounts.** You can select All to specify all transactions regardless of amount; or you can select Less Than, Equal To, or Greater Than, and enter an amount.

- **Include Unrealized Gains.** Enable this option to include unrealized capital gains on your investments in your report. Clear the check box to have Quicken exclude unrealized gains from the report.

- **Tax-Related Transactions Only.** If you want to create a report of your tax-related transactions, check this option. (You'll learn more about what constitutes a tax-related transaction in the next session.)

- **Transaction Types.** You can select All Transactions or restrict your report to just Payments, Deposits, or Unprinted Checks.

- **Status.** Use these three check boxes to select transactions based on their reconciliation status. You can choose to include transactions that are Blank (new, not yet cleared), Newly Cleared, Reconciled, or some combination of these. Placing check marks in all three status options effectively selects all transactions regardless of their reconciliation status.

- **Transfers.** This option allows you to determine how you want to handle transactions that transfer funds from one Quicken account to another. You can choose between Include All, Exclude All, and Exclude Internal. The first two options do exactly what their names imply. The Exclude Internal option allows you to suppress the display of transfers between accounts included in the report (they cancel each other out anyway) but still show transfers to and from other accounts.

- **Subcategories.** Use this option to control how subcategories and subclasses appear in your report. Your choices are Display, Hide, or Reversed. Choose Display to show subcategories listed under their parent categories. Choose Hide to suppress the display of subcategory detail and include subcategory amounts in their parent categories. Choose Reversed to display subcategories and subclasses as if they were top-level categories with the normal categories grouped under them like subcategories. (Sounds confusing? Here's how it works. Suppose you have clothing, recreation, and education expense categories subdivided into expenses for John and Jane. Choosing the Reversed option would create a report in which John and Jane appear as categories with clothing, recreation, and education subcategories.)

After adjusting the report customization settings to your satisfaction, click on the Create button. This will close both the Customize dialog box and the Create Report dialog box and instruct Quicken to generate a report using those settings.

• •

NOTE Whether you change the report customization settings while creating a report or from the report window, the settings will apply only to the report you're working on at the time. Unlike changes in the Report Options settings, any changes you make in the Customize dialog box will not affect previously created reports in other windows or other reports that you might create in the future.

• •

Changing Report Options

To change the Report Options settings, follow these steps:

1. Open a report window.

2. Click on the Options button in the Button bar at the top of the report window. This will open the Report Options dialog box, as shown in Figure 5.17.

3. Adjust the settings in the Report Options dialog box as desired. The available options are as follows:

    ✿ **Account Display.** Choose to display the account name, description, or both where your Quicken accounts appear as items in your reports. The account name is often abbreviated.

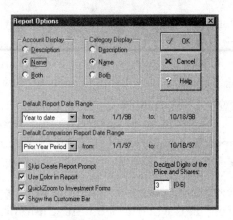

Figure 5.17

The settings in the Report Options dialog box become the defaults for any new reports you create.

As a result, the description is usually more meaningful—provided you supplied a description when you created the account. If some of your accounts are missing descriptions, edit them—or choose Both to make sure *some* account label appears.

☼ **Category Display.** Choose to display the name, description, or both where categories appear in your reports. Again, choosing Description is usually better if you entered descriptions when you defined your categories.

☼ **Default Report Date Range.** Select a date range from the list box to be the default value when you create new reports. Of course, you will be able to override the default when you create a report, but this setting gives you the opportunity to make the date range you use most frequently Quicken's default. That way, you won't have to override the default as often.

☼ **Default Comparison Report Date Range.** Select a date range from the list box to be the default date range for comparison dates in reports. Again, you will be able to override this default value when you create a new report.

☼ **Skip Create Report Prompt.** Check this option to instruct Quicken to forego displaying the Create Report dialog box after you choose a report title from Quicken's Reports menu.

Quicken will generate the report immediately using the default settings. You can then customize the report in the open report window if necessary.

- **Use Color in Report.** Checking this option causes Quicken to display negative numbers and corresponding labels in red.

- **QuickZoom to Investment Forms.** This option controls what happens when you use QuickZoom on an investment transaction in a report. If the option is checked, Quicken will open the investment form you filled in for the transaction. If this check box is cleared, Quicken will open the investment account register and select the transaction there. I think working in the account register is a little more efficient (I like to see the preceding and following transactions), but the investment form is easier to use for editing an individual transaction.

- **Show the Customize Bar.** Check this option to display the Customize Bar—the date range list boxes and the Update button—at the top of the report window. I use the Customize Bar to fine-tune almost every report I create, so I have a hard time imagining doing without it in order to make room for one more row of report data onscreen.

- **Decimal Digits of the Price and Shares.** Enter the number of decimal places you want Quicken to use for the shares owned and price per share values in your investment reports. A value of 2 or 3 is usually sufficient, but you can increase this if you feel the need to track tiny fractions of a share.

4. After setting the options in the Report Options dialog box, click on OK to close the dialog box and record your preferences. Quicken will apply the settings to all open reports and to the new reports you create in the future. The settings will remain in effect until you open the Report Options dialog box and change them.

Take a Break

This would be a good time to stop and take a break. Get up, stretch, and walk around for a few minutes. Refill your cup of coffee or tea. Just get away from the computer screen for a little while. Then, when you return, you'll be ready to learn how to create meaningful financial graphs in Quicken.

Graphs: Getting the Financial Picture

Reports are essential tools for extracting precise information from your financial data. But when it comes to visualizing trends and relationships, you can't beat a good graph. Graphs can turn a stack of dry numeric data into an easy-to-understand picture of your finances.

Quicken can produce five basic graphs. Although they are not as numerous as the many Quicken report formats, Quicken's graphs can be valuable aids to understanding your financial situation.

- **Income & Expense**. A bar graph on top shows separate bars for income and expenses for each month. A pie graph displays savings and expense categories as a percentage of income.

- **Budget Variance**. The top bar graph plots the difference between actual and budgeted net income for each month. The bottom bar graph plots budget and actual values for each category.

- **Net Worth**. A single graph plots assets and liabilities for each month as bars overlaid with a line showing your net worth.

- **Investment Performance**. The top bar graph shows total portfolio value for each month with each bar segmented to indicate the securities that make up the total. Another bar graph shows average annual return for each security.

- **Investment Asset Allocation**. A pie graph showing investment classes as a percentage of the whole portfolio (this graph is useful only if you have assigned classes to your investments).

● ●

NOTE In addition to the graph reports covered in this section, you will find snapshot graphs on each of the Financial Center pages (from the menu bar choose Features, Centers). You can right-click on any of these snapshots to manipulate them in the same way as you manipulate any graph. The snapshots only appear if you have entered data into that particular area. For example, the Budget snapshot will not appear until you set up a budget.

● ●

Creating a Graph

The process of creating a Quicken graph is very similar to the procedure for creating a report. You issue the command to create a graph, select the graph format, define a date range, and then let Quicken do all the work to display your financial data graphically as bar segments, pie slices, or trend lines.

To create a Quicken graph, simply follow these steps:

1. From the menu bar, choose Reports, Graphs, and then any of the graph types listed. The Create Graph dialog box appears (see Figure 5.18).

2. Select a graph format (such as Income and Expenses) from the list box in the middle of the Create Graph dialog box.

3. Specify the date range (such as Year To Date) for the graph by making a selection from the Graph Dates drop-down list box or by

Figure 5.18

It takes only a couple of selections in the Create Graph dialog box to define a Quicken graph.

entering starting and ending dates in the From and To boxes. (You can type in a date or click on the button at the right end of the From or To box and select a date from the shortcut calendar.)

◆ ◆

CAUTION You won't be able to create a budget variance graph until you first create a budget. (Creating a budget is covered later in the Sunday evening session.)

◆ ◆

4. Once you have selected the graph format and set the date range for the graph, click on the Create button to close the Create Graph dialog box and generate the graph image. Quicken displays the graph in its own window, as shown in Figure 5.19.

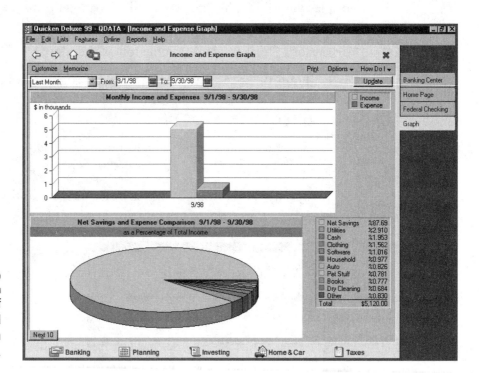

Figure 5.19

This is just one of the five standard graphs Quicken can produce.

NOTE In addition to creating custom graphs, you can create graphs in response to a few of the EasyAnswer questions or by clicking the Report button in an account register and selecting Expense Summary Graph.

Viewing and Using Graphs

The graph window is usually simple. The entire graph and its supporting keys often appear on a single page. Some graphs, such as the Investment Performance Graph shown in Figure 5.20, include buttons to provide access to other graph pages depicting different views or variations of the basic graph.

For example, the Investment Performance Graph normally shows the performance of your investments by security, but Quicken can also show graphs of your investment performance by investment type, goal, account (see Figure 5.21), or asset class. If there are too many categories to show in one

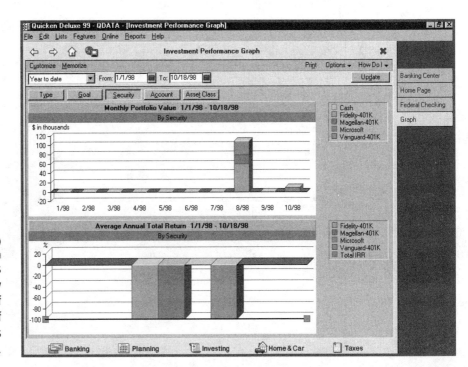

Figure 5.20

Many of Quicken's graphs are actually composed of a couple of separate graphs plus their keys.

graph (as is often the case in the Investment Performance Graph by Security), Quicken will graph ten categories and lump the remaining categories together under the Other label. Clicking on Next 10 will display a graph that plots the categories that made up the Other category in the previous view of the graph.

CAUTION

✦ ✦

Graphs are intended to be viewed in a Quicken application window that is maximized to occupy the entire screen. If you reduce the size of the Quicken window, the graph may be truncated—and there are no scroll bars on a graph window that you can use to bring the truncated portions of the graph into view. To view the entire graph, just maximize the Quicken application window.

✦ ✦

There is one special trick hiding within the graph window—a sort of QuickZoom for graphs that shows the values of each graph element. You

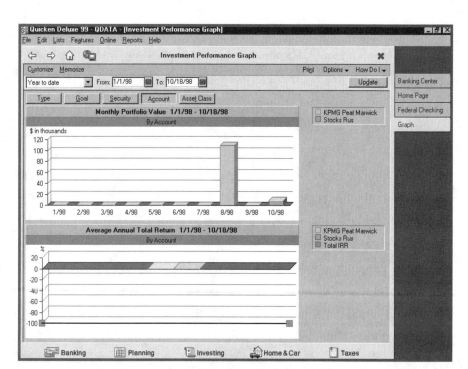

Figure 5.21

Buttons in the graph window give you access to alternate versions of some graphs.

can use this feature to see a shortcut label giving information about one graph element—a bar segment or pie slice—at a time. To use this feature, simply move the mouse pointer across the graph window and point to a graph element you're interested in. When the pointer is over a graph element for which a label is available, it changes from an arrow to a magnifying glass. To see the label, click on the graph element (or just let the pointer sit still for a moment); the label will appear in a small shortcut box like the flyover help boxes in Quicken's toolbars (see Figure 5.22).

Printing Graphs

Printing a graph is a straightforward proposition. You select the printer, page margins, and fonts in the Printer Setup for Reports and Graphs dialog box (which you saw in the section on printing reports earlier). Unlike report printing, graph printing doesn't involve any other options you need to select before printing each graph.

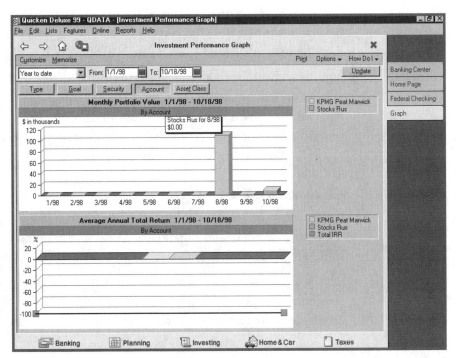

Figure 5.22

Shortcut labels display detailed information about selected graph elements.

To print a graph, first create the graph. If necessary, use the buttons in the graph window to display the variation you want to print. Then just click on the Print button in the Button bar at the top of the graph window. Quicken will print the graph immediately. Quicken resizes the graph to take advantage of the size and shape of the printed page. A printed graph is often more attractively proportioned than the on-screen graph from which it came.

Modifying Graphs

Graphs can be modified and customized in the same ways that you modified and customized reports. When you create a graph, you can click on the Customize button to control all aspects of your graph. Or, while viewing a graph, you can change the date range or click on the Customize button on the Button bar.

Updating a Graph

While you are viewing a graph, you can change the date range in the Customize Bar (just below the Button bar) at any time. After you change the date, be sure to click on the Update button to redraw the graph.

You can also use the Zoom feature to display detailed graphs and eventually the underlying Transaction report (see Figure 5.23). Once in the report, you can drill down further as needed, right to the registers. If you change any data in your registers, click on the Update button in the respective report or graph zoom windows to see your change reflected.

Customizing a Graph

Clicking on the Customize button in the Button bar of a graph view or in the Create Graph window opens the Customize Graph dialog box, as shown in Figure 5.24.

The Customize Graph dialog box is simpler than its counterpart for customizing reports. Graphs are best suited to visualizing summaries and trends, so there's no need for the level of transaction selection detail that is

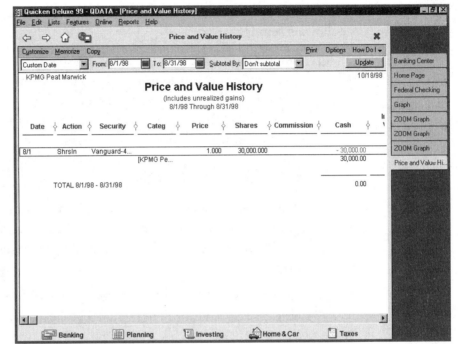

Figure 5.23

Behind each great graph is an even greater report.

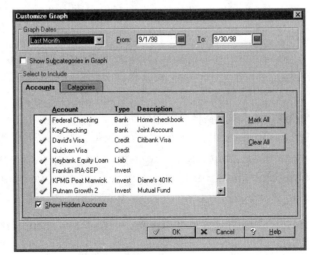

Figure 5.24

The Customize Graph dialog box lets you define the accounts and categories that will be included in the graph.

available for reports. You can customize your graph by adjusting any of the following settings:

- **Graph Dates.** The Customize Graph dialog box provides yet another opportunity to adjust the date range of the data Quicken will use to create the graph. Depending on the kind of graph you're customizing, the date settings may vary slightly. For most graphs, there'll be a drop-down list box where you can select a date range, plus From and To boxes where you can enter specific dates. For the Investment Asset Allocation graph, there will be only a single date box.

- **Show Subcategories In Graph.** Check this option to graph subcategories as separate bar segments or pie slices. Leave it unchecked to simplify your graph and show categories without subcategory breakdowns.

- **Accounts.** In the Accounts list, a check mark beside an account name indicates an account will be included in the graph. Click on account names to toggle the check marks on and off.

- **Categories.** Select the categories to be included in the graph from the list in this tab. Like the Accounts list, a check mark beside an item indicates a category to be included in the graph. Click on the category name to toggle the check mark on and off.

After adjusting the settings in the Customize Graph dialog box, click on the OK button to generate a new (or revised) graph using those settings.

Changing Graph Options

The Graph Options allow you to hide the Customize Bar, change the graph-drawing settings, or create multiple graphs in separate windows. To access the Graph Option settings, click on the Options button in the Button bar. The drop-down menu provides you with the following default options:

- **Hide Customize Bar.** Removes the Customize Bar from the Graph view windows.

- ✿ **Draw in 2D (faster).** Displays the graph as a two dimensional object instead of the default three dimensions (3D).

- ✿ **Draw in Patterns.** Displays the graph using black and white patterns (as used for printing on a black and white printer) instead of the default color display.

- ✿ **Create Graphs in Separate Windows.** For graphs with multiple views, opens a new window for each graph view.

Saving Reports and Graphs

After you invest time and effort in customizing a report or graph to include just the information you want, it can be disconcerting to think that you might have to repeat the entire process to reproduce the same effect again in the future. After all, report and graph customization settings are not permanent—the settings revert to their default values when you create the next report or graph.

Fortunately, Quicken allows you to memorize (save) a customized report or graph definition and reuse it any time you like. In effect, you can add your customized reports and graphs to Quicken's repertoire. Once you've done that, using the memorized reports and graphs is as simple as selecting one of Quicken's standard report or graph formats.

Memorizing a Report

To memorize a report so you can reuse it in the future, follow these steps:

1. Create and customize the report you want to memorize.

2. Click on the Memorize button in the Button bar at the top of the report window. This will open the Memorize Report dialog box, as shown in Figure 5.25.

3. In the Title box at the top of the Memorize Report dialog box, type a name for the memorized report. This is the name that will appear in the list of available report formats when you create a new report. It's not necessarily the title that appears at top of the report page.

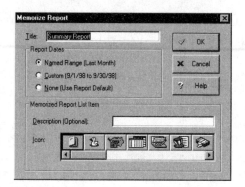

Figure 5.25

When you
memorize a report,
you'll need to give
it a descriptive
name.

4. In the Report Date section, select Named Range, Custom, or None to instruct Quicken on how to save date information for your memorized report. Choose Named Range to memorize the report using the preset date range such as Year to Date. Choose Custom to memorize the report using date settings from the From and To boxes. Choose None to memorize the report without date information, and use the default date settings in force when you create a new report based on this memorized format.

5. In the Memorized Report list item area, type a short description of the report to help identify it. Then select an icon to appear beside this item in the memorized report list.

6. Click on OK to close the Memorize Report dialog box and add this report format to Quicken's list of available reports.

Once a report is memorized, you can use the report at any time by opening the Create Report window and selecting the memorized report from the list on the Memorized tab. While you have a memorized report selected, you can click on the Edit button to open the Edit Memorized Report Item dialog box, where you can quickly change the title, description, and icon associated with the memorized report. You can also click on the Delete button to remove a memorized report from the list in the Create Report dialog box.

TIP You can also open the Create Reports dialog box to the Memorized tab by clicking on Reports in the menu bar and choosing Memorized Reports.

Memorizing a Graph

The procedure for memorizing a graph is essentially the same as the one for memorizing a report. The difference is that you need to enter less information describing a memorized graph. Here are the steps:

1. Create and customize the graph you want to memorize for future use.

2. Click on the Memorize button in the Button bar at the top of the graph window. This will open the Memorize Graph dialog box.

3. Type a descriptive name for your graph in the Graph Name text box.

4. Click on OK to close the Memorize Graph dialog box and add the current graph to Quicken's list of memorized graph formats.

Using a memorized graph format to create a new graph is a simple process—it's just a little different from the process of creating one of Quicken's standard graphs. To create a graph based on a memorized graph format, follow these steps:

1. Open the Create Graph dialog box.

2. Click on the Memorized button found at the bottom of the Create Graph dialog box to open the Memorized Graphs dialog box, as shown in Figure 5.26.

TIP Another way to open the list of memorized graphs is to pull down the Reports menu, point to Graphs, and choose Memorized Graphs from the cascading menu that appears. If you use this technique, the Memorized Graphs list appears in a Quicken window instead of a dialog box, but it functions the same.

Figure 5.26

Select a graph title
from this list of
memorized graphs.

3. Select a memorized graph from the Graph Title list.

TIP

While you have the Memorized Graph dialog box open, you can select a graph title and click on the Edit button to edit the entry. Selecting a graph title and clicking on the Delete button will remove the memorized graph from the list.

4. Click on the Use button in the Button bar at the top of the Memorized Graph dialog box. Quicken opens the Recall Memorized Graph dialog box, which is essentially identical to the Customize Graph dialog box.

5. Adjust the date range and other settings to customize the graph if necessary, and then click on the Create button to close the Recall Memorized Graph dialog box and create the graph.

What's Next?

If the family is hanging around asking when you'll be done so you can take them out to lunch, just show them all the reports you generated. Then explain how it's their treat because of all the work you've been doing. Don't let on how much fun you've been having! When you come back after lunch, you'll learn how Quicken can make short work of tax return preparation and planning.

Managing Your Taxes

- ✿ Exploring Tax-Related Categories
- ✿ Preparing Your Tax Return from Quicken Reports
- ✿ Using Quicken with Tax Software
- ✿ The Tax Deduction Finder
- ✿ Planning for Next Year's Taxes

H ere it is, Sunday afternoon and you're probably wondering why bother with this section on taxes? You may have an accountant who does your taxes for you, or perhaps you have a very simple tax return that you prepare on your own the day before it's due. Besides, April 15th seems so far away, and that new movie is playing over at the super-duper surround sound cinema.

Well, you might want to stick around because Quicken makes keeping accurate tax records and managing your tax expense so easy it's almost fun. In fact, most of the work is done already—just by entering your transactions into Quicken and assigning categories. Knowing how much you owe during the year and properly planning for your tax liabilities is an important part of managing your finances. In fact, managing your taxes is just another way to properly invest your money.

This afternoon, you'll learn how to use Quicken to do the following:

- ⚙ Keep good tax records
- ⚙ Track taxable transactions
- ⚙ Print tax reports
- ⚙ Set up a tax calendar
- ⚙ Minimize tax expense
- ⚙ Plan for future taxes

Keeping Good Tax Records

Tax authorities require you to keep accurate records of your income and expenses for 7 to 10 years, depending on the jurisdiction and your situation. The records must include source records (such as a receipt for a deductible expense) and a trail that shows how and where this number appears on your tax return. For example, suppose you claimed a deduction for a contribution you made to a charity. Good tax record keeping would require that you keep the canceled check, a receipt or letter from the charity acknowledging your contribution, and a list that adds up to the charitable deduction taken on your tax return.

♦ ♦

The exact record keeping requirements vary based on the transaction type and amount involved. For example, charitable contributions over $250 each and contributions of property require more record keeping than cash contributions of less than $250 each. For more in-depth coverage of records retention rules and issues, see IRS publication 552, "Record Keeping for Individuals" available on the Web at **http://www.irs.ustreas.gov/ prod/forms_pubs/pubs/p552toc.htm**. Of course, an accountant who specializes in individual income tax (or business taxes if that's what you need) in your state or locality is the best source of late-breaking news on tax rules and how they apply to your situation.

♦ ♦

If you haven't already, you might consider setting up a file system that allows you to keep source documents such as receipts, 1099 forms, and other tax documents by topic and by year. For example, you might create a folder labeled "Charities 1998" and another one labeled "Medical Expenses 1998." Although Quicken can help you track and list the taxable transactions, it cannot help with the source document record keeping requirement. This unfortunately is a burden we all must bear the old-fashioned way (at least until computer scanning of documents becomes acceptable to tax authorities).

Having provided you with that bit of bad news, I can now lighten up your day with nothing but good news. Quicken can help you do all the rest. As you enter your day-to-day transactions into Quicken, you assign each transaction a category (or several categories through the Splits window)—this is nothing new, you do it for your own information, assuming you've been following the advice in this book. So when you write a check to donate money to a charity there's no extra work involved in assigning the category Charity. But at the end of the year, you can print a report that lists all transactions for the category Charity and voilà, you have a clear audit trail to the total amount to be deducted on your tax return for charitable contributions. You don't need to sort through receipts and canceled checks to find the deductible transactions, and you don't have to add columns of numbers to calculate the amount of a deduction. Quicken does all that for you.

To automate this process even further for you, Quicken allows you to mark categories as tax-related and even link them to a specific tax form. If you use tax preparation software, Quicken can export your tax-related financial information in a format you can import into the tax preparation software electronically. You won't even need to type the information from Quicken's reports into the tax preparation software.

Exploring Tax-Related Categories

As you may remember from Friday evening's session, categories can be marked as being tax-related or not. Press Ctrl+C now to review your Category & Transfer List. Figure 6.1 shows my category list. Notice the Tax column to the far right. Some of the categories have the letter T in the Tax column and some do not. Those marked with the letter T are tax-related categories. The default categories that Quicken created for you when you first set Quicken up were already marked as tax-related where applicable. Any categories that you added yourself only have the T in the Tax column if you checked the Tax-related box in the Set Up Category dialog box.

Some income and expense categories are obviously tax-related. For example, salary income is undoubtedly a tax-related item for nearly everyone. Similarly, the income and property taxes you pay are potential tax deductions, as are expenses such as mortgage interest and medical bills. On the other hand, expenses such as groceries, personal clothing, and cable TV service are normally not tax-related.

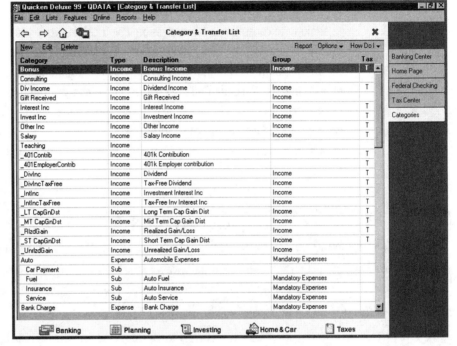

Figure 6.1

You can spot the tax-related categories easily.

The hard part is identifying those transactions that may or may not have tax consequences, depending on your particular situation. For example, utility bills are normally not flagged as tax-related because they are not a deductible expense for a typical family. But if you operate a small business and have a qualifying home office, you will need to track utility bills as a tax-related expense because a portion of your utility payments can be assigned to the home office—a tax-deductible business expense. The Tax Deduction Finder (which you'll learn about later in this session) can help you identify some potential tax deductions and set up categories to track them.

◆ ◆

 **CAUTION**

Quicken can help you keep track of tax-related income and expenses. However, the Quicken program cannot determine which income and expense items should be placed in which categories—tax-related or not. That responsibility is yours! If you have any question about whether or not an item belongs in a tax-related category, you should consult a CPA or other tax professional before submitting it on your tax return.

◆ ◆

■■■■■■■■■■■■■■■■■■■■■■■■■■■■■■■■■■■■■

TIP In addition to consulting a tax professional, you can improve your understanding of the tax law by reading tax publications written in plain English, such as J.K. Lasser's *Your Income Tax* or Ernst & Young's *Tax Savers Guide.* Both publications explain the tax law, provide Internal Revenue Code references, and guide you through the calculations and rules. Often, your tax adviser can advise you better when you understand the rules and what is possible within the scope of the law.

■■■■■■■■■■■■■■■■■■■■■■■■■■■■■■■■■■■■■

TAX-RELATED WEB SITES

If you have access to the Internet, the World Wide Web has over 1,000 tax sites waiting for you. Almost every tax jurisdiction from state income tax departments to the federal government has a Web site. In addition, most large public accounting firms and professional accountants' organizations offer free tax research information and forms for you to download. Here are a few of my favorites:

✿ **IRS** (Uncle Sam's own tax Web site, where you can download forms, read publications, and read the latest tax news)—**http://www.irs.ustreas.gov**

✿ **TaxWeb** (with links to zillions of federal and state tax sites)—**http://www.taxweb.com**

✿ **AICPA** (a professional society of licensed CPAs whose site includes tax information and ways to find a CPA in your area)—**http://www.aicpa.org**

✿ **ACT** (a professional society of corporate tax automation professionals whose site offers good links to tax and computer sites)—**http://taxact.org**

✿ **ABA's Tax Site State Links** (a great list of all state tax sites including tax forms online)—**http://www.abanet.org/tax/sites.html#state**

✿ **J.K. Lasser's Links** (includes links to the Big 6 public accounting firms in the world)—**http://www.jklasser.com/links.html**

✿ **Intuit's TurboTax** (tax preparation and planning software that works very well with Quicken's data files)—**http://www.turbotax.com**

As you scroll down the Category & Transfer list, you'll notice that most of the income categories are tax-related. When you get into the expense categories, you'll find fewer tax-related entries. That makes sense—almost all forms of income must be reported whereas only a limited number of expenses are tax deductible. The standard list of categories created when you install Quicken includes categories defined with tax-related links for most of the common tax-deductible items. For example, Charity and Childcare are tax-deductible types of expenses (but only if you meet the tax requirements specified in the tax law).

Assigning Tax-Related Status to a Category

In cases where you have created your own new categories or subcategories, you'll need to define the tax-related status for those new categories. You can do so when you create a new category, or by editing an existing category.

To assign tax-related status to an existing category, follow these steps:

1. Select the category you want to edit from the Category & Transfer List.

2. Click on the Edit button in the Button bar at the top of the Category & Transfer List window. This will open the Edit Category dialog box, as shown in Figure 6.2.

3. Check the Tax-related box at the bottom of the dialog box.

4. Click on OK to close the dialog box and save your changes.

Figure 6.2

You can assign or remove tax-related status by editing a category.

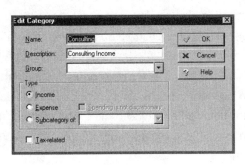

TIP If you need to change the tax-related nature of many categories, save time by using the Tax Link Assistant discussed later in this chapter.

Using Tax-Related Categories

In your day-to-day tax work with Quicken, you assign your transactions to categories just the same as before. The only difference is that when you select a category to assign to a transaction, you must ask yourself a new question: "Does this transaction generate taxable income or a potential tax deduction?" If the answer is yes, then you must assign the appropriate tax-related category.

For example, if you get a bonus check from your boss, you need to classify that deposit as a taxable receipt of income in a category such as Salary or Bonus (which would be reported on the Form 1040 W-2 Salary and Wages line). If by accident you classify that deposit to the wrong category, such as Cash, which is not tax related, your tax reports (and consequently your tax return) would be incorrect.

TIP Although computers can help you track and manage your finances, they cannot do what humans do best: review for reasonableness. Never take a computer printout as absolute truth. Always review the reports for mistakes, omissions, and errors. At tax time, I always print a full-year, all-account Itemized Categories report with full details. Although it runs to 60 or so pages, it's an invaluable record of everything I entered into Quicken and thus a complete listing of all my financial transactions. I then review the printout looking for odd items such as uncategorized transactions, items in the wrong category, and mystery transfers between accounts. Then I compare any tax forms such as 1099s, charitable receipts, and estimated tax payments to the printout. I circle and make notes on tax-related categories such as Salary, Medical Expenses, and specific categories that enter into my home office and Schedule C computations. In a few hours (yes, it is worth the few hours), I feel a complete confidence in the financial data and their validity on my tax return.

Linking to Tax Forms and Schedules

At this point, you can print reports for tax-related categories sorted by category names. This is fine, but IRS and state tax forms are not organized alphabetically by category name. So Quicken has another nifty feature to help you transfer your Quicken data to your tax return—it's called the Tax Link Assistant.

The Tax Link Assistant (see Figure 6.3) allows you to control the tax-related feature of all categories and point each tax-related category to a specific tax form line number or to a tax schedule. You can view, create, and change tax links for several categories, one after another, without closing the Tax Link Assistant dialog box.

To use the Tax Link Assistant to edit or assign tax links for your categories, follow these steps:

1. From the menu bar, choose Features, Taxes, Set Up for Taxes. The Tax Link Assistant dialog box appears.

2. Scroll down the Category list box on the left side of the Tax Link Assistant dialog box. There you'll see a list of all the active categories in your Quicken file. If a category is defined as tax related, the tax form and line item to which it is linked will appear in the Assigned Line Item column. Select a Category.

Figure 6.3

The Tax Link Assistant is a convenient place to view and manage all the tax links defined for your active categories.

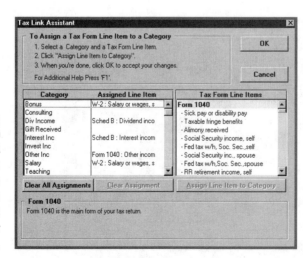

3. If the Category is already linked to a Tax Form line item and you wish to remove the link, click on the Clear Assignment button.

4. If the Category has no Tax Form Line item assignment yet, scroll down the Tax Form Line Items list box until you find the desired tax form line item. When you click on a form name, a description appears at the bottom of the dialog box. Then, click on the Assign Line Item To Category button.

● ●

NOTE Identifying the correct tax schedule and line item for each tax-related category is the hardest part of setting up tax links. Quicken tries to help by offering a list of tax schedules and line items, complete with brief descriptions, for you to choose from. If those descriptions aren't enough, dig out last year's tax return and check the schedules and instructions for more information. Better yet, when you discuss a particular tax deduction with your CPA, ask what form to use for claiming the deduction, then use that information to create the tax link when you set up a Quicken category to track it.

● ●

5. To change the assignment of a tax line item, simply choose the new tax form line item and then click on the Assign Line Item To Category button. The new assignment will appear in the Assigned Line Item list box (see Figure 6.4).

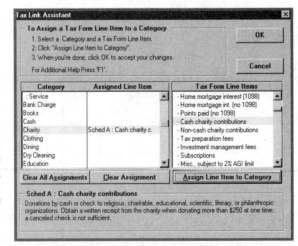

Figure 6.4

The Tax Link Assistant provides a brief description of each tax form line item.

◆ ◆

CAUTION In addition to the Clear Assignment button, which will dissolve the tax link for the selected category, the Tax Link Assistant dialog box also includes a Clear All Assignments button. Clicking on the Clear All Assignments button (and then confirming the action) will simultaneously remove all the tax links that are currently defined. Then you would need to rebuild all the tax links one by one. Make sure you don't hit the Clear All Assignments button by mistake!

◆ ◆

6. When you finish, click on OK to save your changes or on Cancel to exit without saving (Quicken will prompt you to verify the cancellation).

■ ■

TIP If you make some mistakes editing tax links in the Tax Link Assistant dialog box, you can just close the dialog box without implementing your changes. Simply click on the Cancel button in the Tax Link Assistant dialog box. Then, when Quicken presents the small dialog box that says "Save Tax Schedule Changes before Exiting?" just click on No.

■ ■

Setting the Tax Link Option

By default, Quicken hides the tax form links in the Category Setup and Edit dialog boxes. If you would like to see and manage tax form links when you set up or edit your Categories (highly recommended), follow these steps:

1. From the menu bar, choose Edit, Options, Quicken Program.

2. Select the General tab and check the first box, Use Tax Schedules with Categories (see Figure 6.5).

3. Click on OK to close the dialog box and edit your category.

Now, when you edit or add new categories you will be able to view and edit the tax-related category box and tax form link (see Figure 6.6).

Figure 6.5

If you want to manage tax form links in the Category windows, you need to check the Use Tax Schedules With Categories box.

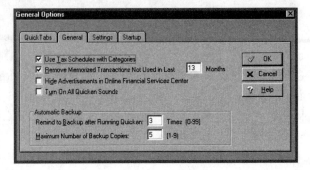

TIP If you would like to see the tax form links in the Category &Transfer List, choose Options from the Button bar and check ShowTax Item.

Preparing Your Tax Return from Quicken Reports

Throughout the year, you carefully enter your financial data into Quicken and assign your transactions to the appropriate categories. Quicken will take care of the chore of keeping your information intact and well-organized. (Now, if only they could get Quicken to file all the receipts and other financial records too!)

When the time comes to gather your tax records so you can fill out your tax return, you won't need to sit down and laboriously thumb through a box or file drawer full of receipts and statements to compile a list of deductible

Figure 6.6

You can now assign tax form links when you set up or edit a category.

expenses. Instead, you can simply create a couple of Quicken reports to have all the data compiled, subtotaled, and available at your fingertips. The task is done in a matter of minutes!

> **NOTE** You can run Quicken's tax reports at any time, and you might want to do so periodically throughout the year to get a preview of your tax situation (and perhaps discuss it with your accountant). However, you probably won't be able to run the final version for preparing your tax return until a month or more after the end of the tax year. It usually takes that long to get all the bank and credit card statements and other documents covering the final month of the year.

If you intend to use tax preparation software, I recommend that you print the tax reports in Quicken first and review the data. That way, when you import the data into the tax software, you can be assured of the correctness of the source data. If you plan to use Intuit's TurboTax, you will be happy to know that TurboTax reads the Quicken data file directly and launches the Tax Link Assistant to help you further detail out your data (with TurboTax, you do not need to export a Quicken Tax File first).

Creating Tax Reports

As you learned this morning, Quicken provides several tax reports that you can use and customize to meet your needs. There are three main tax reports:

- **Tax Summary report.** Groups and subtotals your tax-related transactions by category, from taxable income to deductible expenses.

- **Capital Gains report.** Groups and subtotals your tax-related realized gains on securities sold by security.

- **Tax Schedule report.** Groups and subtotals your tax-related transactions by tax form or tax schedule line.

You create the tax reports just like any other Quicken reports. Just choose Reports, Taxes from the menu bar, and then select a tax report. The Create Report dialog box will appear. You'll find the Tax Summary report and Tax

Schedule report on the Home tab; the Capital Gains report is on the Investment tab.

Be sure you give Quicken the correct date range. If you are preparing an estimated tax return for the past three months, then you need to specify the three-month time frame. If you are preparing your tax return for the last year, and you are a cash basis taxpayer on a normal calendar year, you need to specify the "Previous Year" date range. If you are preparing an annual tax return for a business with a fiscal year that ends on June 30, you need to specify the date range for the proper year from July 1 to June 30.

The Tax Summary report (see Figure 6.7) is designed to give you a quick summary of your taxable income before special tax rules are applied. The Tax Summary report does not take into account adjustments to gross income, tax limitations imposed on business and partnership income or expenses, or ceilings on tax deductions or tax exemptions. But, if all you

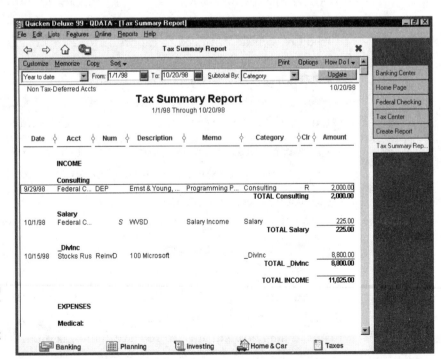

Figure 6.7

The Tax Summary report provides a convenient overview.

are looking for is the big picture on the general income on which you may be taxed, the Tax Summary report can be handy. Since the report is organized by category name, it helps you track down transaction details and verify that you have chosen your tax-related categories wisely.

The Tax Schedule report (see Figure 6.8) subtotals your tax data by tax form or schedule, which makes it the best report to assist you in filling out your tax return. The Tax Schedule report uses the tax link information you defined for each tax-related category. It groups all your transactions assigned to each category under a heading that shows the tax form and line item where the transactions in that category should be entered.

The Tax Schedule report provides you with a good audit trail since it lists the detailed transactions as well as the totals that you need to use on the tax return. For example, my Tax Schedule report lists the transaction details (check number, payee, date, and so on) for each medical expense as well as the total amount that should go on the Schedule A Medical and Dental Expenses line of my Form 1040.

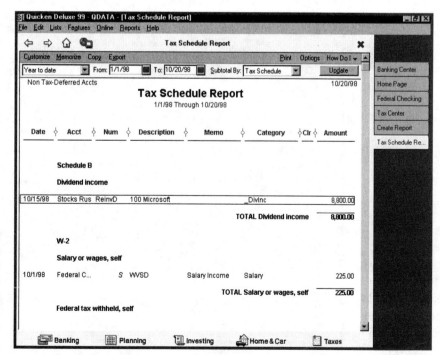

Figure 6.8

The Tax Schedule Report gives you most of the information you'll need to fill in your tax return.

Furthermore, when you review the Tax Schedule report, you can easily pinpoint incorrect links by comparing the description, memo, and category to the tax schedule name. Once I even found a trip to the food store accidentally posted to Schedule A! When I investigated, I found that only one medical item was deductible. A simple adjustment to the category split window and voilà, a correct tax report without all the correction fluid!

NOTE To see your tax data by tax schedule, you need to link tax-related categories to specific tax lines (as covered earlier in this session). By default, Quicken enables the Tax Schedule feature. To verify that the Tax Schedule feature is enabled, choose Edit, Options, Quicken Program. Select the General tab and make sure there is a check in the box, Use Tax Schedules with Categories. Click on OK to close the dialog box.

The Capital Gains report (see Figure 6.9) is useful if you've realized a gain from the sale of securities, or a home, or something of that sort. If you

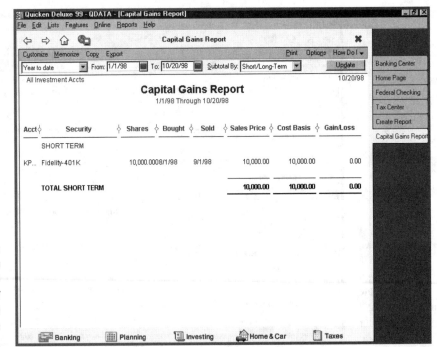

Figure 6.9

The Capital Gains report is a must for active investors who sell taxable securities.

didn't sell any investment property, then you won't need to print the Capital Gains report.

CAUTION The tax laws surrounding the sale of investment property are very complex and change frequently. You should consult a tax professional well-versed in the taxability of investments for assistance on whether and how much (if any) of your investment sales are taxable. This is one road you don't want to walk alone.

NOTE The Quicken Home & Business edition includes an extra tax report—the Schedule C report—for small business owners.

Before you begin entering data from your Quicken tax reports into your tax return, you'll need to go over those reports in detail and find and correct any miscategorized items. In addition to the Tax Schedule report and Capital Gains report, you'll probably want to create an Itemized Categories report and study it to identify tax-related items that were mistakenly assigned to non–tax-related categories.

TIP If you use a tax professional to prepare your tax returns, be sure to provide copies of the Quicken tax reports, Itemized Categories report, and your bank statements for the same period. In some cases, tax preparers may even ask for a copy of your Quicken data file (use File, Backup) so they can bridge your tax data directly into their tax software!

When you locate a miscategorized item in one of the reports, you can use the QuickZoom feature (which you learned about this morning) to drill down to the register entry for the offending transaction and edit it—assigning it to the correct category. Searching for and correcting miscategorized items in Quicken is much faster and easier than sorting through folders full of paper receipts!

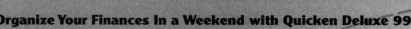

After you finish correcting any miscategorized items that you find, you can simply update your Quicken reports and print out the final copies of the Tax Schedule report and Capital Gains report that you will use to complete your tax return.

NOTE   It's not uncommon for your Quicken records of salary received and taxes withheld to differ slightly from the official W-2 form you receive from your employer. If the differences are small, it's probably not worth the trouble to track down the paycheck entries that account for the discrepancies. Just be sure to use the numbers from the W-2 form on your tax return and not the numbers on your Quicken Tax Schedule report. On the other hand, if you do find any significant differences, be sure to contact your employer's payroll department. Even W-2 software has bugs in it!

Filling Out Your Tax Return

When you're ready to complete your tax return, you'll need to gather all your tax information, that is:

- Your tax return forms and schedules

- The W-2s, 1099s, and other tax documents from your employers, banks, and so on

- Final versions of your Quicken tax reports—Tax Schedule report and Capital Gains report

When you have these documents in hand, you're ready to complete your tax return. If you're preparing your tax return yourself, you just need to begin entering data from the various tax documents and reports into the proper boxes on the tax forms and schedules. Fortunately, the Quicken Tax Schedule report brings most of the information you need together in one convenient location. You won't need to go on a scavenger hunt for receipts and canceled checks to find out how much you spent on some tax-deductible expense—it'll be right there on the Tax Schedule report. The organization of the Tax Schedule report, with your transactions grouped and subtotaled under headings that identify the tax form and line item

they apply to, makes it easy to enter the amounts in the proper place on your tax return.

If you have your tax return prepared by a CPA or other tax preparer, your Quicken tax reports should help make the process go faster and smoother. Having a neat, well-organized report of your tax-related income and expenses will certainly save the tax preparer some time. As a result, you might get a little better rate, or at least a little better service, than someone with a shoebox full of old-fashioned paper tax records.

Using Quicken with Tax Software

Quicken is not a tax preparation program. It cannot calculate your taxes (at least, not in precise detail) or prepare and print your tax return for submission. For that, you'll need a separate tax preparation program.

There are several good tax preparation software packages available. Intuit, the developer of Quicken, also makes TurboTax, the leading tax preparation program (and my personal favorite). Naturally, Quicken and TurboTax are designed to work together very nicely. TurboTax can automatically pick up tax-related financial data from Quicken and fill in your tax return. But you don't have to stick with TurboTax just because you use Quicken. Other options for tax preparation software include programs such as Kiplinger TaxCut, Personal Tax Edge, and U.S. Tax. These other tax preparation programs may not enjoy the close integration with Quicken that TurboTax does, but they can also use Quicken data to prepare your taxes—the process just isn't quite as automated.

Any of these programs will simplify and automate the process of preparing your tax return by letting you fill out tax forms onscreen and then handling all the calculations and the tedious cross-referencing of numbers from one form to another. Most of them include on-screen interviews that help you identify potential tax deductions and enter all your tax data without having to deal directly with the arcane tax forms. The tax preparation programs also provide ready access to on-screen explanations of tax terminology and rules. After you enter all your data into a tax preparation program, you can use it to print out your completed tax return, ready for submission.

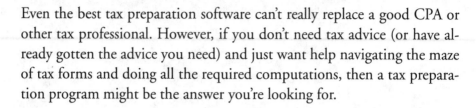

Even the best tax preparation software can't really replace a good CPA or other tax professional. However, if you don't need tax advice (or have already gotten the advice you need) and just want help navigating the maze of tax forms and doing all the required computations, then a tax preparation program might be the answer you're looking for.

Transferring Information from Quicken to Your Tax Program

If you decide to use a tax preparation program, you'll need to get your tax-related financial data entered into the program in the appropriate places. Of course, if you've been using Quicken for the full year, you already have that information stored in your Quicken file. The question is, what is the best way to transfer data from Quicken to your chosen tax preparation software?

Obviously, one way to get tax-related data from Quicken into the tax preparation software is to do exactly the same thing you would to if you were preparing your tax return manually. Just go into Quicken and print out the Tax Schedule report and the Capital Gains report. Then you can simply refer to the reports and type in the appropriate amounts when prompted to do so by the tax preparation software.

An even better solution is to use Quicken's ability to export the Tax Schedule report or Capital Gains report to a data file that you can then import into most of the popular tax preparation software packages. Importing the tax data file into the tax preparation program will eliminate most of the need to type in numbers manually, thus reducing the chance of errors and saving time.

NOTE ●
If you use TurboTax, you won't need to go through the process of exporting Quicken data to a tax information file and then importing it into the tax preparation program. TurboTax can read tax information directly from your Quicken data file—as you will learn in the next section.
● ●

To export tax data from Quicken into a file and import it into a tax preparation program (other than TurboTax), follow these steps:

1. Create the Quicken tax report—Tax Schedule report or Capital Gains report—that you want to export. (Refer back to the Sunday Morning session for detailed instructions on creating Quicken reports.) Make sure the report covers the correct time period (the full tax year) and that the information in the report is accurate, complete, and up to date. (Figure 6.10 shows part of a completed Tax Schedule report open in Quicken.)

2. When you're confident that the report is ready to be exported, click on the Export button in the Button bar at the top of the report window. This will open the Create Tax Export File dialog box shown in Figure 6.11.

Export tax files here

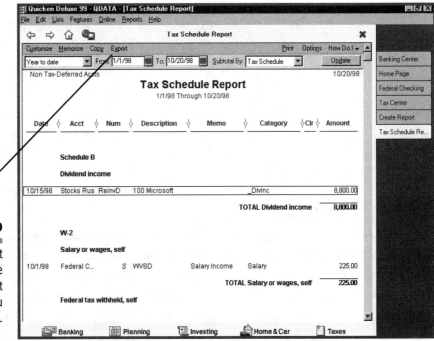

Figure 6.10

Notice an Export button is available in the report window when you view a tax report.

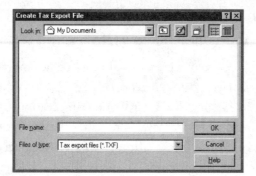

Figure 6.11

Most of the popular tax preparation programs can read Quicken's tax export files.

3. In the File Name box of the Create Tax Export File dialog box, enter a filename for the tax data file. Be sure to use a filename that you can remember and identify easily. Quicken will automatically add the .TXF extension to the filename when it creates the file. If necessary, change the location where a file will be created by selecting a different drive and folder.

4. Click on OK to close the Create Tax Export File dialog box and create the file.

5. Open your tax preparation program and follow its procedure for importing data from a tax export file. You'll need to remember the location and filename of the tax export file you created in Quicken so as to specify the correct file to import into the tax preparation program.

Transferring Tax Information from Quicken to TurboTax

Because Quicken and TurboTax are both Intuit products, the two programs enjoy a special family relationship. The programs complement each other very well and they are particularly adept at sharing information. Consequently, if you use TurboTax as your tax preparation software, you will not only be able to transfer tax data electronically from Quicken to TurboTax, you'll be able to do it without going through the steps required to create an export tax file in Quicken and import that file into TurboTax.

CAUTION

The feature of TurboTax that automatically reads and helps you import Quicken data is called TaxLink (sounds familiar, doesn't it?). TaxLink is great and easy to use, but you should know one very significant limitation: you can't specify the tax year. TaxLink assumes you are a calendar year taxpayer whose tax year begins on January 1 and ends on December 31. If you have a short tax year, or a different tax year, you will need to use the Tax Exchange Format (.TXF) file method discussed in the last section.

TurboTax can read the tax data in your Quicken data file and import the information directly into the tax return you are working on in TurboTax. The details of the process change slightly from year to year as each new version of TurboTax comes out and the links between TurboTax in Quicken get stronger and easier to use. Recent versions of TurboTax have been able to detect your Quicken program installation, locate the Quicken data file currently in use, and import tax-related data automatically, after receiving nothing more from you than a confirmation that you would like to import Quicken data.

Even after you have imported tax data from Quicken into TurboTax, the program maintains links back to the Quicken data file. If, as you work on your tax return in TurboTax, you find that you need to recategorize tax-related items or reassign a tax-related category to a different tax form or line item, you can open TurboTax's version of the Tax Link Assistant and make the changes. If necessary, TurboTax can automatically open Quicken so you can edit individual transactions and then automatically update the corresponding data when you return to TurboTax.

Before importing your Quicken data into TurboTax, you should make sure Quicken is configured to link categories to tax schedules. To do this, choose Edit, Options, Quicken Program and select the General tab. Make sure the Use Tax Schedules With Categories option is checked.

In addition, if you have prior year TurboTax data that you want to roll over into this year's tax return data file, be sure to transfer that data *before* you import Quicken data.

TIP Did you get multiple tax documents (such as two W-2s for the same person)? The best way to handle that in Quicken is to create a class for each taxpayer and a subclass for each tax document issuer. For example, if you have two W-2s, you could categorize them as Salary/Me:Job1 and Salary/Me:Job2.

To start the import procedure from TurboTax, choose Import from the EasyStep menu and then click on Quicken. The TurboTax TaxLink window appears and displays your Quicken data. Review the links between your Quicken data and the tax forms in TurboTax. You can add, change, or remove links and edit Quicken data as needed. After the import is completed, you can review your imported data in TurboTax by choosing Tools, My Tax Data. The imported data is flagged with the label Import. If you want to see the data on the form, click on the data item. If the data item appears to be on the wrong form, choose Interview and EasyStep will walk you through the process of correcting the posting.

Take a Break

Ah ha! Caught you looking out the window. This would be a good time to take a short break. Set the book aside and get away from the computer screen for a few minutes. Don't even think about Quicken and taxes again until you've had a chance to stretch, walk around, and get a snack. Me, I'm heading for that box of chocolate-covered cherries I've been hiding in the cupboard.

Exploring the Tax Center

As with the other key financial areas (Banking, Planning, Investing, and Home & Car), Taxes has its own page called the Tax Center (see Figure 6.12). You can use the Tax Center to get the big picture or as a launch pad to the various tax features in Quicken.

Some of the key topics in the Tax Center include:

⚙ **Projected Tax.** Provides a summary of your estimated tax liability, plus tax advice and access to the Quicken Tax Planner.

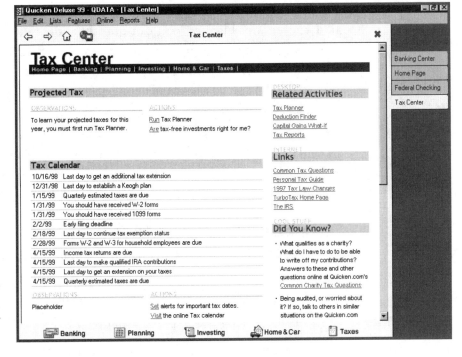

Figure 6.12

The Tax Center helps you get a handle on your tax situation.

⚙ **Tax Calendar.** A listing of upcoming tax deadlines, tax events (such as receiving your W-2 statements), and tax election due dates (such as the last day to make an IRA contribution).

⚙ **Income and Deductions.** A summary listing of the year-to-date taxable income and tax deductions. Provides access to the Quicken Deduction Finder, Net Worth report, tax advice, and online resources.

In the column on the right side, you will find the familiar Related Activities (access to Quicken features), Links, and Did You Know? sections filled with tax-related items. Take some time now to review and become familiar with the Tax Center. Note that all of these items are also available through the menu bar.

Planning for Taxes

When dealing with taxes, it often pays to think ahead. And Quicken includes a valuable feature to help you do just that. The Quicken Tax Planner

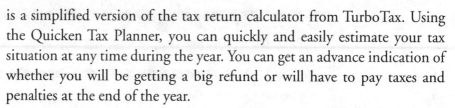

is a simplified version of the tax return calculator from TurboTax. Using the Quicken Tax Planner, you can quickly and easily estimate your tax situation at any time during the year. You can get an advance indication of whether you will be getting a big refund or will have to pay taxes and penalties at the end of the year.

In addition to keeping track of your projected tax situation, the Quicken Tax Planner lets you test and compare various scenarios to see what their tax impact will be. For example, the Quicken Tax Planner can help you estimate whether or not you will save enough taxes on mortgage interest to be able to afford a larger house payment.

Estimating Tax Liabilities

To use the Quicken Tax Planner to estimate your taxes, follow these steps:

1. From the Tax Center page, click on Projected Tax Actions, Run Tax Planner (or choose Features, Taxes, Tax Planner). The Quicken Tax Planner dialog box appears, as shown in Figure 6.13.

2. Select your filing status and the tax year from the Status and Year drop-down list boxes.

3. Click on the Rates button to open the Tax Rates For Filing Status dialog box shown in Figure 6.14. The tax rates, brackets, exemp-

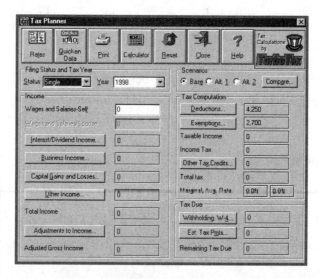

Figure 6.13

Use the Quicken Tax Planner to estimate your tax liability.

Figure 6.14

If the tax law changes or if you want to do some tax planning, you can change the tax rates here.

tions, and so forth are all preset to the rates in effect when the Quicken software was published. If tax laws have changed (or you want to test the effects of some possible changes that are being discussed) you can adjust the tax rates and brackets as needed. Click on OK to close the Tax Rates For Filing Status dialog box and return to the Quicken Tax Planner.

TIP

When you update Quicken online, Quicken automatically checks for the latest tax rates and tax calculations, downloading any updates as needed. If you have online access, you should do the update prior to using the tax planner (every time).

NOTE

If you prefer to enter amounts in the Quicken Tax Planner manually instead of importing data from your Quicken data file, you can skip Steps 4 through 6.

4. Click on the Quicken Data button at the top of the Quicken Tax Planner dialog box. After a brief delay while Quicken scans your data file, the Preview Quicken Tax Data dialog box appears, as shown in Figure 6.15.

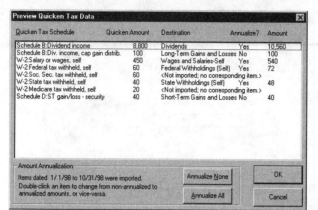

Figure 6.15

Preview the data being imported from your Quicken data file into the Tax Planner.

5. The Preview Quicken Tax Data dialog box will display a list of the tax-related categories found in your data file. The categories are listed by tax schedule with the amount and destination in the Tax Planner. The Amount Annualization section lets you decide whether you want to see the numbers as they are now or as they'd be at the end of the year if your present income and expenditure levels stay steady. You can do this for all the amounts at once by clicking the Annualize None or Annualize All buttons, or you can toggle the categories individually by double-clicking on them. That way, you can project your salary for the full year while keeping Quicken from expanding things that were one-time payments or expenses. You can leave this at the default value for now and get a pretty good idea of what's happening, and play with it later as you get more comfortable with the program.

6. After adjusting the annualization status of the imported categories (if you decide to do so), click on OK to close the Preview Quicken Tax Data dialog box and insert the imported data into the corresponding fields of the Quicken Tax Planner dialog box.

NOTE To arrive at annualized amounts for the imported Quicken data, the program assumes that the amounts in each category will continue to accumulate at an average rate based on the year-to-date figures and calculates the annualized figure for each category based on those averages. For example, if the year-to-date figure in a given category after six months was $500, the annualized amount would be $1,000.

7. In addition to importing data from your Quicken data file, you can enter amounts (or estimates) directly into the Quicken Tax Planner. You can type amounts directly into the Wages And Salaries Self and Wages And Salaries Spouse boxes. To enter amounts in the other fields, you must click on the button beside each amount box to open a dialog box that serves as a worksheet where you can enter amounts for various tax categories that make up the item on the main Tax Planner dialog box.

   For example, clicking on the Adjustments To Income button in the lower left corner of the Quicken Tax Planner dialog box opens the Adjustments To Income dialog box shown in Figure 6.16. There you can enter amounts for tax items such as Allowable IRA Deduction and Moving Expenses. Quicken totals your entries automatically. After entering the amounts in the dialog box, click on OK to close the Adjustments To Income dialog box and enter the total amount into the corresponding field in the Quicken Tax Planner dialog box.

   Repeat the process for each of the buttons in the Income, Tax Computation, and Tax Due areas of the Quicken Tax Planner dialog box.

8. The Quicken Tax Planner recalculates its results automatically each time you enter new information. You can view the results of the calculation in the Remaining Tax Due box in the lower right corner of the Quicken Tax Planner dialog box. When you are through with the Tax Planner, click on the Close button to close the Quicken Tax Planner dialog box and return to the main Quicken program.

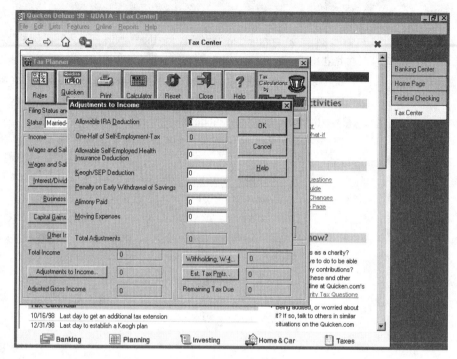

Figure 6.16

This dialog box is a worksheet where you can enter the various items that make up the main Adjustments To Income entry.

Comparing Tax Scenarios

As great as the Quicken Tax Planner is at providing a quick estimate of your projected tax situation, it becomes even more valuable when you use it to compare the tax impact of different financial scenarios. To create and compare an alternate tax scenario with the Quicken Tax Planner, follow these steps:

1. Open the Quicken Tax Planner and prepare an estimate of your taxes as outlined in the preceding sections. Be sure the Base option is selected in the Scenarios area when you do this.

2. Click on the Alt 1 or Alt 2 option in the Scenarios area to begin defining an alternate tax scenario. Quicken opens a small dialog box asking if you want to copy the current scenario. Click on Yes if you want to copy the amounts from your base scenario into the alternate scenario you're creating. This will save you time if you want to change

just a few amounts and keep everything else the same. Click on No if you want to start from scratch.

3. Import Quicken data, enter estimated amounts, or edit existing amounts as necessary to create your alternate scenario.

4. When your alternate scenario is complete, click on the Compare button in the Scenarios area of the Quicken Tax Planner dialog box. Quicken opens the Tax Scenario Comparisons dialog box, as shown in Figure 6.17.

When you're through comparing the tax scenarios, click on OK to close the Tax Scenario Comparisons dialog box and return to the Quicken Tax Planner dialog box. Click on the Close button to close that and return to the Quicken program.

Using the Tax Calendar

Nothing is worse than that feeling when you've missed an important deadline, or missed a cut-off date for enrolling in a special program. Nothing

Figure 6.17

This dialog box gives you a quick side-by-side comparison of the key figures from the three alternate tax scenarios.

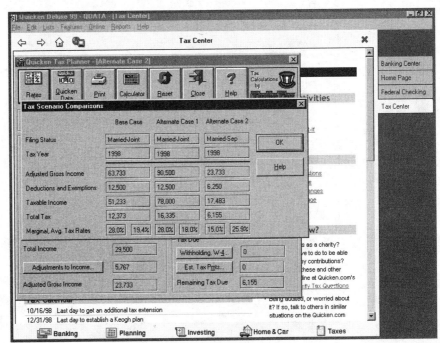

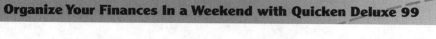

that is, except knowing you've missed a tax return due date or the cut-off for beneficial tax election that would have saved you thousands of dollars. But now that you have Quicken, you don't need to worry about missing tax deadlines or any tax-reduction opportunities.

On the Tax Center page, Quicken provides a listing of important tax dates including deadlines for tax returns and tax elections in the Tax Calendar area (see Figure 6.18).

In the Tax Calendar Actions area, you can click on Set Alerts For Important Tax Dates to update or edit the Tax Calendar. The familiar Set Up Alerts dialog box appears. On the General tab, select the Important Tax Dates alert option. The right side of the dialog box now provides you with several tax date options (see Figure 6.19). If you want reminders for quarterly estimated taxes and self-employment tax reporting and election dates, check the corresponding box. When you finish, click on OK to save your changes.

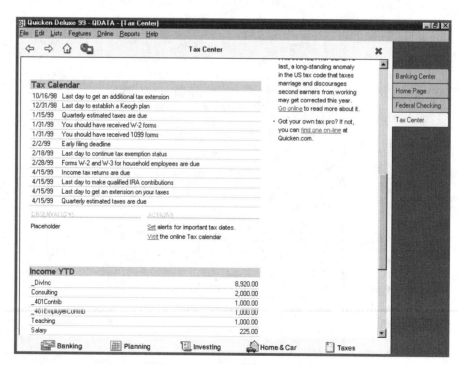

Figure 6.18

Use the Quicken Tax Calendar to keep current on your tax filings and elections.

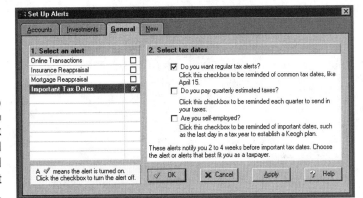

Figure 6.19

You can set up tax
alerts for estimated
tax payments and
self-employment
tax deadlines.

Finding More Tax Deductions

The Quicken developers weren't content to just provide you with tools you need to maintain records of your taxable income and the deductible expenses you already know about. They also included the Tax Deduction Finder to help you identify potential tax deductions you might have overlooked and set up categories and tax links to track those expenses so you can take advantage of the deductions.

To use the Tax Deduction Finder, follow these steps:

1. In the Tax Center, click on the Desktop Related Activity Deduction Finder (or from the menu bar select Features, Taxes, Tax Deduction Finder). Quicken will open the Deduction Finder window. If this is the first time you've used the Deduction Finder, the Introduction To Deduction Finder dialog box will appear superimposed over the Deduction Finder window, as shown in Figure 6.20.

NOTE   Another dialog box, warning about possible recent changes in the tax law, may precede the Deduction Finder window onscreen. Click on OK to acknowledge the warning and display the Deduction Finder. Then, at the first opportunity, download the Quicken software update that brings the Tax Deduction Finder up to date with the latest changes in the tax law.

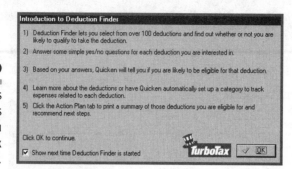

Figure 6.20

Quicken displays these instructions before you enter the Tax Deduction Finder.

2. Read the instructions in the dialog box. If you don't want to see these instructions again in the future, clear the check box beside the Show Next Time Deduction Finder Is Started option in the lower left corner of the dialog box. Click on OK to close the Introduction to Deduction Finder dialog box. This will give you full access to be Deduction Finder window, as shown in Figure 6.21.

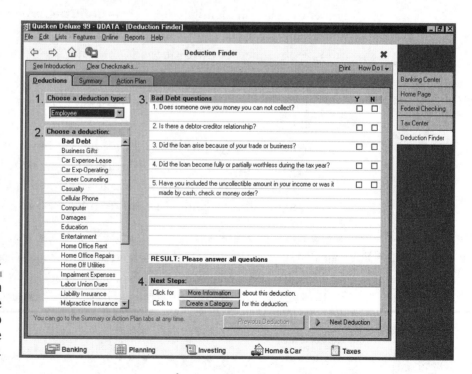

Figure 6.21

Select a deduction and answer the questions to determine your eligibility.

3. On the Deductions tab, select one of the general deduction classifications from the Choose A Deduction Type drop-down list box.

4. Click on one of the items in the Choose A Deduction list.

5. Answer each of the questions in the Questions box (box number 3) by clicking on the Y (Yes) or N (No) boxes beside each question. Scroll down if necessary to answer all questions. Based on your answers to the questions, the Deduction Finder will try to determine whether or not you might be eligible for the deduction and display its best guess in the Result line at the bottom of the box. The program also places a check mark beside the deduction in the Choose A Deduction list to indicate that you have answered the questions about this deduction (see Figure 6.22).

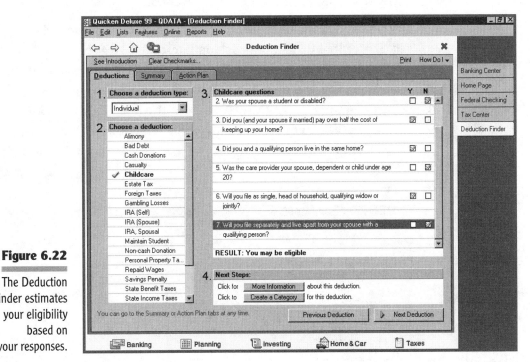

Figure 6.22

The Deduction Finder estimates your eligibility based on your responses.

CAUTION

Just because the Deduction Finder indicates that you may be eligible for a deduction doesn't mean that a CPA or the tax authorities will agree. However, it does mean that you have passed the initial screening questions for eligibility for the deduction and it's probably worth your while to track your expenses in this area.

6. If you want to find out more about this particular deduction, click on the More Information button in the Next Steps area at the bottom of the Deduction Finder window. Quicken will display a More Information dialog box similar to the one shown in Figure 6.23. You can read information onscreen or click on the Print button to make a hard copy of the information. When you're through reading about the potential deduction, click on OK to close the More Information dialog box and return to the Deduction Finder window.

7. If you want to create a category to track expenses related to this potential deduction, click on Create A Category in the Next Steps box at the bottom of the Deduction Finder window. When you do, Quicken will open a dialog box similar to the one shown in Figure 6.24 to give you the details about the category you're about create. The dialog box shows the name and description of the category and, since it will be a tax-related category, the tax form and line item to

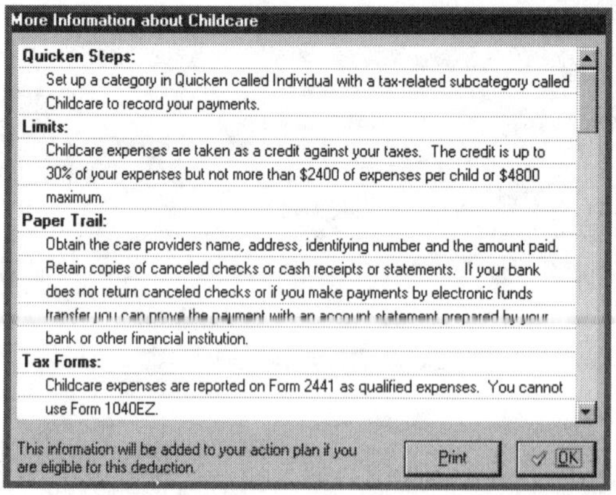

Figure 6.23

Quicken can provide detailed information about potential deductions and what you will need to do to qualify for them.

> **More Information about Childcare**
>
> **Quicken Steps:**
> Set up a category in Quicken called Individual with a tax-related subcategory called Childcare to record your payments.
>
> **Limits:**
> Childcare expenses are taken as a credit against your taxes. The credit is up to 30% of your expenses but not more than $2400 of expenses per child or $4800 maximum.
>
> **Paper Trail:**
> Obtain the care providers name, address, identifying number and the amount paid. Retain copies of canceled checks or cash receipts or statements. If your bank does not return canceled checks or if you make payments by electronic funds transfer you can prove the payment with an account statement prepared by your bank or other financial institution.
>
> **Tax Forms:**
> Childcare expenses are reported on Form 2441 as qualified expenses. You cannot use Form 1040EZ.
>
> This information will be added to your action plan if you are eligible for this deduction.   [Print]   [✓ OK]

Figure 6.24

Quicken can
automatically create
a tax-related
category to help
you keep track of
each deductible
expense.

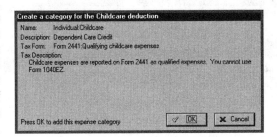

which the category will be linked. Click on OK to close the dialog
box and create the category as described.

8. Return to the Deduction Finder window and repeat Steps 3 through
7 for the next deduction. You can go through the process for as
many, or as few, deductions as you like.

NOTE   To be very thorough and explore all the possible deductions, you would need to go through
each deduction presented by the Deduction Finder. However, it's more likely that you will
simply go through the list of deductions looking for the ones that might pertain to your
situation or that you have some question about—if you have no kids, you don't need
Quicken to tell you that the Childcare deduction probably won't be much use to you. You
can return to the Deduction Finder and check out other deductions at any time.

9. After going through a batch of deductions in the Deduction Finder
window, you can click on the Summary tab to see a status report
showing how many of the available deduction questions you've answered and how many of those the Deduction Finder determined
that you are eligible for (see Figure 6.25).

10. Click on the Deduction Finder's Action Plan tab to see a detailed
report (see Figure 6.26) listing information about the deductions
that the Deduction Finder has determined that you look eligible for.

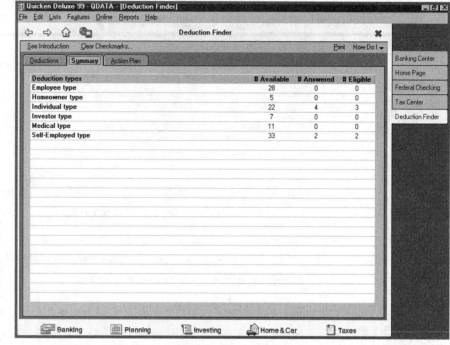

Figure 6.25

Quicken keeps track of which Deduction Finder questions you've answered and which deductions you may be eligible for.

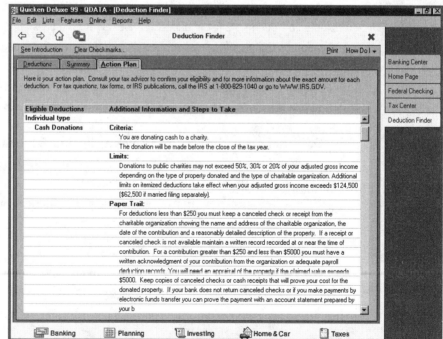

Figure 6.26

For each deduction the Deduction Finder finds, it gives you detailed information on the Action Plan tab.

What's Next?

Dinner. I can smell it cooking, which is good since that means I don't have to cook. See how Quicken helps you out! When you return, you will learn about Quicken's budgeting and planning tools. You'll learn how to use Quicken to create a budget and discover the specialized calculators Quicken provides to help you plan for life events such as buying a house and saving for retirement.

Planning for the Future

- ✿ Saving and Managing Your Budgets
- ✿ Living with a Budget
- ✿ Creating a Savings Plan
- ✿ Saving for Major Financial Events
- ✿ Taking On or Consolidating Debt

Wow! What a weekend, huh? Just think back to Friday night when you were so unsure of where to go and what to do. You should be very proud of yourself and what you have accomplished in these few hours at the keyboard. You've learned how to set up Quicken to track your bank accounts, credit card accounts, and even investments. You've learned how to enter transactions and reconcile accounts. You've learned about online banking, managing investments, creating reports, and how Quicken can help you at tax time.

Now it's time to look ahead to the future. In this session, you'll learn about the following:

- ⚙ Creating and working with a budget
- ⚙ Setting up savings goals
- ⚙ Forecasting your finances
- ⚙ Planning for retirement
- ⚙ Reducing and consolidating debts
- ⚙ Creating what-if scenarios to evaluate financial opportunities (such as saving for college, estate planning, and buying a home)

Who Cares about Tomorrow—My Bills Are Due Today!

How often have you heard someone make a comment like that? How often have you said it yourself? Undoubtedly, there is a feeling of urgency as you worry about how to pay bills that are due today. There's a natural tendency to go into crisis management mode to deal with immediate problems, and long-term plans get pushed to the back burner to be dealt with later "when you have time."

The trouble is that it's easy to get caught up in each new crisis and lose sight of your overall goals. That's when you need to step back and look at the bigger picture. As a bonus, you may find that the situation isn't so bad after all. Often, even in the midst of crisis, you'll discover that most things are really all right; it's just a few things that are causing the trouble.

Goals and plans can be valuable guides as you work with your personal finances. Goals remind you of why you are doing this in the first place. (After all, most people wouldn't have to work as hard on their finances if the only goal was to provide minimal food and shelter for themselves.) Plans provide a road map of how to achieve your goals. Not only that, good planning can help avoid crises and can provide management strategies to deal with crises when they come up.

So there are ample reasons to look beyond the immediate situation and do some long-range planning. Most people understand and agree with this in principle. The problem is finding the time to do it. That's where Quicken comes to the rescue with a handful of helpful tools to make budgeting and planning fast and easy.

You no longer have an excuse to avoid financial planning because it takes too long. So, in the words of the commercial, just do it. You'll be glad you did.

Exploring the Planning Center

Perhaps more than any other financial center, the Planning Center (see Figure 7.1) provides you with easy access to Quicken's planning features and an overview of your financial plans. In the Actions area, you can

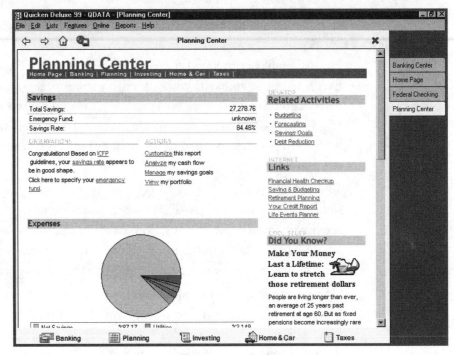

Figure 7.1

The Planning Center provides you with a good summary of your financial plans and gauges how you're doing on reaching your planning goals.

customize graphs, analyze your spending, or get help on changing your spending (by setting up Alerts for monthly expenses by category).

- **Budgets.** Provides information on how you are doing compared to your budget (if you've set one up). In the Actions area, you can customize the budget report, analyze your spending, change your budget, and get help on controlling spending (by setting up Alerts for monthly expenses by category—same as in the Expense area).

- **Net Worth.** Displays your current net worth (assets minus liabilities), complete with a Net Worth graph. You can customize the graph, analyze your net worth, view your account list, or forecast your future net worth based on your financial history.

In the right-hand column, the familiar areas for Related Activities, Links, and Did You Know? list more Quicken financial planning features.

SUNDAY EVENING   Planning for the Future   299

Start to Take Control with a Budget

A budget is a plan like a road map, designed to help you get where you want to go. The process of creating a budget is similar to the process of planning a trip. When you plan a trip, you pick your destination (your goal) first, along with the time you need to arrive. Then you make plans for how you'll get there by selecting your mode of travel and finally the specific route you need to follow to reach your destination. No doubt, you will note some checkpoints along the way that will show you're making progress toward your destination. When planning a budget, you start with a goal and the time you have to reach it. Then you plan a series of steps that will take you from where you are to where you want to be. By comparing your actual results to your budget, you can measure your progress toward your goal.

Quicken provides the tools that enable you to create a budget quickly and easily. More important, Quicken shows you how your actual numbers (income and expenses) compare to the budget amounts, allowing you to set Alerts and helping you to stay on target or adjust your budget as needed to meet your changing lifestyle.

Creating a Budget

You create a budget by entering amounts for each category to show the activity you expect in that category each month, quarter, or year. The budget shows how much you *expect* to spend on items such as groceries, rent, utilities, and dining out each month.

Naturally, it's easier to create a budget if you have information about your existing income and spending habits. You start with what you've done before and then make adjustments in the budget to show what you plan to do differently in the future. If you have a fair amount of financial data in your Quicken file, you can have Quicken automatically create a budget based on that data. However, if you don't have enough information in your Quicken data file to create a budget automatically, you can still create a budget by entering your own estimates for each category.

TIP

To make your budget as meaningful as possible, you'll need reasonably accurate esti-mates of the amounts in each category. If you don't have enough data in your Quicken file, look at your tax returns, bank statements, canceled checks, and credit card state-ments from last year—they're good sources for the information you'll need. Gathering the information manually is a chore, but the effort will be rewarded in the advantages of a good budget. (Also, the experience will really make you appreciate Quicken's Autocreate feature when you have enough data entered to use it for your next budget.)

To begin working with your Quicken budgets, click on the Budgeting item in the Planning Center's Related Activities section (or point to the Plan-ning icon on the Activity Bar and choose Budget My Spending). If this is your first time entering the Budgeting area, Quicken displays a First Time In Budgets dialog box (see Figure 7.2). Quicken is letting you know that it is automatically creating a budget for you based on your existing data and that any category with an amount of less than $100 will not appear in your budget.

Of course, you can modify and update the resulting budget (see Figure 7.3) however you wish. The budget is laid out like a spreadsheet with rows for categories and columns for months (or other periods, such as quarters). You use the scroll bars to view different categories and months. The bot-tom three rows and the right column show totals and remain fixed onscreen so your totals are always in view.

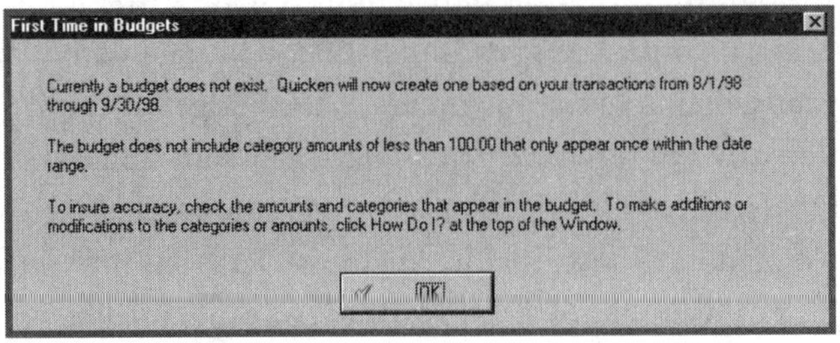

Figure 7.2

For newcomers to Budgeting, Quicken automatically fills in a budget based on existing data.

First Time in Budgets

Currently a budget does not exist. Quicken will now create one based on your transactions from 8/1/98 through 9/30/98.

The budget does not include category amounts of less than 100.00 that only appear once within the date range.

To insure accuracy, check the amounts and categories that appear in the budget. To make additions or modifications to the categories or amounts, click How Do I? at the top of the Window.

OK

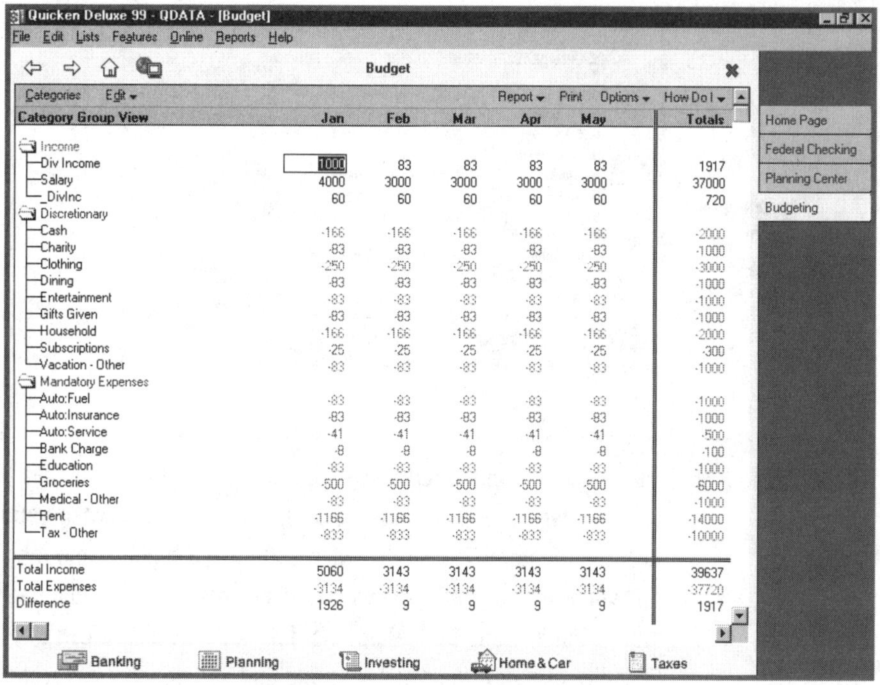

Figure 7.3

By default, the Budgeting QuickTab shows your income and expenses by month.

You can view your budget with columns displayed for months, quarters, or years. To change views, just click on the Options button in the Button bar at the top of the Budget window and choose Display Months, Quarters, or Years from the menu that appears. The default view is Months. Personally, I like to set up my budget on a yearly basis and let Quicken alert me on a day-to-day basis when I go over budget.

To add other Categories to your Budget, click on Categories in the Button bar. The Select Categories To Include dialog box shown in Figure 7.4 appears. You can check the specific Categories to include, or use the buttons Mark All, Clear All or Clear 0 Amounts (removes all categories with zero as a budget amount) as needed. Click on OK to save your settings and return to Budget view.

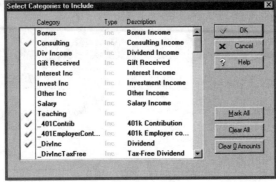

Figure 7.4

You can select the categories to include in your budget.

CAUTION

The whole purpose of creating a budget in Quicken is so that you can compare your actual numbers to the budget and set Alerts to notify when you go over budget on an item. This feature only works when you have a budget amount assigned to a category that you use for actual amounts. In other words, if you spend money on a category named Movies but have no budget amount for Movies, Quicken can't help you stay on budget. Periodically review your budget setup and update it for new categories—and weed out the old categories you no longer use.

You develop the budget by entering amounts you expect to receive or spend in each category each month. The simplest way to enter a budget amount is to click on the cell where a category row and month column intersect and type in the appropriate number. For example, if you have a regular salary of $36,000 per year ($3000 per month), you would click on the *0* in the *Jan* column of the *Salary* row and type **3000**. Then press Tab or click on the *Feb* Salary cell to highlight it in the budget and enter **3000** there as well. Repeat the process until you have entered an appropriate salary amount for each month.

TIP

To build budgets faster, switch to Year view (Options, Current Year) and enter the total amounts. Later, you can click on Month or Quarter view and Quicken will do the division for you!

Autocreating a Budget

At any point, you can use the Autocreate feature to prepare a budget based on your existing Quicken data. If you don't have data for a full previous year to use as the basis for developing a budget, the Autocreate feature can create budget entries based on data from another time period. If necessary, you can use a couple of months of data from the current year.

● ●

 Quicken allows you to have multiple budgets. This lets you keep prior-year budgets and budgets for home versus business, and play around with different budgets until you get the one you want to keep and use.

● ●

To create a budget using the Autocreate feature, follow these steps:

1. Click on the Edit button in the Button bar at the top of the Budget window, and then choose Autocreate from the menu that appears. This will open the Automatically Create Budget dialog box shown in Figure 7.5.

2. At the top of the Automatically Create Budget dialog box, define the date range for the data you want to import by making selections in the From and To boxes. (You can type a date in the From or To box using the MM/YY format or click on the button at the right side of the box to open a mini-calendar and select the date you want by using the arrow buttons to display the desired month on the calendar.)

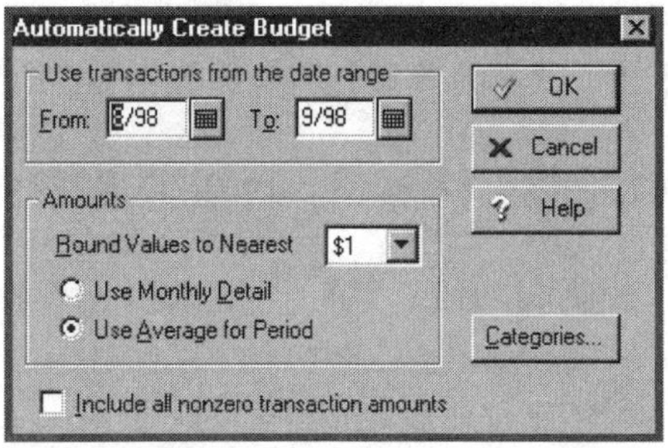

Figure 7.5

This deceptively simple dialog box gives you a lot of control over how Quicken imports data into your budget.

3. In the Amounts area of the dialog box, select a value from the Round Values To Nearest list box. You can choose from $1, $10, or $100. When calculating the budget entries, Quicken will round them off as instructed here.

4. Choose either the Use Monthly Detail or the Use Average For Period options (see the sidebar titled "Autocreate Timing" for more information).

AUTOCREATE TIMING

When you use Autocreate, you can have Quicken create a budget based on your actual amounts as a consistent average, or as a monthly total. If you select the Use Average For Period option, Quicken totals all the transactions in each category for the entire date range and then divides by the number of months in the date range to arrive at a monthly average for each category. The average amount is inserted into your budget and repeated for each month.

If you select the Use Monthly Detail option, Quicken enters the total amount per month into your monthly budget. In some cases, there won't be much difference between averaged results and monthly detail. For example, a monthly salary or basic cable TV subscription will be the same from month to month anyway. On the other hand, income from seasonal overtime or sales commissions and expenses such as utility bills and semiannual insurance premiums might look very different when averaged.

You might want to create the budget both ways and print both versions out so you can review the information. Chances are that a combination of the two methods will give you the most realistic budget.

TIP Using monthly detail in your budgets for seasonal income and expenses can be an invaluable aid in planning cash flow to handle predictable peaks and valleys.

---

5. Click on the Categories button to open the Select Categories To Include dialog box. When you have selected the categories you want to include, click on OK to close the Select Categories To Include dialog box and return to the Automatically Create Budget dialog box.

6. When you are satisfied with the settings in the Automatically Create Budget dialog box, click on OK. Quicken will close the dialog box, scan the specified data in your Quicken file, calculate the budget entries, and enter them into the Budget window, as shown in Figure 7.6.

Of course, you probably don't want your budget for this year to exactly match last year's actual income and expenses. So, after using the Autocreate feature, you'll want to go back into the budget and adjust the amounts in some categories to reflect changing goals and priorities and different spending habits. However, entering historical data into the budget is a good way to get started.

Figure 7.6

Quicken automatically creates budget entries based on the criteria you specified.

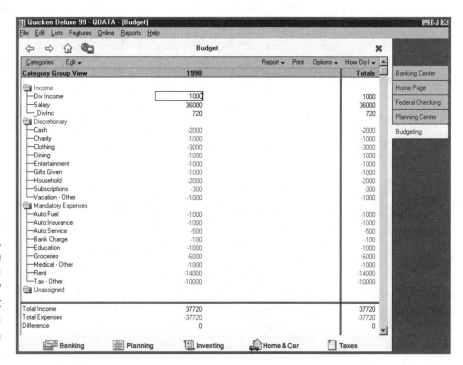

TIP You're not locked into autocreating your entire budget with the same settings. You can run Autocreate several times in the same budget and select different categories and settings each time. For example, you might want to create most of your budget using average amounts based on last year's data. Then, for some categories, you could create monthly detail entries based on last year's data. For other categories, you might want to establish budget amounts based on the average of the first three months of the current year.

Editing a Budget

Quicken's Autocreate feature is a great way to get a lot of information into your budget fast. The trouble is that Autocreate generates budget entries based on existing data in your Quicken file. That's good for telling you where you have been in the past or where you are at present, but a budget is a plan for the future—it should represent your financial goals and expectations, not just a simple projection of the status quo. While many budget items will stay the same from month to month and year to year, others will change, increasing or decreasing from their historical values as your priorities, plans, and predicaments change. For example, you might have found that you spent $500 a month on dining out last year, but after taking a cooking class, you're determined to cut that amount to $200 a month this year. Of course, that also means you'll need to increase your grocery budget category compared to last year. Naturally, you'll need to edit entries in your budget to reflect those anticipated changes.

Of course, as I mentioned earlier, you can simply click on a budget entry in the Budget window and change it by typing in a new number. And, in fact, that is the fastest and easiest way to edit individual budget entries. But making the same change in every monthly column would quickly get tedious. Fortunately, Quicken includes budget editing tools to help you avoid such tedium.

Filling Rows and Columns

Whether you are creating a budget manually from scratch or editing and refining budget items that were entered by Quicken's Autocreate feature, perhaps your most common editing task will be to enter a budget amount for a category and repeat it in each monthly column. To avoid having to type the number over and over, you can follow these simple steps:

1. Suppose you want to change all amounts for a category from January on. Right-click on the cell that contains the data to be changed and choose Fill Row Right from the shortcut menu (see Figure 7.7).

2. A confirmation dialog box appears asking if you want to fill the row to end of year with the selected cell's budgeted amount. Click on Yes to continue, or on No to cancel.

3. After you click on Yes, Quicken copies the contents of that cell to each of the cells to the right on that row. Now you have identical budget amounts entered for that category in each month column.

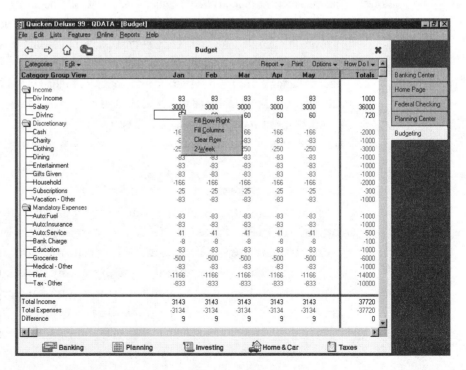

Figure 7.7

The shortcut menu gives you easy access to the budget editing features.

NOTE The Fill Row Right editing command does exactly what it says: it fills budget cells to the right of the selected cell. It does not change cells to the left of the selected cell. This makes it easy to pick a month in midyear where some budget item should change (such as the date when you expect that big raise to affect your salary category) and project that change forward to the end of the year without altering the budget entries for the prior months. However, if you want to change an entire row, you must be careful to select the first (January or First Quarter) column as the basis of your change.

Quicken not only enables you to copy amounts from column to column along a row, but also copy an entire column in much the same way. Just right-click on any cell in the desired column and choose the Fill Columns option. The Fill Column command copies the contents of the first column into the remaining columns for the rest of the year.

TIP You can enter one annual budget amount and let Quicken do the calculations to spread it out across the 12 months. Just make the entry while viewing your budget in Year mode. Here are the steps in a nutshell: Click on the Options button and choose Display Current Year; click on a category budget entry and type in the annual budget amount; click on the Options button and choose Display Months to return to the normal Monthly view. You'll notice that Quicken has divided the annual budget amount by 12 and entered that amount in each of the monthly columns for the category.

Clearing Unwanted Entries

If you make mistakes or change your mind while editing your budget, you can recover easily. For example, if you start editing a budget entry and realize that you are working in the wrong cell, you can cancel the changes and return the cell to its original value by simply pressing Esc. This technique works as long as you catch the error before you freeze the new value by pressing Enter or selecting another budget cell.

If you make one or more changes to your budget and then decide that you would rather return everything to the way it was before your last batch of edits, you can do so by clicking on the Options button in the Button bar at the top of the Budget window and choosing Restore Budget Options. Quicken will open a small dialog box asking you to confirm your action and warning you that restoring the budget will overwrite your current changes. If you go ahead and click on Yes, Quicken will restore all the budget amounts to their values as of the last time you saved the budget. This will effectively undo any changes you have made since the last save.

Quicken includes a couple of budget editing commands that enable you to quickly erase budget amounts and return them to a value of zero. To quickly zero out the budget amounts for an individual category, follow these steps:

1. Right-click on any cell in the row for the budget category in which you plan to erase the values.

2. Choose Clear Row from the shortcut menu that appears.

3. Click on the Yes button in the confirmation box that appears next. When you do, Quicken will erase the budget amounts for the selected category and replace them with zeros in all columns.

If you're really desperate, you can wipe out an entire budget with one command. This is a radical step, but you might want to do it to quickly create a budget template by erasing all the values in a budget. To erase all budget amounts and fill the entire budget with zeros, follow these steps:

1. Click on the Edit button in the Button bar at the top of the Budget window and choose Clear All from the menu that appears. Quicken displays a small dialog box asking, "Clear All Budget Amounts?"

2. If you click on Yes, Quicken will close the dialog box and erase all the budget amounts for all categories in your budget and replace them with zeros. If you decide that's not what you want to do, click on No.

Setting Up a Two-Week Budget Item

Most budget categories fit nicely into the yearly, quarterly, or monthly time frames. But some budget categories defy such pigeonholing. One of the most troublesome examples is the common two-week pay period. Most months will have two two-week pay periods, but some months will include three pay periods. This kind of schedule plays havoc with a traditional monthly budget because the budget amount never matches the actual amount if you use averages. Even if you use actual amounts from the previous year as the basis for your budget, it may not match the actual amounts because the extra payments may not fall in the same months in successive years. Fortunately, Quicken includes a special feature to help you set up a budget category that operates on this kind of two-week cycle. Here are the steps to follow:

1. Right-click on any cell in the row for the category that you want to set up on a two-week cycle.

2. Choose 2-Week from the menu that appears. Quicken opens the Set Up Two-Week Budget dialog box, as shown in Figure 7.8.

3. In the Amount box, type in the amount of the income or expense as it occurs every two weeks.

4. Select a starting date in the Every Two Weeks Starting box.

5. When you click on OK, Quicken will close the Set Up Two-Week Budget dialog box, calculate the impact of the two-week schedule on the budget for the category, and enter the appropriate monthly budget amounts into your budget.

Figure 7.8

Quicken provides help with the problem of fitting two-week pay periods into a monthly budget.

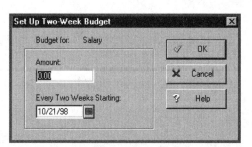

Viewing by Category Group

You may have noticed the heading Category Group View just above your category names. (If your Budget window doesn't show this, choose Options, Show Category Groups from the Button bar.) You can assign individual categories to groups and then view your budget at the more summarized group level instead of the detailed category level. For example, you could assign all of your household expenses such as electricity, rent, and lawncare to a Category Group called Household. By default, Quicken comes with three predefined Category Groups: Discretionary, Income, and Mandatory Expenses. This is another fine way to manage your budget. Categories such as rent and food are Mandatory Expenses that you cannot control, whereas categories such as Dining and Vacation are Discretionary expenses that you can control (or so the accountants say . . .).

To manage Category Groups and assignments, follow these steps.

1. From the Button bar choose Options, Category Groups. The Assign Category Groups dialog box appears.

2. Select a Category from the left list.

3. Select a Category Group from the right list.

4. Click on Assign Category to Group to associate the category with the selected Category Group. Or, to remove an assignment, click on Clear Assignment.

5. If you want to create a new Category Group, click on the New button and type in a name for the new Category Group. Click on OK to continue.

6. To edit an existing Category Group, select the Category name, click on the Edit button, and change the name as needed. Click on OK to continue.

7. To delete a Category Group, select the name and click on the Del button.

8. Click on OK when you finish to save your changes, or on Cancel to exit without saving your changes.

NOTE Any categories that have not been assigned to a Category Group will appear in a folder named Unassigned. You can use the Assign Category Groups dialog box to take care of these unassigned categories.

Saving Your Budget

Quicken saves your budget data automatically when you close the Budget QuickTab window. But if you are making many changes to your budget, you might want to manually save your budget as you work. To save the current budget, click on Options in the Button bar and choose Save Budget (this option is only available after you've made a change to your budget).

Working with Multiple Budgets

You're not restricted to only one budget. In fact, Quicken gives you the option of creating several different budgets. You can develop separate budgets for different contingency plans or create a series of budgets as your plans change so you can look back and compare your latest budget to your original plans.

To create a new budget, just follow these steps:

1. Click on Options in the Button bar at the top of the Budget window and choose Other Budgets. This will display the Manage Budgets dialog box shown in Figure 7.9.

2. Click on the Create button. The Create Budget dialog box appears (see Figure 7.10).

3. Type a name and a description for your new budget into the respective boxes in the Create Budget dialog box.

4. Select one of the options in the Create Budget Options area. Your choices are as follows:

Figure 7.9

The Manage
Budget dialog
box allows you to
create new
budgets, view
existing budgets,
and rename or
delete budgets.

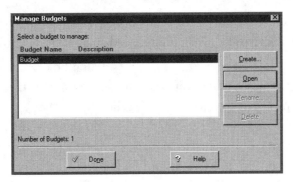

- **Autocreate Budget.** Quicken will open the Automatically Create Budget dialog box, where you can specify how you want to create budget entries based on your existing Quicken data.

- **Copy Current Budget.** Quicken will make a duplicate of the current budget under another name, which you can then edit to create a variation of your current budget.

5. Click on OK to close the Create Budget dialog box and create the new budget. The new budget appears in the Budget window in place of the budget you were working on previously.

Although you can create several separate budgets, Quicken's Budget window can display only one budget at a time. You'll need to select which of your budgets you want to view and work on.

To select a budget to work on, click on the Options button in the Button bar and choose Other Budgets. When the Manage Budgets dialog box appears, select the budget you want to work on from the Budget Name list,

Figure 7.10

When you create a
new budget, you'll
typically want to
make a copy of the
current budget—
but that's not
your only choice.

and then click on the Open button. Quicken will close the Manage Budgets dialog box and display the selected budget in the Budget window.

While you are in the Manage Budgets dialog box, you can do more than just select which budget you want to display. You can rename one of the budgets in the list by selecting it and clicking on the Rename button. Or, if you want to discard a budget that you don't need any longer, select the budget from the list in the Manage Budgets dialog box and click on the Delete button. (The Rename and Delete buttons won't work on a budget that is currently displayed on the screen.)

Using Your Budget

To get the most from your budgets, you'll probably want to do more than simply view them in Quicken's Budgets window. You may want to print your budget or create reports that compare actual results to your budget plan. Quicken can even display bar graphs to monitor your progress compared to a couple of selected budget categories.

Printing a Budget

If you want to print a copy of your budget to have on hand for easy reference, the procedure is simple. Just follow these steps:

1. Open the Quicken Budget window and display the budget you want to print. Choose the budget view—Years, Quarters, or Months—that you want to see on the printout.

2. Click on the Print button in the Button bar at the top of the Budget window. The familiar Print dialog box appears.

3. Adjust the options in the Print dialog box as needed and then click on OK. Quicken will close the Print dialog box and print your budget using the same settings it uses for printing reports and graphs.

Budget Reports

Click on the Report button on the Button Bar for quick access to the budgeting reports. The Budget report (see Figure 7.11) lists your actual and budget amounts by category group. As with any Quicken report, you

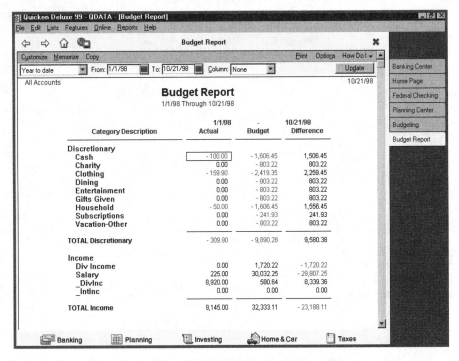

Figure 7.11

The Budget report compares your actual income and expenses to your year-to-date budget amounts.

can use the Customize bar to change the date range or column setup. Or use the Customize button to change any of the report settings.

If you need to know more details, choose the Monthly Budget Report from the Reports button. This report, shown in Figure 7.12, compares actual monthly amounts to your monthly budget amounts.

If you prefer to study a graphic representation of your budgeting success or failure, choose the Budget Variance graph shown in Figure 7.13. The graph uses bars to show the magnitude of the difference between your budgeted and actual amounts. The top graph shows the total budget variance per month and the bottom graph shows budget variations broken down by category.

 NOTE

Refer to this morning's session for detailed instructions on how to further customize these reports and graphs.

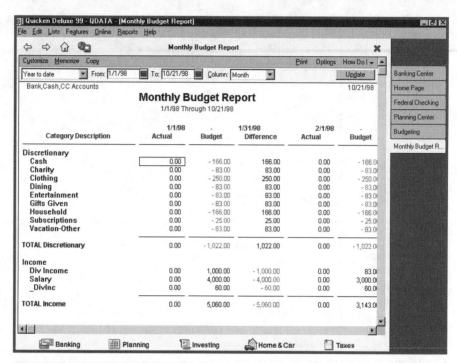

Figure 7.12

Check out this report to see how you're doing compared to your annual budget.

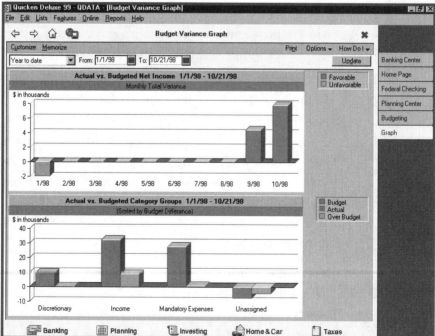

Figure 7.13

The taller the bar, the bigger the difference between your budget and actual amounts.

One last report you can use to manage your budget is the Snapshot report on the Planning Center page. Click on the QuickTab to return to the Planning Center and scroll down to the Budgets section. Now that you have set up a budget, this section contains a very informative Budget Snapshot report (see a sample in Figure 7.14). You can click on Customize This Report to change the layout and appearance of the Snapshot report (such as the date range, categories to include, and category groups).

Progress Bars

If you want to monitor your progress relative to a couple of key budget items, Quicken's Progress bars might be just the tools you're looking for. When Progress bars are enabled, Quicken displays two horizontal bars at the bottom of the screen that show how actual results compare to budgeted amounts for two selected budget categories. Progress bars keep a graphical representation of a couple of budget categories onscreen where they serve as constant reminders of how you're doing. In addition to specific budget

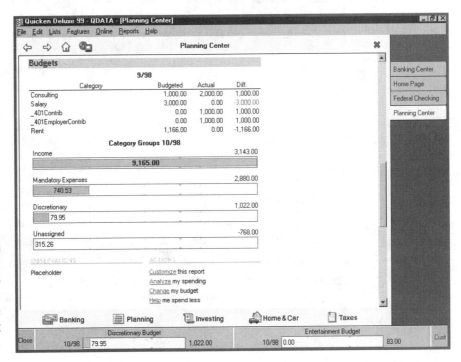

Figure 7.14

The Planning Center Budgets section provides you with a quick picture of your budget goals.

categories, Progress bars can show supercategories—groups of several related categories that are lumped together and subtotaled for convenience. For example, you could use one Progress bar to keep tabs on a specific budget category, such as Dining Out, and use the other Progress bar to monitor a supercategory, such as Discretionary Expenses.

To set up and use Progress bars, follow these steps:

1. Click on the Features menu, point to Planning, and choose Progress bars from the drop-down menu that appears. This will add the Progress bars to the bottom of the Quicken window, as shown in Figure 7.15.

2. To customize the Progress bars to show the budget items of your choice, click on the Cust button at the right end of the Progress bars. This will open the Customize Progress Bar dialog box shown in Figure 7.16.

Progress bars

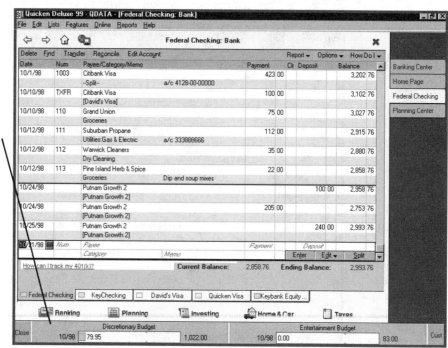

Figure 7.15

Progress bars can help you visualize how you're doing compared to your budget.

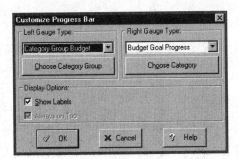

Figure 7.16

Progress bars can display progress toward either budget categories or supercategories.

3. In the Left Gauge Type list box select Category Group Budget (to see how an overall Category Group is doing), Budget Goal Progress (to see how a specific Category is doing), or Savings Goal Progress (to see how your savings plan is doing—covered later today).

4. Click on the button under the list box (depending on your selection in the list box, the button might be labeled Choose Category or Choose Category Group). This will open a dialog box similar to the one shown in Figure 7.17.

5. In the Choose Category dialog box (or Choose Category Group dialog box), select a date range for the Progress bar from the Date Range list box. You can choose from Current Month, Current Quarter, and Current Year.

6. Select a category (or category group) you want to monitor from the list in the dialog box and then click on OK. Quicken will close the Choose Category dialog box and return to the Customize Progress Bar dialog box.

Figure 7.17

You can select the date range and category Quicken will display in each Progress bar.

7. Repeat Steps 3 through 6 in the Right Gauge Type area.

8. If you would like to see the labels, click on Show Labels.

9. If you would like the gauge to always appear on the screen as long as Quicken is open, click on Always On Top.

10. Click on OK when you finish to save your settings, or on Cancel to exit without saving.

As you enter transactions and work in Quicken, the Progress bars give you a constant visual readout of your actual results for the current period in the selected categories compared to the budgeted amounts. It's a handy way to keep tabs on problem areas in your budget.

If you want to get rid of the Progress bars, simply click on the Close button at the left end of the Progress bar at the bottom of the Quicken window.

Creating a Savings Plan

Nearly everyone has been lectured on the importance of saving—setting aside some money to go toward future large purchases and creating an emergency fund for the proverbial rainy day. Since most people agree with the basic idea, I won't restate the obvious here. Suffice it to say that saving is not only a good idea, it's an essential part of a sound financial plan.

There are many ways to save. You can choose from passbook savings accounts, money market accounts, or certificates of deposit—from your bank, credit union, savings and loan, brokerage house, or other financial institution. You can make contributions to your savings by manually depositing funds in the appropriate account. Or, to help encourage and enforce the habit of saving, there are numerous programs available that will automate the process of transferring funds into your savings account on a regular basis. For instance, credit unions typically make savings contributions available as payroll deductions—your savings come out of your check before you see it. Many banks will automatically transfer funds from your checking account to your savings account every month if you request the service. If your employer offers direct deposit of your paycheck, you can usually instruct it to deposit a portion of the funds in a savings account and deposit the remaining portion in your regular checking account. All these options, and many more that I haven't mentioned, are excellent savings mechanisms.

Keeping track of your savings in Quicken is a straightforward proposition. You simply create a Quicken savings account to correspond to the savings account at your bank or financial institution. You record deposits and withdrawals in a savings account just like any other transactions. (If the funds you are depositing are being transferred from another Quicken account, you can enter the transaction in either account. Selecting the other account name as the category assigned to the transaction will ensure that the transaction is appropriately recorded in the other account.) If you use direct deposit or payroll deduction to deposit funds from your paycheck into a savings account, you can handle the deposit just like the other splits that record payroll deductions.

If your bank automatically transfers funds from your checking account to your savings account, you can set up a scheduled transaction in Quicken to make the corresponding entries in your Quicken accounts. Just enter the transfer manually the first time, then memorize the transaction. After you have memorized the transaction for the transfer, you can set up a scheduled transaction to repeat the transfer each month without bothering you. (See the Saturday Morning session for more information on setting up scheduled transactions.)

Don't forget to include savings deposits when you develop a budget. In most cases, the savings deposit will take the form of a transfer from another Quicken account or from an income category. You'll want to make sure you can see and work with transfers in your budget. To do so, click on the Options button in the Button bar at the top of the Budget window and make sure there is a check mark beside the Transfers option in the menu. This will instruct Quicken to display transfers between accounts in your budget as well as the regular income and expense categories.

Quicken's Savings Goals

In addition to all the usual savings accounts, Quicken includes a special feature—called *Savings Goals*—that enables you to keep track of funds that you want to set aside for a special purpose. The nice thing about Quicken savings goals is that they operate entirely within Quicken—you don't have to go down to the bank and open a separate savings account in which to store the funds you are setting aside.

Savings goals give you the electronic equivalent of fictitious entries in your checkbook account register—they let you create a hidden cushion of extra funds that doesn't show up in the running balance. The problem with doing this in a paper account register is that it is easy to get confused and lose track of how much extra money is in the account. Furthermore, reconciling the account register to your bank statement can be extremely difficult if your paper account register contains bogus entries. But Quicken doesn't get confused. The program can keep track of multiple savings goals accounts funded with contributions from several different Quicken accounts. When you view your Quicken accounts, you can see them with or without the effect of the savings goal contributions. And there's no problem reconciling accounts because Quicken keeps track of where all the funds really are.

Basically, savings goals let you set up one or more *pretend* accounts and fund those accounts with transfers from other Quicken accounts, such as your checking account. The savings goal accounts exist in Quicken but—unlike your checking and regular savings accounts—they have no counterpart in the real world. Savings goal accounts have account registers that you can use just like any other Quicken account. In addition, you can make contributions and withdrawals to and from savings goal accounts in a special window where Quicken also tracks your progress toward the goal you established for the account.

TIP A savings goal account is a good way to set aside money each month to make sure you have sufficient funds on hand when a big semiannual or annual bill is due.

To create a savings goal account, follow these steps:

1. In the Planning Center's Related Activities section, click on Savings Goals. Quicken opens the Savings Goals window, as shown in Figure 7.18.

2. Click on the New button on the Button bar at the top of the Savings Goals dialog box. This will open the Create New Savings Goal dialog box shown in Figure 7.19.

3. Fill in the Goal Name, Goal Amount, and Finish Date boxes in the Create New Savings Goal dialog box. (The goal name can be anything you want—normally it's a descriptive name that identifies the purpose of the account. The goal amount is the total amount of money you expect to eventually accumulate in the account. The finish date is the date by which you need to reach the goal amount.)

4. Click on OK to close the Create New Savings Goal dialog box and add the new savings goal to the Goal Name list in the Savings Goals window, as shown in Figure 7.20.

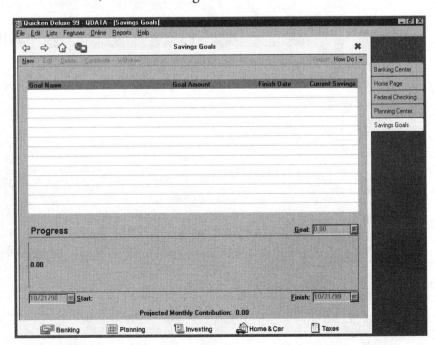

Figure 7.18

The Savings Goals window looks a little barren until you create some savings goals.

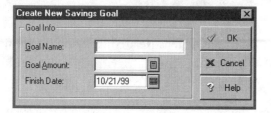

Figure 7.19

Use this dialog box to define a new savings goal.

Since there are no funds in the selected savings goal account, the Progress bar in the lower half of the window is sitting at 0.00. That will change as you make contributions to the goal account. Note the Start, Finish, and Goal boxes around the Progress bar. You can use them to adjust the start date, finish date, and goal amount for the selected savings goal. Also note the Projected Monthly Contribution at the bottom of the window. Quicken calculated that amount for you as a guideline for future monthly contributions to the goal.

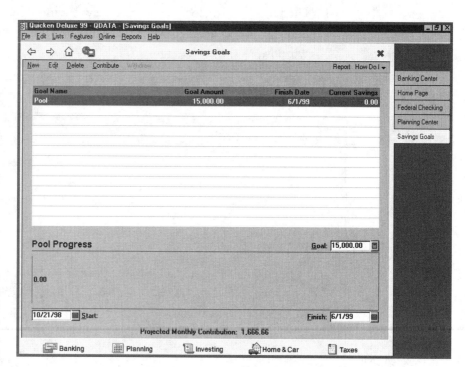

Figure 7.20

A savings goal added to the Savings Goal window

To add money to a savings goal account, follow these steps:

1. Open the Savings Goals window and select from the Goal Name list the item to which you want to contribute.

2. Click on the Contribute button in the Button bar at the top of the Savings Goals window. This will open the Contribute To Goal dialog box shown in Figure 7.21.

3. In the From Account drop-down list box, select the account from which you want to take money.

4. Enter the date and the amount of the transaction in the Date and Amount boxes, respectively.

5. Click on OK to close the Contribute To Goal dialog box and record the transfer of money from the selected account into the savings goal account. As shown in Figure 7.22, Quicken updates the Savings Goals window to show the total savings for the goal in the Goal Name list and in the Progress bar. Quicken also recalculates the projected monthly contribution that will be needed to attain the goal on schedule.

In addition to tracking your progress on savings goals in the Savings Goals window, Quicken also enters regular transactions into your account registers for each savings goal contribution or withdrawal. For example, Figure 7.23 shows a checking account register with a savings goal transaction visible.

Figure 7.21

Use this dialog box to transfer money from another account into the savings goal.

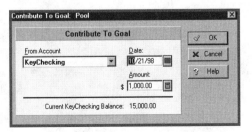

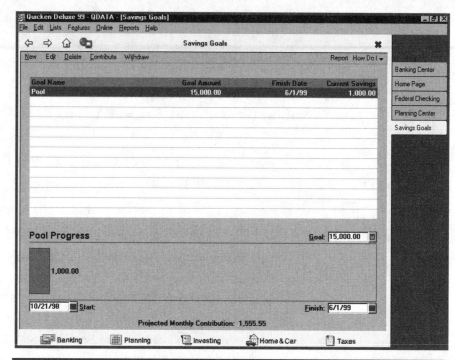

Figure 7.22

The Savings Goal window helps you track your progress toward attaining your savings goals.

Savings goal transaction

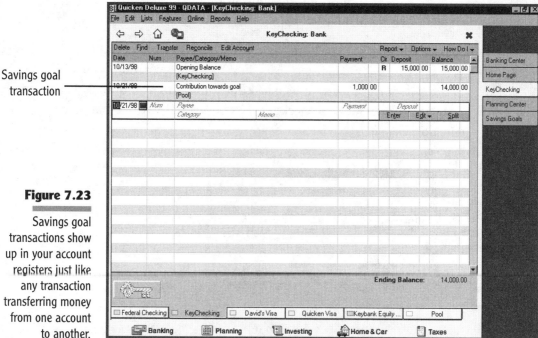

Figure 7.23

Savings goal transactions show up in your account registers just like any transaction transferring money from one account to another.

NOTE

• •

To withdraw money from a savings goal, you follow basically the same procedure as outlined above for making contributions to a goal. Just be sure to click on the Withdraw button instead of on the Contribute button in the Savings Goals window. Quicken will reduce the balance in the savings goal account by the amount you specify. The transaction will look like a deposit when you view it in the account register for the account to which you returned the funds.

• •

At first glance, savings goal transactions look like any other transfer of money between accounts. They appear in the account register and have the expected effect of increasing or decreasing the account balance. However, unlike transfers where money actually moves from one account to another, savings goal transactions are really fictitious entries that refer to pretend accounts—no money actually moves. So Quicken keeps track of them internally and gives you the option of displaying savings goal transactions in your account register or hiding them so that the account register shows the real balance without adjustments for the money set aside for your savings goal.

TIP

■ ■

You don't have to make all of your contributions and withdrawals to savings goals in the Savings Goals window. If you prefer, you can simply enter the transaction into the account register for the account you want to transfer money to or from. It's just like entering any other transfer transaction. You just choose the savings goal account as the transfer category.

■ ■

You can toggle on or off the display of savings goal transactions in an account register. To suppress the display of savings goal transactions in an account register, click on the Options button in the Button bar at the top of the account register window and choose Hide Savings Goals from the menu that appears. To show the effects of savings goal transactions in the account register, repeat the procedure and choose Show Savings Goals. (The Hide Savings Goals or Show Savings Goals commands don't appear on the shortcut menu that appears when you click on the Options button unless the account register you're viewing contains transfers to or from a savings goal.)

TIP

You can use Quicken's scheduled transactions to automate the process of making contributions to a savings goal. Just enter the first contribution to the goal manually. Then open the account register for the account from which the money was transferred to the savings goal, locate the savings goal contribution in the account register, and memorize the transaction. After you have memorized the transaction for the transfer, you can set up a scheduled transaction to automatically repeat the contribution to the savings goal each month. (See the Saturday Morning session for more information on setting up scheduled transactions.)

Back in the Planning Center, the Savings section (see Figure 7.24) has come alive with your savings goal and progress information.

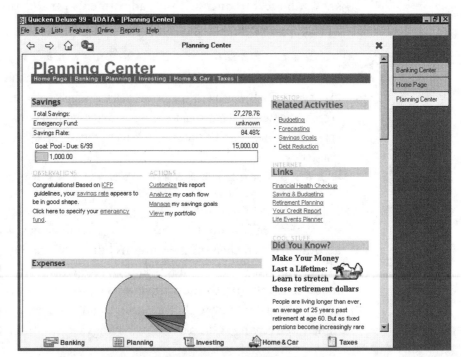

Figure 7.24

The Planning Center shows you the savings goal and progress at a glance.

Take a Break

Okay, enough financial planning for a moment. It's time for a break! Get up and stretch; step outside and enjoy the evening air for a few minutes. When you return, you'll see how Quicken can help you plan for life events such as college tuition and retirement.

Evaluating Financial Opportunities

Quicken provides a broad assortment of tools to help you keep track of your savings and investments. But that's not the only way the program helps you prepare for the future. Quicken also includes a set of what-if scenario tools and financial calculators that can be invaluable aids in helping you analyze your future needs and calculate what you'll need to save to achieve your goals.

The what-if scenarios walk you through the process of determining what you need to do now to finance your children's education, plan for your own estate, and figure out if you can afford to buy a home. The planning calculators help you with analyzing a loan, evaluating refinancing options, and saving for your own retirement.

Quicken's planning calculators do more than perform simple calculations to determine the monthly contribution you would need to accumulate a given amount by some future date. Instead, Quicken's planning calculators go a step further to do things like help you take stock of your existing resources, predict the resources you will have available in the future, and factor the impact of investment return and inflation into the calculations of your savings goals.

Opening the Scenario Index

Point at the Planning icon on the Activity Bar and choose Evaluate Financial Opportunities. The Scenario Index QuickTab shown in Figure 7.25 appears. Like the Planning Center pages, the Scenario Index is set up like a Web page with hypertext links to more information. Under the heading "Coming Soon," Quicken lets you know that you can download new what-if scenarios when you update Quicken and provides you with a link to click for instant updates.

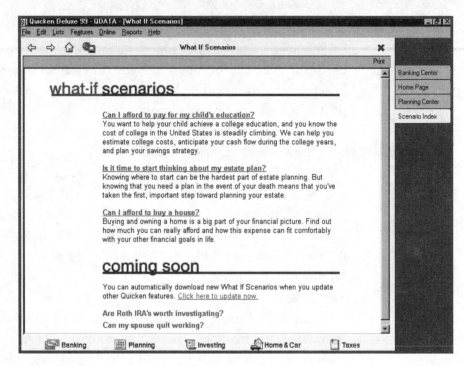

Figure 7.25

The Scenario Index provides you access to the what-if scenario assistants in Quicken.

Planning For College Costs

Open the Scenario Index and click on the what-if scenario that asks, "Can I afford to pay for my child's education? The College Scenario QuickTab shown in Figure 7.26 appears. The page is arranged into a calculator, a welcome to saving for college section, and an advice for your next steps section.

The College Calculator helps you estimate how much you need to save each year to afford your child's education. You can then use the Next Steps section to get advice on how to set up a savings plan to meet your savings goal. You can use the College Calculator to compute any of the following:

- **Annual College Cost.** To find out how much you will be able to afford given your current savings and planned contributions.

- **Current College Savings.** To find out what kind of one-time contribution you would need in order to meet your cost and contribution goals.

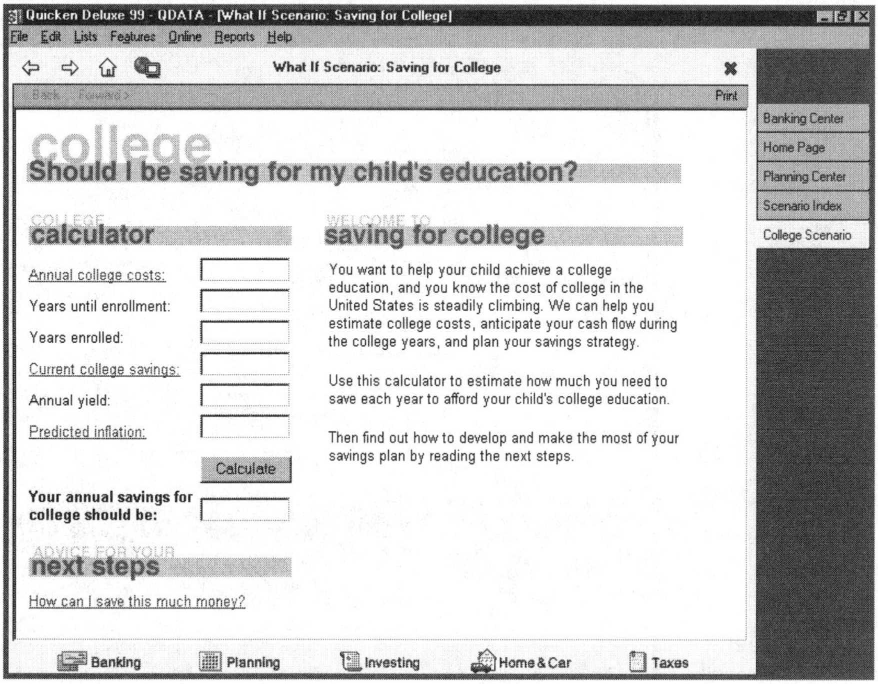

Quicken Deluxe 99 - QDATA - [What If Scenario: Saving for College]

File   Edit   Lists   Features   Online   Reports   Help

What If Scenario: Saving for College

Back   Forward >   Print

Banking Center

Home Page

Planning Center

Scenario Index

College Scenario

college
Should I be saving for my child's education?

COLLEGE
calculator

WELCOME TO
saving for college

Annual college costs:

Years until enrollment:

Years enrolled:

Current college savings:

Annual yield:

Predicted inflation:

Calculate

Your annual savings for college should be:

You want to help your child achieve a college education, and you know the cost of college in the United States is steadily climbing. We can help you estimate college costs, anticipate your cash flow during the college years, and plan your savings strategy.

Use this calculator to estimate how much you need to save each year to afford your child's college education.

Then find out how to develop and make the most of your savings plan by reading the next steps.

ADVICE FOR YOUR
next steps

How can I save this much money?

Banking   Planning   Investing   Home & Car   Taxes

Figure 7.26

The College Scenario page includes a college planning calculator.

⚙ **Annual Contribution.** To find out the yearly savings contributions you need to make to meet anticipated college costs.

You can adjust the expected annual yield for your college savings, change the percentage predicted for inflation, and tell whether to increase your planned contributions by the inflation factor.

To use the College Calculator, follow these steps:

1. Click on the first hypertext item, Annual College Costs. Quicken displays help text to the right of the calculator (see Figure 7.27) explaining how to estimate college costs and reporting the cost results from the most recent Annual Survey of Colleges.

2. Enter the annual college costs.

3. Enter the number of years until enrollment.

4. Enter the number of years your child will be enrolled.

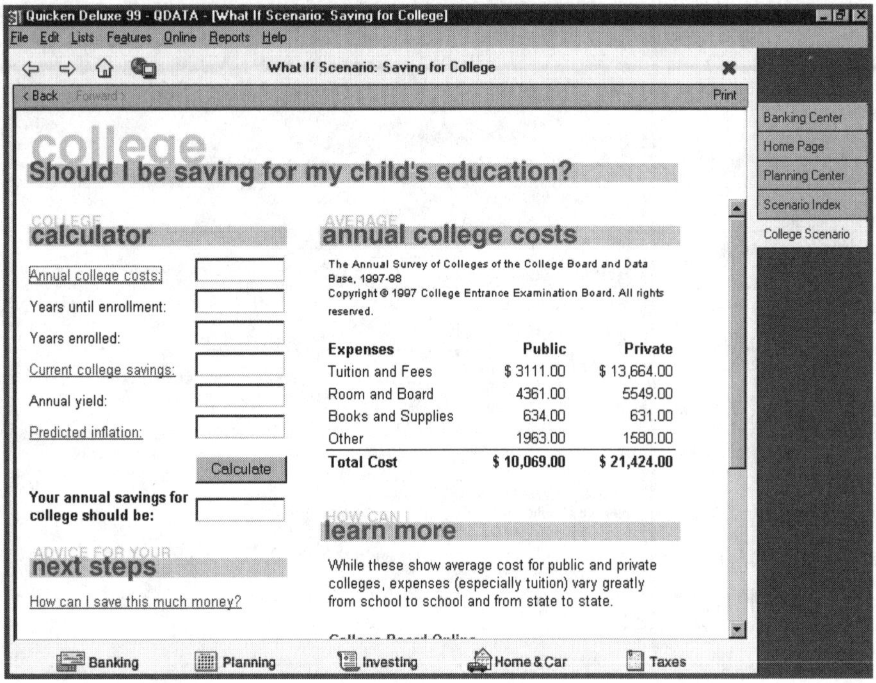

Figure 7.27

When you click on hypertext words in the calculator, Quicken displays help text on the right.

5. Click on the hypertext Current College Savings. Quicken displays your current savings and investment portfolio data so you can determine the savings available. How convenient!

6. Enter the current savings (if any) that you want to put aside for college costs.

7. Enter the annual yield (interest percentage that your savings plan will pay you). For example, you would enter 6 for a CD that pays you 6 percent on your investment.

8. Click on the hypertext Predicted Inflation. Quicken displays help text on the right explaining how you estimate inflation and providing an online resource. Enter the Predicted inflation factor as a number (for example, 4 for 4 percent).

9. Click on the Calculate button. Quicken computes and displays what you need to save each year in order to cover your college costs.

10. Click on the various hypertext items under Next Steps for assistance on setting up a savings plan, budgeting your spending, and discovering sources of financial aid (see Figure 7.28).

11. Close the College Scenario planner when you are done.

TIP For families with several college-bound children, it is best to go through the College Calculator for each child, one at a time. Then add up the amount you need to save monthly to arrive at your total monthly savings goal.

Estate Planning

Return to the Scenario Index and click on the what-if scenario "Is it time to start thinking about my estate plan?" The Estate Scenario QuickTab shown in Figure 7.29 appears. The Estate Scenario planner is arranged into multiple pages, with a table of contents in the top left corner. You can click

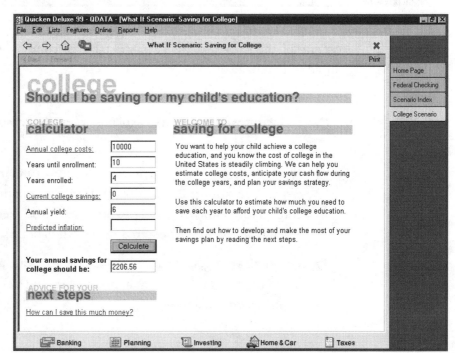

Figure 7.28

Use the Next Steps hypertext for easy access to online resources like getting financial aid.

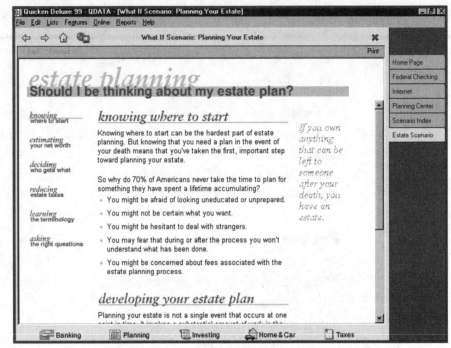

Figure 7.29

The Estate Scenario page teaches you about estate planning while walking you through the financial issues.

on any of the hypertext items in the table of contents to quickly jump ahead to that page or topic.

Estate Scenario topics include:

- **Knowing where to start.** Explains when to develop an estate plan and what is involved.

- **Estimating your net worth.** Explains how to compute your gross estate (also known as net worth), shows you your estate value (as entered into Quicken), and provides you with a Net Worth Calculator in case you haven't entered net worth data into Quicken yet.

- **Deciding who gets what.** Explains how to create a will, how a will protects you, and how to establish a trust, and also provides online resources on these topics.

- ✿ **Reducing estate taxes.** Explains the estate tax rules and provides ideas on how to limit or eliminate estate taxes. A Learning More Online section contains links to federal estate and gift tax sites.

- ✿ **Learning the terminology.** Defines the buzzwords in plain English, provides advice on topics such as avoiding probate, and lists online links for even more information.

- ✿ **Asking the right questions.** Lists estate planning questions meant to provoke your thought process and guide you in evaluating your own personal needs and issues. It also includes links to online topics such as making funeral plans, the process of events after the death of a loved one, and a very handy checklist designed to help you organize and finalize financial issues in a time of sorrow.

The pages provide you with a plain-talk, down-to-earth description of the issues and rules surrounding estate planning. Each page provides links to online resources where you can learn more or download forms. Estate planning jargon is defined in an understandable way, with plenty of real-life examples to help you understand the issues and consequences. Information you have entered into Quicken appears as needed so that you can make decisions based on your own data (see Figure 7.30).

If you haven't had time to enter your net worth data into Quicken, you can use the Estate Planning Calculator to compute your estate's value. Just click on the hypertext link Estimating Your Net Worth and scroll down to the bottom. In the Taking A Closer Look section, you'll see the Use Our Calculator hypertext link. Click on the link and Quicken will display the Estimating Your Net Worth Calculator shown in Figure 7.31. Fill in the asset and liability information and click on the Estimate Net Worth button. Quicken will calculate and display your net worth. When you finish, you can use the Back button to return to the prior page, or choose a different Estate topic to view.

Buying a House

Becoming a homeowner can be the highlight of a lifetime, but the financial issues of the actual purchase can seem overwhelming. You need to

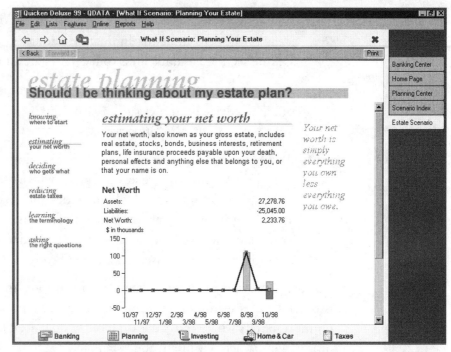

Figure 7.30

Quicken displays
your net worth
information so you
can quickly see
the worth of
your estate.

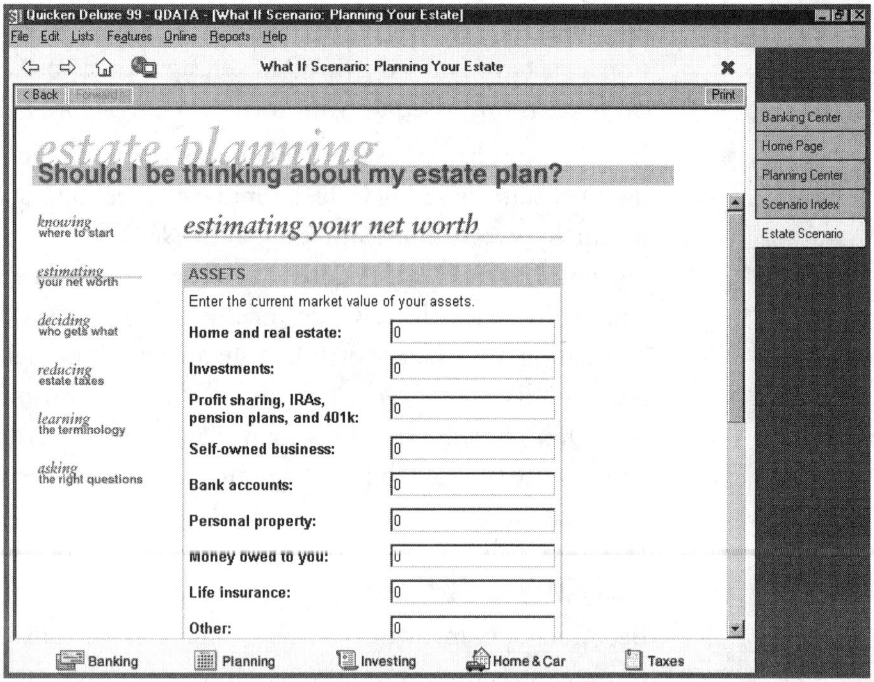

Figure 7.31

Use the Net Worth
Calculator to
determine
the value of
your estate.

apply for a mortgage, save for a down payment, get a favorable interest rate, decide between mortgage products (fixed rate, variable, balloon, and so on), and above all else be able to make your monthly mortgage payment and all the other demands on your checkbook and attention. Property taxes, school taxes, and zoning issues can take the joy out of your little piece of Earth.

Quicken's House Scenario helps you by guiding through this process from analyzing your financial goals to researching mortgage rates to the annual tax savings you can expect on your tax return each year. To open the House Scenario, return to the Scenario Index and click on the hypertext item Can I afford to buy a house?

As you can see in Figure 7.32, this scenario is similar to the Estate Scenario in that it consists of many pages. You can navigate the pages by clicking on the number line that appears across the top of the page. As you point to each number, the description of that page appears beneath the number. A hypertext link for the glossary and a map of this scenario appears to the

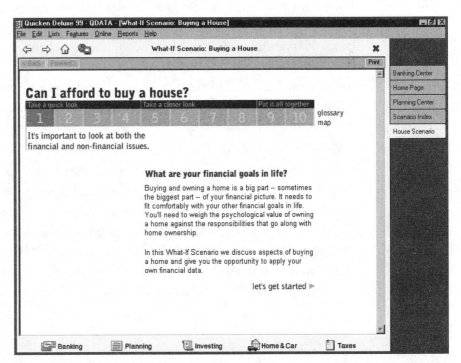

Figure 7.32

The what-if scenario for buying a house covers all financial aspects of house buying.

right of the number line. You can also click on Let's Get Started at the bottom of the page (a similar link appears at the bottom of each subsequent page) to go to the next page.

Take some time now to page through this section to familiarize yourself with the contents and issues involved. Click on the hypertext links within each page to see your financial situation and explore your house-buying options.

Planning for Retirement

Quicken Deluxe 99 provides you with two retirement planners: a basic retirement calculator and a more in-depth lifelong retirement planner. I'll show you the more comprehensive retirement planner first.

Using the Quicken Financial Planner for Retirement Planning

To access the Financial Retirement Planner, point at the Planning icon on the Activity Bar and choose Plan For Retirement. The Financial Retirement Planner is actually part of another Quicken product, the Quicken Financial Planner. (An abridged version of the Quicken Financial Planner is included free as part of the Deluxe version of Quicken 99.) The first time you open the Quicken Financial Planner, a software license agreement dialog box appears. Read over the agreement and click on Accept to continue. When the Quicken Financial Planner window appears (see Figure 7.33), click on the Open button.

Take a moment to review the Welcome screen that appears (see Figure 7.34). The tabs down the right side (Personal, Income, and so on) are the steps you need to complete in order to review your results and create an action plan. The information requested on each tab is minimal, just a few items per page. Go ahead and click on the first tab, Personal. Fill in the information for you and your spouse. Then continue to the next tab and so forth until you've entered all of the background information needed.

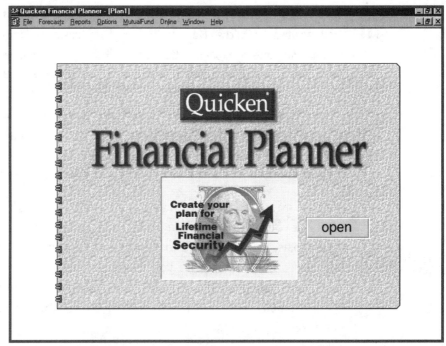

Figure 7.33

The Quicken
Financial Planner
helps you with
retirement
planning.

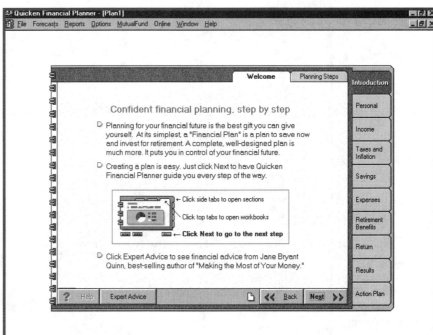

Figure 7.34

The Quicken
Financial Planner is
organized by the
tabs on the
right side.

You can open the Quicken Financial Planner at any time by clicking on the Windows Start button and choosing Programs, Quicken, Quicken Financial Planner.

If you are uncertain of the information being requested, click on the Help button or Expert Advice button for assistance.

At the end, the Action Plan tab (see Figure 7.35) provides you with a summary of your financial situation, lists action steps you need to take to meet your goals, and allows you to print your action plan. The Upgrade tab (at the top of the page) gives you a chance to purchase the full version of Quicken's Financial Planner. When you finish, choose File, Save to save your financial plan. You can then close the Financial Planner to return to Quicken Deluxe.

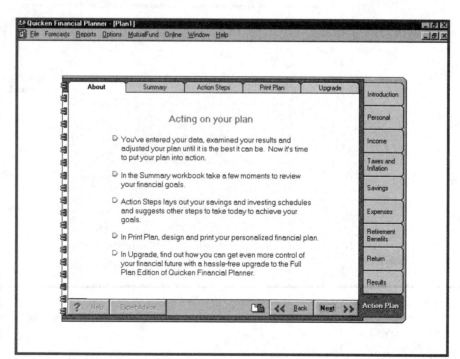

Figure 7.35

The action steps help you achieve your retirement goals.

NOTE Quicken.com also provides a Retirement Planner for you (modeled after the Quicken Financial Planner) that you can use online. To access this feature, go to **http://www.quicken.com/retirement/planner**.

Using the Retirement Calculator

The simpler, more basic retirement planner is one of the Quicken planning calculators. To open the Retirement Calculator, choose from the menu bar Features, Planning, Financial Calculators, Retirement. The Retirement Calculator shown in Figure 7.36 appears. Enter the retirement information as applicable to you and your situation. Click on the Calculate button to compute one of the following:

- How much current savings you need to meet your retirement income goal with your planned annual contributions

- The annual contribution you need to meet your retirement goal

- The annual retirement income you can expect, given your current savings and planned contributions

To fine-tune your calculations, you can adjust the expected annual yield of your investments and the predicted inflation rate. You can choose whether

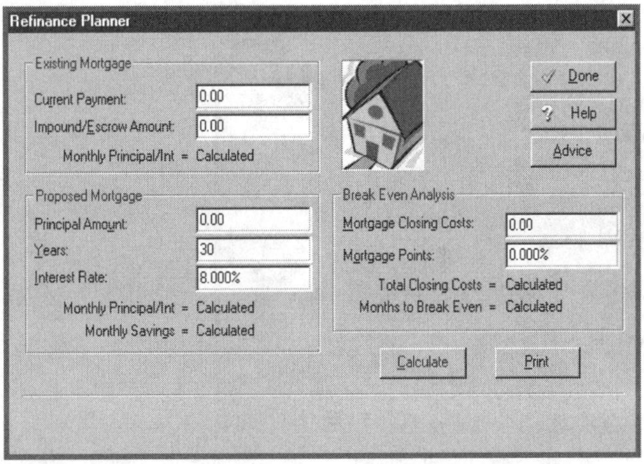

Figure 7.36

The Retirement Calculator can help you plan for retirement by showing you what kind of retirement income to expect from a combination of current savings and annual contributions.

to increase your planned contributions by the inflation factor and you can elect to show your planned retirement income in today's dollars (check the Annual Income In Today's $ option) or in inflation-devalued dollars. You can also adjust the calculations to allow for the impact of taxes. You can adjust the calculations by selecting boxes labeled Tax Sheltered Investments or Non-Sheltered Investments, and also Current Tax Rate and Retirement Tax Rate (that is, for what you pay now and what you expect to pay when you retire).

NOTE One weakness of the Retirement Calculator is that it assumes that all your retirement funds are equal—that they all share the same tax-sheltered or taxable status and earn the same annual yield. If you need to do more complicated retirement planning, you might want to consider using the Quicken Financial Planner as covered earlier.

For more information on tracking and analyzing retirement plans in Quicken, refer back to the Investment session (Saturday Evening).

Using the Investment Savings Planner

To open the Investment Savings Planner, choose from the menu bar Features, Planning, Financial Calculators, Savings. The Investment Savings Planner (shown in Figure 7.37) appears. You can use it to predict the growth

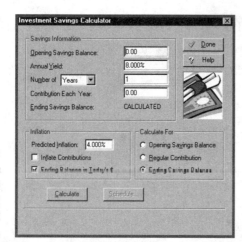

Figure 7.37

Predict the performance of a savings investment with this calculator.

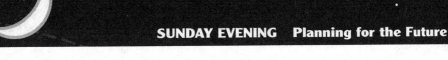

of an investment or to calculate the contributions needed to achieve a certain balance at a future time.

You can calculate either the Opening Savings Balance, the Regular Contribution, or the Ending Savings Balance. (You need to supply two of the three amounts to calculate the third. However, one of the amounts you supply can be zero.) You can adjust the Annual Yield of the investment and the number and frequency of contributions to the investment. You can also instruct Quicken to adjust the contributions or the ending balance for inflation of a percentage you specify.

Using the Investment Savings Planner is easy. Just select the value you want to calculate, enter the information in the various boxes in the dialog box, and then click on the Calculate button. The Investment Savings Planner will show the result beside the appropriate label in place of the CALCU-LATED legend. You can change the settings and redo the calculation as many times as you like to try out various scenarios. To see a schedule of your planned contributions, click on the Schedule button.

Taking On or Consolidating Debt

Most financial planners agree that saving for major purchases and other needs is almost always preferable to borrowing money to meet those needs. After all, you're generally going to be better off earning interest on money that you are saving, rather than paying (higher) interest on money that you've borrowed.

However, there are situations where borrowing money makes good financial sense. Buying a home is a good example. After considering the favorable tax treatment of mortgage interest and the typical appreciation of real estate investments, it may be cheaper to borrow the money to buy a house than to pay rent while saving the money you would need to buy a similar house.

More often, the reason for borrowing money isn't that it makes good financial sense to do so, but that borrowing money enables you to make a purchase or do something—whether it's buying a car or taking a vacation cruise—that you wouldn't be able to do until much later if you waited to save the money to do it. And many people are willing to pay for the privilege and convenience of getting immediate gratification.

Sometimes, the choice to take on debt is made willingly. Other times the choice is forced by circumstances. Credit cards come to the rescue for situations such as having to replace the transmission in the car when there's barely enough money in the checking account to cover groceries, and they are all too convenient for dining out and making impulse purchases. Whatever the reasons for borrowing, most families are carrying some debt and many have come to accept it as a fact of life.

Quicken can help you manage your debt load by helping you analyze your options. Using Quicken's planners, you can estimate the costs of loans and compare home mortgages and refinancing options. Quicken Deluxe even includes a feature to help you develop a plan to pay off your debts.

Using the Loan Calculator

Quicken's Loan Calculator enables you to do quick calculations for the kinds of loans typically used for such things as automobile purchases, mortgages, and signature loans. To open the Loan Calculator, choose from the menu bar Features, Planning, Financial Calculators, Loan. The Loan Calculator (shown in Figure 7.38) appears.

The Loan Calculator lets you figure the estimated payments for a loan if you know the amount of the loan and terms. Or you can figure the loan amount you can get with a given payment and terms. To calculate a loan,

Figure 7.38

Can you afford the payments on that new car? Find out with this calculator.

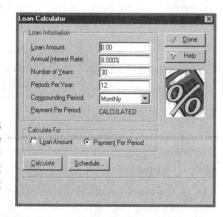

you'll need to fill in the boxes labeled Annual Interest Rate, Number of Years (how long the loan is for), the Periods Per Year (how many payments you'll make each year), and the Compounding Period. You also need to fill in either the Loan Amount or the Payment Per Period box. After entering the information, click on the Calculate button and the results will pop up on the screen. By changing the settings and recalculating the results you can quickly see the effect of changes in the terms of the loan. As with all the calculators, you can click on the Schedule button to open a separate dialog box where you can view (and print) a schedule of payments for a loan after it is calculated. This is especially useful with loans because the schedule shows what portions of each payment go toward principal and interest and also what the outstanding balance will be after each payment.

♦ ♦

The Loan Calculator does a good job of estimating loan amounts and payments. But the figures may not match your financial institution's numbers exactly. Also, the Loan Calculator doesn't handle loans that include balloon payments, adjustable rates, deferred interest, or other special provisions.

♦ ♦

Thinking about Refinancing Your House

Refinancing your house to get a mortgage with a lower interest rate can save you significant money each month in lower mortgage payments. But the closing costs and points charged by mortgage lenders complicate the calculations you need to do to compare a proposed mortgage to what you are paying now.

The Refinance Calculator is designed to facilitate the sometimes difficult task of evaluating whether a proposed mortgage refinancing is a good deal. The Refinance Calculator looks at your current monthly payment and compares it to the estimated monthly payment for the replacement mortgage to figure the monthly savings (if any). The Refinance Calculator will also figure how many months of those lower payments it will take to break even after paying points and closing costs for the refinancing.

CAUTION   The Refinance Calculator concerns itself with monthly payments only. It does not figure the total long-term cost of refinancing. So if you extend the term of your mortgage, the refinance may look great in terms of lowering your monthly payment—but it could dramatically increase your total cost over the life of the mortgage and slow your accumulation of equity. Of course, if you plan to sell the house in a few years, that may not matter.

To open the Refinance Calculator, choose from the menu bar Features, Planning, Financial Calculators, Refinance. The Refinance Calculator (shown in Figure 7.39) appears. To compare mortgages, follow these steps:

1. In the Current Payment box, enter the total amount of your current monthly mortgage payment. In the Impound/Escrow Amount box, enter the portion of your payment that goes to an escrow account to pay insurance and taxes. The Refinance Calculator figures the combined monthly principal and interest payment.

2. In the Principal Amount box, enter the amount you plan to finance with the proposed mortgage. Then enter the term of the proposed mortgage in years and the interest rate in the appropriate boxes. The Refinance Calculator will figure the monthly payment for the proposed mortgage and the monthly savings compared to your current mortgage payment. (If the Monthly Savings is a negative number, it

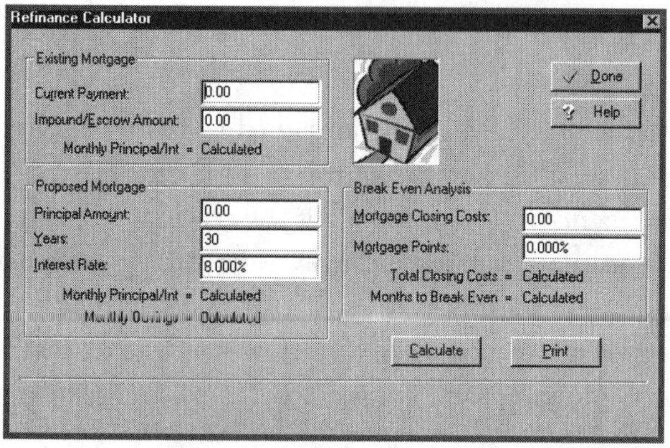

Figure 7.39

Calculate how long it will take for a lower monthly mortgage payment to break even with the closing costs that go along with refinancing your home.

means the proposed mortgage will cost more than your current mortgage costs each month.)

NOTE Presumably, your monthly contribution to an escrow account for taxes and insurance will be the same for both your current mortgage and the proposed mortgage. If so, the amount of the escrow payment is not a factor in comparing the mortgages. Just don't forget that you will need to add the escrow payment to the Monthly Principal/Int amount the Refinance Calculator comes up with to find your new mortgage payment.

3. In the Break Even Analysis area of the Refinance Calculator, fill in the boxes for Mortgage Closing Costs (that is, the total of the various appraisal and processing fees) and Mortgage Points. The calculator figures the total closing costs and then tells you how many months of lower payments it will take to pay yourself back for those closing costs.

Creating a Debt Reduction Plan

If you're like many Americans, you may have succumbed to the temptation and convenience of credit cards and used those dangerous pieces of plastic a little too freely. As a result, you may have accumulated a sizable debt. It's all too easy to do. And once the debt builds up, it can be difficult to get it back under control. For one thing, if your debt is spread out among several credit cards and other accounts, it's tough to get a good picture of just where you stand.

With credit card statements and other bills coming in at various times of the month, all with different interest rates and minimum payment requirements, it can be confusing and very difficult to come up with an intelligent plan for paying off your debt. You probably know that it will take many years (and a fortune in finance charges) to pay off credit cards and similar debt if you pay only the minimum payments, so you do pay more than minimums. But if you can't pay the full outstanding amount on all your credit cards, what's the best strategy for apportioning your payments among the various credit card accounts?

Quicken's Debt Reduction feature can walk you through the process of developing a plan to pay off your debts. It helps you take stock of what you're paying on your debt now, plus what other resources you can put toward reducing your debt. Then it helps you develop a plan to pay off your debt as efficiently as possible. You can print out a copy of the plan to follow as you pay your monthly bills and track your progress toward becoming debt free.

The goal of Quicken Debt Reduction is to reduce the total long-term cost of carrying the debt. It does this by developing a plan to pay off the accounts with the highest interest rates first while making only the minimum payments on other accounts. As soon as one account is paid down to zero, you take the money you were paying each month on that account and apply it to the next account, and so on until all your debts are paid off. The total amount you pay on debt reduction remains the same throughout the duration of the plan. The allocation of those payments is what changes.

Your debt reduction plan can encompass debts that you don't normally track with Quicken as well as those for which you have established Quicken accounts. The Quicken Debt Reduction feature is composed of two parts. First, there is the Debt Reduction wizard, which leads you through the process of developing your plan. Then there is the Debt Reduction window, where you can see a chart of your debt reduction plan and monitor your progress. You can revise your plan from time to time as needed.

TIP Before you begin developing your debt reduction plan, you'll need to gather detailed information such as current balances, interest rates, and minimum payments on all your debts. You can usually find the necessary information on credit card statements and similar documents.

The Debt Reduction wizard includes extensive multimedia instructions and support to guide you through the necessary steps to create your debt reduction plan. You'll see just an outline of the general process in the following steps:

1. Point to the Planning icon on the Activity Bar and choose Create A Debt Reduction Plan from the shortcut menu that appears. This will open the Debt Reduction dialog box to the first page, as shown in Figure 7.40. (If the Debt Reduction window appears but the wizard doesn't start automatically, it's probably because a debt reduction plan already exists. In that case, you can rerun the wizard by clicking on the New Plan button in the Button bar at the top of the Debt Reduction window.)

2. Make sure your Quicken Deluxe CD is in your CD-ROM drive and click on Next to begin working through the process. The Start page introduces you to the Debt Reduction Wizard with three on-screen movies.

3. Click on Next to proceed to the Debts page, as shown in Figure 7.41. Here you will develop a list of your debts. The wizard has already imported some information from the debts you track in Quicken.

   ✪ If you need to add debts to the list, click on the Add button to open the Edit Debt Reduction dialog box. Enter the requested information into the appropriate boxes and then click on OK to close the dialog box and return to the wizard.

   ✪ Select each of your debts in the list in turn and click on the Edit button. This will open the Edit Debt Reduction dialog

Figure 7.40

The opening screen of the Debt Reduction wizard's dialog box

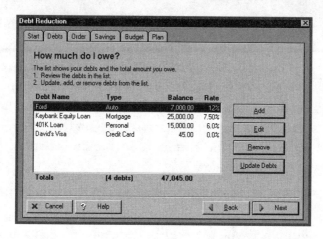

Figure 7.41

First, you must develop a list of the debts you want to include in your debt reduction plan.

box. The information in the Loan Info area will probably be filled in, but you'll need to enter Monthly Payment and Interest Rate information. Click on OK to close the dialog box and return to the wizard.

❂ If a debt appears on the list that you don't want to be part of your debt reduction plan, select the debt and click on Remove.

❂ Click on the Update Debts button to import the data from Quicken again.

4. When your list of debts is complete, click on Next. The Debt Reduction wizard will calculate your total debt, the total monthly payments you currently make, and display how long it will take to get out of debt and how much interest you will pay.

5. Click on Next twice to proceed to the Order tab of the Debt Reduction wizard. The wizard calculates the optimal order in which to pay off your debts and displays a list like the one shown in Figure 7.42. Normally, you'll want to accept the wizard's recommendation. But if you want to change the order, you can click on the Change Payment Order check box and then click on Next to go to another page where you can select debts and move them up or down in the payment order list.

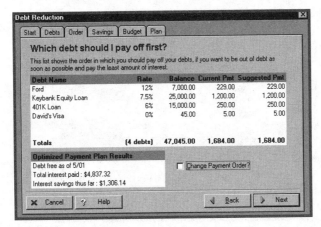

Figure 7.42

The wizard determines the optimal order to pay off the listed debts.

6. Click on Next to proceed to the Savings tab and listen to the instructions, and then click on Next again to reach a screen where the Debt Reduction wizard suggests using some of your savings to reduce your debt.

TIP ■
Since banks and credit card companies almost always charge higher interest rates than your savings earn, it can make good financial sense to use savings to pay off a portion of your debt. You avoid having to pay interest on the debt you pay off with savings, so it's almost like investing those funds at the higher interest rate charged on the debt—and you save on income taxes if the savings interest was taxable, too!
■ ■

7. If you decide to use some of your savings to reduce your debt, enter the amount in the box and click on Recalculate. (This is a one-time payment; it's not something you'll continue to do every month.) The wizard shows you the effect of the payment on your debt.

8. Click on Next to move to the Budget tab and listen to the instructions. Then click on Next again to open the Budget page shown in Figure 7.43.

9. The wizard searches your Quicken data file and automatically locates your four highest expense categories and shows how much

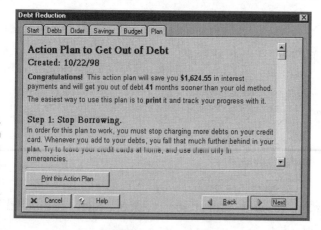

you've been spending in each of those categories. The idea is to identify some areas where you can curtail your spending somewhat and then apply that money toward reducing your debt. You can select different categories in the Quicken Categories boxes and then enter an amount in the Amount To Cut Back boxes beside each category. You can also enter an amount that isn't tied to a category in the Other row. Click on Recalculate to see the effect on your debt.

10. Click on Next to go to the Plan tab of the Debt Reduction wizard, as shown in Figure 7.44. The wizard summarizes the debt reduction steps you've worked out in a detailed report that you can read onscreen or print out (just click on the Print This Action Plan button).

11. Close the Debt Reduction dialog box and go to the Debt Reduction window shown in Figure 7.45. The chart and the summary boxes below it show a comparison between your debt reduction plan and your old payment habits, and give you the debt-free date and total interest paid. You can change the amounts in the Current Plan area and click on Recalculate to see a quick preview of how the change would affect your plan.

✿ Click on Update Debt Balances to import data from your Quicken data file.

✿ Click on Payment Schedule to view an updated schedule of debt reduction payments. You can print the schedule if desired.

✿ Click on New Plan to rerun the Debt Reduction wizard and make revisions in your plan.

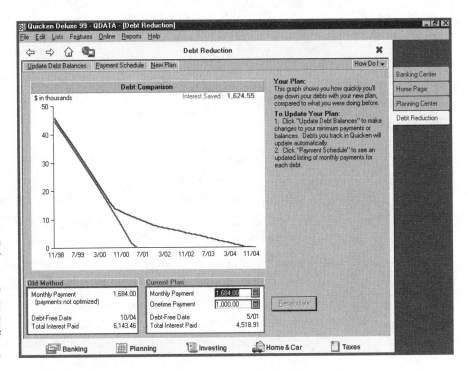

Figure 7.45

Quicken charts your debt reduction plan to make it easy to see how following the plan will get you out of debt sooner.

QUICKEN HANDLES THE YEAR 2000

No doubt, you've heard about the *millennium bug* that threatens to crash computer systems around the globe when we reach the year 2000. Well, you don't need to worry about your Quicken data being affected—Quicken is not infested with the millennium bug.

The so-called millennium bug is a result of the once-common computer programming practice of using just the last two digits to keep track of the year in dates. For example, 1998 is entered simply as 98. That works as long as the first two digits don't change, as has been the case ever since computers were invented. But now, as we approach the year 2000 and beyond, two-digit dates are a potential problem. The 00 for the year 2000 would be interpreted as 1900 instead. All calculations based on such dates would be wrong.

Fortunately, Quicken is well-prepared to enter the next century. The program stores date information with four digits for years so all the date calculations will be correct—even those that extend beyond the year 2000. Quicken may display two-digit years in notations such as 10/15/01 (October 15, 2001), but all dates are stored within the program with full four-digit years.

What's Next?

Congratulations, you've made it! You've reached the end of the book and the end of your weekend project.

By now, you have developed a basic familiarity with the tools Quicken provides for organizing your finances. Hopefully, you've had time to put some of this information to use and enter at least some of your financial data into Quicken. Now it's up to you to apply what you've learned to help you manage your finances.

You should be able to see some improvements immediately as you get a handle on aspects of your finances that may have previously eluded you. Just getting all your financial information together in one place where you can have easy access to it can make a big difference. You'll find that you can manage your finances better with better access to your financial information—and the bonus is that you can spend less time doing it.

But be patient, too. Some of the reporting, budgeting, and tax features don't come into their own until you have accumulated more than a year of financial data in your Quicken file. So some of the advantages of working with Quicken won't materialize until you have worked with the program for a while—but many others are at your fingertips right now!

Installing Quicken Deluxe 99

- ✿ What You Need
- ✿ Problems to Watch Out For
- ✿ Installing Your Quicken Program
- ✿ Registering Your Software
- ✿ Moving On

I f you haven't had a chance to install or update to Quicken Deluxe 99, this appendix will walk you through that process. In most cases, it is very straightforward, but if you have an unusual hardware or software environment, have already installed a newer version of Internet Explorer, or have another Quicken product (such as QuickInvoice) already on your computer, you may run into some difficulties.

In this appendix, you will find out:

⚙ What hardware and software you need

⚙ What hazards and potential conflicts you may face

⚙ How to install Quicken Deluxe 99

This appendix takes you to the point where Quicken prompts you to set up a new user data file or open an existing data file (for those who are upgrading). After installing, please continue with the Friday Evening session to set up a new data file or open or convert existing Quicken data.

What Do You Need?

Intuit lists the basic system requirements for installing and running Quicken Deluxe 99:

⚙ IBM-compatible 486 or higher PC.

⚙ Windows 95 or 98, Windows 3.1 running in enhanced mode with MS-DOS 5.0 or higher and MS-DEX 2.2 or higher (a CD-ROM driver), or Windows NT 4.01 or higher.

⚙ At least 8MB of RAM.

⚙ 30MB of free hard disk space.

⚙ Double speed CD-ROM drive or faster (sound board and speakers are recommended).

⚙ A monitor and video board capable of displaying 256-color VGA.

This is the bare minimum. If your PC lacks one of these basic items, you will be missing out on many of Quicken's features and many functions may run slowly. But for core operations such as automating bank accounts, Quicken runs just fine under these conditions.

For optimal performance, I recommend you have the following system configuration:

⚙ Pentium PC with 32 MB or more of memory so you can get your work done faster.

⚙ Windows 98 to get the fastest 32-bit processing and optimal performance.

⚙ A laserjet or deskjet printer to provide the best quality printing for checks and reports.

⚙ Sound board and speakers so you can enjoy the audio help features and that wonderful cash register "cha-ching" as you pay bills!

⚙ An additional 4-6MB of hard disk space and the fastest Hayes-compatible modem you can afford. (14.4K is the minimum speed at which Quicken will connect to the Internet, but 28.8K is probably the minimum that you can endure). With the extra hard disk space and faster modem, you can enjoy all the online features of Quicken such as program updates and bug fixes, online banking, online bill paying, and online investing.

⚙ A comfortable workstation with proper support for your wrists (such as wrist rests for the keyboard and mouse) and good lighting. Proximity to refrigerator and TV optional.

Problems to Watch Out For

As with any software, there are always unexpected problems and conflicts. You can get a list of the most recent issues by using the Intuit Fax-Back service or visiting the Web site. To access the Fax-Back service, call 800-644-3198 and request an index of available documents. When you receive the index, scan for topics that include the word "install" or names of hardware or software that you use. For example, if you use Windows NT, you should read over any documents that discuss problems running Windows NT. To access the Quicken Web site, point your Web browser to **http://www.intuit.com/support/Quicken**. Again, search for topics that deal with Quicken 99 installation issues or names of products you use.

FIND IT ▶
ONLINE

At the time this book was written, Quicken listed the following issues:

⚙ QuickInvoice and QuickPay 3.0 are not compatible with Windows NT 4.0. For QuickInvoice, you could switch to Quicken 99 Home & Business, which includes invoicing. For QuickPay, you could switch to QuickBooks, which includes payroll functions. Or, for QuickPay, you could install the Windows 3.1 16-bit version of Quicken 99 with QuickPay on Windows NT 4.0, but you won't get online account access or be able to connect to the Internet.

⚙ Install fails if you have your TEMP directory set to a RAM drive.

⚙ Online Billing is not available on the Windows 3.1 version.

⚙ When updating Quicken from Home Inventory (covered Saturday morning), you may need to restart Quicken to see the update.

⚙ Quicken will not install from a networked CD-ROM drive. You will need a local CD-ROM drive, or you should order diskettes from Quicken. (The diskettes are free, you just pay a small shipping charge.)

⚙ You must register your software (by phone, fax, or modem) before Quicken will allow you to update your software online. After an

online update, Quicken seems to leave .TMP files in the TEMP directory. You can erase these files.

✿ Once you install the Home & Business edition of Quicken, you may experience problems if you decide to revert back to the Quicken Deluxe edition. Even though you uninstall the Home & Business edition and reinstall Quicken Deluxe, Quicken still displays the Home & Business logos and options. Contact Quicken to see if a fix has been developed. Meanwhile, you can ignore the Home & Business portions, as they won't interfere with the normal Deluxe features.

Installing Your Quicken Program

If you are upgrading from a prior version of Quicken, I recommend that you open the older version of Quicken and back up your data to a new folder on your hard disk AND to floppy diskettes. Having two backups is the safest way to go. Nothing is worse than announcing to the family that you'll be upgrading, then finding out that something went wrong and your backup diskettes are damaged!

Now, you are ready to install Quicken.

1. Before you install Quicken, you should save any open data files and close any open programs.

■■■

Unsure as to whether other programs are running? In Windows 3.1, press Ctrl+Esc to display the Task List. Only the Program Manager should be running. In Windows 95 or 98, look at the Taskbar. It should be empty.

■■■

2. Insert the CD into the CD-ROM drive or disk 1 into the disk drive.

✿ If your PC's CD-ROM supports the AutoRun feature in Windows 98, Quicken will ask you if you want to install Quicken 99 now. Click on Yes.

✿ In Windows 95 without the AutoRun feature, click on Start, Run, and then type in the text box the drive letter of your CD-

ROM drive and the program name Install.exe. For example: d:\install.exe where drive D is the CD-ROM drive letter. Click on OK.

⚙ In Windows 3.x, choose File, Run, and then type the drive letter of your CD-ROM drive and the program name Install.exe. For example: d:\install.exe where drive D is the CD-ROM drive letter. Click on OK.

3. The Quicken Deluxe 99 Welcome screen appears (see Figure A.1).

4. Click on Next to continue. The next screen displays the license agreement.

5. Read over the license agreement and click on Yes to continue.

6. Quicken displays the Choose Destination Location dialog box shown in Figure A.2. Here you can specify where on your computer you want to install Quicken. Type in the drive letter and folder path (such as C:\QUICKENW) or use the Browse button to locate the

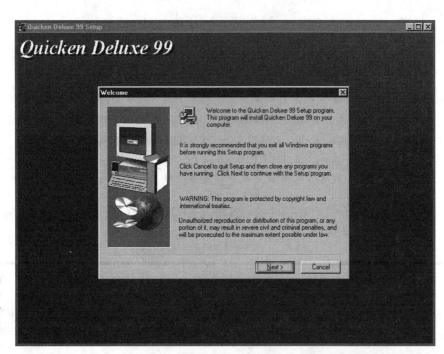

Figure A.1

Quicken reminds you to exit all other Windows programs before continuing.

Figure A.2

You can install Quicken in a specific folder.

folder name. If you type in a folder name that doesn't exist yet, Quicken will give you the opportunity to create the new folder. Click on Next to continue.

7. Quicken displays the Type of Installation dialog box (see Figure A.3). In the Express install, all of the commonly needed features of Quicken are installed. In the Custom install, you can pick and choose which features are installed

NOTE To use all the online features of Quicken, you need to have Internet Explorer installed. Installing Quicken's version of Internet Explorer won't interfere with any other browser that you may already have installed. You can continue to use your current browser for your other Internet activities, but you will need to use Internet Explorer within Quicken to use all of its features. If you decide not to install Internet Explorer, some of the features will appear outside of Quicken in the other browser's window. Furthermore, you will not be able to use the online banking, investment tracking, or online billing features.

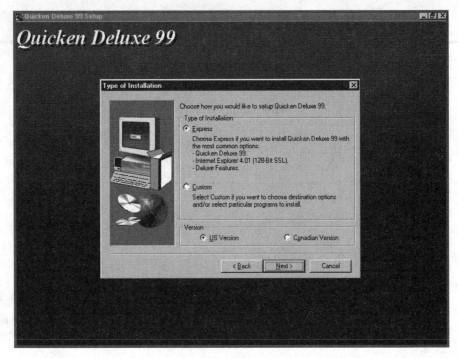

Figure A.3

You can install Quicken quicky by using the Express Setup.

8. If you want to select specific programs to install, click on Custom. Otherwise, leave the Express setup type selected.

9. Select the country as US or Canada. Click on Next to continue.

10. If you're using the the Custom setup, Quicken will display a list of components that you can deselect for installation (see Figure A.4). Note that this screen specifies the space required for each component and provides a listing of the total space available on your hard disk. Check the components you want to install, uncheck those you do not want to install. You can always run custom installation at a later time to install the components that you decide not to install now. Click on Next to continue.

11. Custom installers who deselected Internet Explorer for installation will be reminded of the benefits of Internet Explorer and will need to re-assert their wishes.

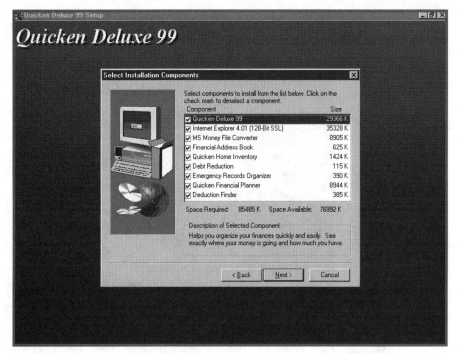

Figure A.4

Custom setup
allows you to select
which programs
to install.

12. Select the Start Menu program folder into which you want to put Quicken (defaults to Quicken) and click on Next to continue.

13. Quicken checks for the required hard disk space and, if enough space exists, displays the Check Settings screen (see Figure A.5). Scroll down to review the current installation settings. If you need to change any settings, use the Back button to move to a prior setup screen. If the settings are OK, click on Start Copying to install Quicken.

■■
TIP   If Quicken finds that you do not have enough hard disk space, you can either use the
Custom setup to install just the basic Quicken program components or click on No to end
the installation until you can clear more space on your hard disk.
■■

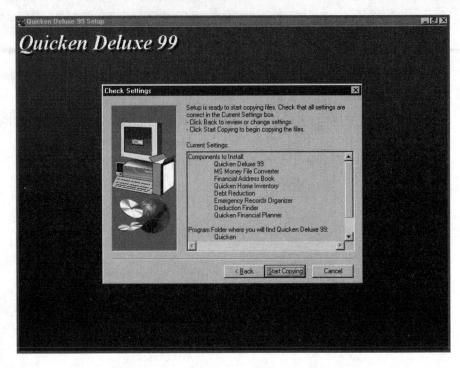

Figure A.5

Figure A.5

Setup lists the
components to be
installed.

14. Quicken will continue with the installation. If you are using diskettes, Quicken will prompt you for the next diskette when needed. Prior to installing Internet Explorer, Quicken will display the license agreement. Read it over, then click on Yes to continue.

15. When the installation process has been completed, click on Yes to restart your computer. Quicken will prompt you to remove any disks from drive A. The system will reboot, and then the Quicken Setup program will run briefly to complete the installation. When it finishes, you will see a Quicken icon on your screen. To start Quicken, double-click on the Quicken icon.

Registering Your Software

When you open Quicken for the first time, the Product Registration dialog box will appear (see Figure A.6).

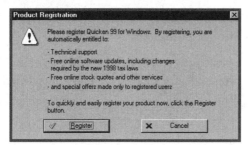

Figure A.6

Registering your copy of Quicken is important.

Registering your program entitles you to technical support and places your name on Intuit's mailing list so that you will receive information about future updates of your software and other related promotions. If you are using the online features of Quicken, you will not be able to receive program updates online until you register your software.

To register now, click on the Register button. If you do not want to register at this time, click on the Cancel button in the Product Registration dialog box. You can always register at a later date by clicking on the Help menu and choosing Register Quicken.

● ●

NOTE   Quicken removes the Register Quicken command from the Help menu once you've successfully registered so you don't accidentally register again.

● ●

The software registration wizard appears and walks you through the registration process. Registration can be done by telephone or online, which will require a modem.

For telephone registration, Quicken displays your serial number and asks you to call a toll-free 800 number. After you provide some basic information and the serial number, the Quicken Customer Service representative will tell you your customer number. You need to enter this customer number in the space provided.

For online registration, you will be asked to provide your name, address, e-mail address, and information about how you plan to use the software.

When ready, click on Next and Quicken will dial up on a secure connection and register your software.

After registration is complete (or after you cancel registration), the New User Setup dialog box will appear. This is the point at which Friday Evening's session picks up. Enjoy!

GLOSSARY

A

Accounts. Quicken organizes your financial information into accounts, which usually resemble your accounts in the real world. With these accounts, you can track your assets and liabilities, such as your checking and saving accounts or mortgage and credit card accounts.

Accounts list. By opening this list, you can get a quick overview of your accounts.

Accrual-basis accounting. Accounting in which expenses are recognized when the obligation is incurred, and income is recognized when the customer is billed.

Adjustable rate loans. Loans with a variable interest rate. When the interest rate changes, Quicken can calculate your new payment amount using the new rate.

Amortize. To write off a regular part of an asset's cost over a specific time interval.

Assets. Items that you own, such as a car, stocks and bonds, or real estate. In business, assets are defined as economic resources with three vital characteristics—a future probable economic benefit, control by the business entity, and results from a prior transaction or event.

Asset Depreciation Range (ADR). The range of depreciable lives allowed by the Internal Revenue Service. Once replaced by the Accelerated Cost Recovery System (ACRS) but revived in the 1986 Tax Reform Act to determine class lives.

B

Balance. The difference between total debits and total credits in an account, such as a bank balance or a loan balance.

Balloon payment. The last payment on a loan if it is significantly more than the prior payments. These types of loan arrangements are also called partially amortized loans.

Billminder. A list of upcoming financial actions, bills to pay, payment instructions, and so on that appears each time Quicken starts.

Blue chip. A high-quality common stock with a long record of paying dividends. These securities are considered good for long-term investment.

Budget. A plan of actions and programs expressed in terms of assets, liabilities, revenue, and expenses. A budget expresses financial plans and goals in terms of specific operational plans.

C

Cash flow. The result of the cash receipts less the cash disbursements for a particular asset or operation over a given period of time.

Categories. Units that provide a method to identify transactions by placing them in related groups, such as entertainment, food, and writing income. You could use an income category to keep track of deposits and an expense category for car insurance payments.

Classes. Ways of identifying transactions in Quicken. You specify such details as to whom, where, and to what transactions apply.

Credit. 1. The entry made on the right side of an account. In double-entry bookkeeping, credits are an increase in the liabilities, equity, and revenue accounts but a decrease in asset and expense accounts. 2. The ability to borrow money or buy things with a promise to pay later.

Credit analysis. A process used to determine the credit standing of a potential creditor to determine his suitability to have credit extended to him, and to decide how much credit should be extended.

D

Debit. An entry made on the left side of an account. In double-entry bookkeeping, a debit is an increase in asset and expense accounts, but a decrease in liabilities, equity, and revenue accounts.

Demand deposit. An account where funds may be withdrawn on demand or transferred on demand to another person by means of a check. An example of this is your checking account.

Disposable income. Your personal income less your personal income tax and any other governmental deductions. It is what most people think of as their take home pay.

Dividend. Money paid to shareholders of a stock, mutual fund, or a money market fund.

E

Embezzlement. The theft of money or property from a business by a person charged with the custody of the item(s) stolen.

Encumbrance. A lien on assets to secure a loan.

Ending balance. The balance of all transactions, including postdated transactions, in the account register.

Exchange rate. The ratio at which one currency or commodity can be exchanged for another.

Expenditure. A payment made with cash or property, or by incurrence of an obligation to pay later, to obtain an asset or service.

Expense. A way of measuring the depletion of an asset, such as depreciation, or the incurrence of a liability, such as an equipment lease. In other words, something that you put out to obtain revenue in the current period.

Excise tax. A tax levied on specific goods or services to collect money for a specified purpose. An example would be the excise tax on gasoline where the funds collected go to repair the building of the road system.

F

Factoring. The sale of a firm's accounts receivable to another party at a discount and without recourse to avoid having to wait until the accounts receivable mature or to avoid collection costs. Some banks and other financial institutions will factor (buy) accounts receivable and then the customer may either pay the factor or pay through the seller indirectly.

Financial statement. A report containing a financial representation of the organization. It is usually comprised of a balance sheet, an income statement, and a statement of changes in financial condition.

Fixed asset. An asset purchased for the use of the organization and not intended for resale with a life of more than one year. Usually property, plant, and equipment are first considerations.

Fixed cost. Costs that remain constant as expenses, regardless of changes in operation, such as rent, insurance, and so on.

G

General partner. A partner who is liable for all debts and obligations incurred by the partnership. General partners have no limited liability.

Graph. Data represented visually, such as a pie chart of your salary.

Gross income. The money earned from the sale of goods or services minus the cost of the goods or services sold. Gross income less the company's operating expenses is net income.

Gross sales. The sum of all sales totaled before adjustment for sales discounts and returns. It is the total number of units sold multiplied by the unit sales price.

Growth stock. The group name applied to companies that have no earnings record from past operations. The valuation of the company is based on speculation about anticipated future earnings. The return can be high because these companies generally do have a faster than normal rise in the market and industry they are in. They are correspondingly risky though because they are speculative in nature and anticipated future gains may not appear.

H

Hidden accounts. Accounts that Quicken uses to deal with accounts that are obsolete or have a zero balance. Hiding them enables you to remove the account and its balance from your accounts list but still retain the transaction information from the account.

I

Income. Money earned during a specific period that increases total assets, including rents, interest, gifts, commissions, salary, and so on. Any excess of revenue over expense (net income).

Individual Retirement Account (IRA). An account for investment of money for retirement that meets government regulations for an account that doesn't generate any taxable income as long as it is in the account.

J

Joint stock company. A group of individuals joined to form and operate a business venture. It has many of the characteristics of a corporation except the investors aren't given limited liability.

Joint tenancy. An arrangement in which property or real estate is deeded to two or more persons who hold an undivided interest in the property. Should one of the persons involved die, the property reverts to the control of the surviving member(s) without going through the estate of the deceased.

K

Keogh plan. A retirement plan for the self-employed who meet certain requirements. A Keogh plan contributor may contribute 25 percent of earnings or up to 30,000 dollars annually.

Kiting. An illegal practice of concealing a cash shortage by taking advantage of the time it takes for a check to clear the banking system.

L

Lead time. The number of business days from the time you send instructions for an online payment until the payment is received by the payee. Quicken automatically computes this time for you when you send payment instructions.

Liability. An amount payable either in dollars (accounts payable) or services. The party having the liability is called the debtor.

Lien. The right of a second party, usually a creditor, to hold, take possession of, or control the property of another party to satisfy a debt or duty obligation.

M

Maturity date. The date when the principal of a debt must be paid.

N

Net worth. Total assets minus total liabilities. This is an individual's personal equity; in a business evaluation this is stockholder's equity.

Non-profit organization. An organization formed to provide goods and services to meet a need structured so that no person (trustee, shareholder, and so on) can share in the profits or losses. These organizations often refer to themselves by the IRS code section that grants them exemption from taxes. This alerts donors to the tax-deductible nature of their donations.

Nontaxable gross income. Money received by a taxpayer that the government does not tax, like a gift of money.

O

Owner's equity. The owner's interest in the assets of the business, as represented by capital contributions and retained earnings.

Operating loss. The amount of money by which the business operating expenses coupled with the cost of goods sold exceeds the operating revenue.

Operating revenue. Net sales plus all of the other regular business income.

Operating risk. The risk posed by a fluctuating operating revenue stream. The higher the operating risk, the higher the instability of the company.

P

Paid-in capital. One of the two things that make up stockholder's equity. Paid-in capital is the result of donations to the company or the resale of treasury or other capital stock at a price above par value, and so on. This is added to retained earnings to make up stockholder's equity.

Par value. The value, assigned arbitrarily by the corporate charter, of one share of stock. This amount is printed on the stock certificate.

Patent. An exclusive right to use, manufacture, or market a process or a product for 17 years without interference or infringement. Patents are issued to a company or individual by the government.

Q

Quicken. Personal finance software by Intuit, Inc.

QuickTabs. A feature that keeps the most-used Quicken windows open and provides a handy tab at the right of the screen to make it easy to shift from one open window to another.

Quickzoom. A feature that enables you to get a more detailed display of a report or graph.

Quoted price. The last transaction price of a listed security or commodity.

R

Recession. A downturn in the economy. Some economists refer to a drop in the gross national product for two consecutive quarters as a recession.

Reconcile window. When reconciling an online account to a statement, this window displays the cleared transactions that occur before the statement end date.

Reconciliation. The process of ensuring that there is agreement between your account register and the statements you receive from financial institutions.

Retirement accounts. Accounts in which income generated by the invested money doesn't incur any tax liability as long as it remains in the account. Retirement accounts are typically coordinated with an employer.

S

Short-term debt. Money owed to a creditor with a repayment date of less than a year.

Shrinkage. The difference between inventory on the books and real inventory on hand.

Simple interest. Interest based on the original principal and not compounded.

Speculation. The process of investing in high-risk ventures to obtain a higher profit from capital gains.

Stock quotes. Continuously updated prices of stocks and securities, available through Quicken with Internet access. Quicken does this through the Portfolio window.

T

Tax credit. A reduction in the taxes payable to the Internal Revenue Service where the basis for reducing the taxpayer's obligation is reduced dollar for dollar by the credit.

Transaction. Any item affecting the balance of an account, such as checks, account fees, service charges, deposits, and so on.

Treasury bill (T bill). An actively-marketed, low-risk, short-term obligation of the federal government, sold without interest at a discount, and usually redeemed in 91 or 182 days at face value. There are also nine-month and 12-month T bills that are sold periodically. Treasury bills range in value from 10,000 dollars to one million dollars.

Treasury bond. 1. A long-term debt obligation issued by the federal government, with maturities of 10 years or more, sold in minimum denominations of 1,000 dollars. 2. A long-term obligation sold by a corporation and then retired (repurchased) by the corporation at a later date.

Treasury certificate. A coupon interest, bearing debt security of the federal government, whose maturity date is one year or less from date of issue.

Treasury note. An actively marketed low-risk obligation sold by the federal government with maturities of one to 10 years.

U

Unappropriated retained earnings. Those funds in the retained earnings account that are free for disbursement as dividends.

Unaudited statement. A statement that an accountant did not prepare by applying the Generally Accepted Auditing Standards (GAAS).

Unit trust. A type of mutual fund whose only investment is in bonds.

Unlimited liability. The liability that applies to the owner or owners in sole proprietorships or general partnerships. In corporations, shareholders have limited liabilities, which means their risk is limited to their investment in the business and doesn't involve their personal assets.

V

Variable costs. Costs that vary in direct proportion to changes in activity. An example is gasoline expense or overtime costs.

Variable annuity. An investment in a portfolio through an investment company or an insurance company, with the periodic payments from the annuity dependent on the performance of the portfolio.

Venture capital. An initial financing source for some new or restructured high-risk businesses that have potential for high return. This riskier sort of financing is often done by wealthy investors, investment clubs, small business investment companies, or limited partnerships.

Vested. Describes an employee's paid-up rights to pension benefits—those benefits that are not contingent on the employee's retention by the employer.

Voucher check. A business check with a voucher page on the side to allow more detail in record keeping.

Vouching. To recognize obligations and to authorize cash disbursements.

W

Warranty. An agreement of a seller or manufacturer to satisfy (for a specific time) any grievances over quality or performance of an item.

Windfall profits. Unexpected earnings usually not due to the efforts or any investment of the person who benefits.

Workers' compensation. A program that provides payments, regardless of a finding of negligence, to a worker with certain job-related injuries.

INDEX

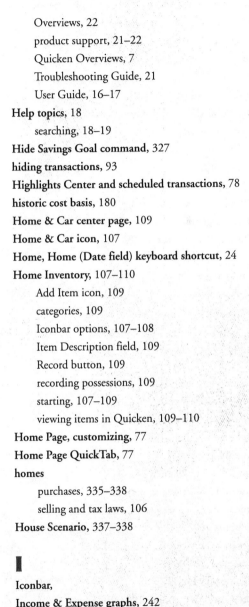

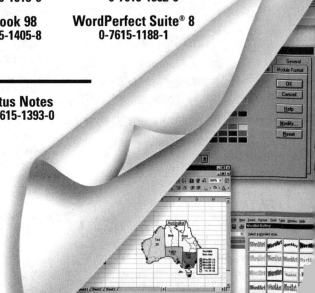